Le Coq

A Journey to the Heart of French Rugby

Peter Bills

FOREWORD BY DAN CARTER

ALLEN&UNWIN

First published in hardback in Great Britain in 2023 by
Allen & Unwin, an imprint of Atlantic Books Ltd.

This paperback edition published in 2024.

Photography credits: Pages 231 and 237,
photographs by Stade Toulousain; all other featured
images courtesy of the author.

10 9 8 7 6 5 4 3 2 1

A CIP catalogue record for this book is available from
the British Library.

Paperback ISBN: 978 1 83895 605 9
E-book ISBN: 978 1 83895 604 2

Printed in Great Britain

Allen & Unwin
An imprint of Atlantic Books Ltd
Ormond House
26–27 Boswell Street
London
WC1N 3JZ

www.atlantic-books.co.uk

*To Gabriel, in the hope he too will come
to love* La Belle France.

*And to my great friends throughout
France whose generosity and kindness
have been omnipresent down the years.*

Peter Bills was chief rugby writer worldwide for
the *Independent* newspaper group, contributing to
publications in London, Dublin, Auckland, Belfast,
Cape Town and Johannesburg.

He was also the Number 2 rugby writer for *The Times*
in London and has been a columnist for *Midi Olympique* in
France and the *Sydney Morning Herald* in Australia.

His most recent book, *The Jersey*, an exclusive inside
account of the All Blacks and New Zealand rugby, has
become an international bestseller.

Contents

CONTENTS

Foreword by
Dan Carter

I fell in love with rugby when I was five years old and it was all off the back of the inaugural Rugby World Cup in 1987. I still remember very vividly the World Cup final, the All Blacks against France. Yes, we went on to win that World Cup and, from that moment, I always wanted to be an All Black. But at the same time, I learned about this French style of play, about Serge Blanco, Philippe Sella and French flair rugby. It captured my imagination. Then fast-forward to 2009 when I got the opportunity to come to play in France. I wanted to experience it for myself.

I was lucky enough to come and play on a short-term contract at Perpignan and it was an amazing insight into the passion of French rugby. I always knew from the TV the style of rugby they played, but I didn't understand the passion of the fans. Going to the holy grail, I remember the stadium in Perpignan, the Aimé Giral, and to see their supporters and the chants and the singing, they just put their heart and soul into the team that they were supporting. That blew me away; I hadn't experienced anything like it.

I decided to go on and help them that season, even though I got injured. I stayed because I wanted to support the team and they went on to win their first Bouclier de Brennus in fifty-four years. I will never forget that night.

The final was played in Paris and then we flew back the next morning to Perpignan. We landed at the airport and there were people all the way from the airport to the city centre, cheering and being so joyful. They wanted to celebrate with us. We went into the city centre to present the Bouclier to the city and there were tens of thousands of people who'd come to celebrate with us.

There were supporters in tears. It was incredible to see how much it meant to them, and in the world we live in it's nice to be able to give the people of the city that you play for so much joy to take their minds off the distractions or difficulties they have in their lives. It was about coming together for a common cause, to support their team and in turn to have success and bring such joy. It's a great part of the game that I really enjoy.

It's so hard to describe in words the feeling, the emotion, it's almost like being a part of the supporters' lives. It was a very proud moment of my career.

That whole experience just ingrained another level of how much passion there is for this game in France and even though it was only a short-term contract, there was a part of me that said I needed to come back and play in France longer.

I went back to New Zealand to continue my career and the opportunity came about again at the end of the 2015 Rugby World Cup when I had finished playing for the All Blacks. At that stage my focus was to come back to France and play for a team that had huge aspirations to be successful and to win titles. I found that with Racing 92.

The Racing Club de France has an incredible history dating way back so when I came to Racing, I was trying to experience this tradition. The best way to do that was to try and win a Top 14 title.

Happily, we managed to do that in the most incredible fashion. Even better, it was in a game in Barcelona at the massive Nou Camp, a stadium that I used to go to all the time when I was living down in Perpignan to watch the Barcelona football games. To be suddenly playing in front of 100,000 people in a Top 14 final was mind-blowing, an amazing experience. I loved being a part of that. To have come to Racing and had success straight away, I could see how much it meant to the club.

For me, the toughest places to go and play rugby in France were down south. Somewhere like Toulon. If I had to play against Perpignan, I'm sure that would be one of them. But Toulon was a very hostile environment. They'd had a lot of success at the time I was playing there. But then every little place has its own character. Like Clermont Auvergne who at one stage, in 2014, had gone seventy-seven matches unbeaten at their Stade Marcel Michelin. You could almost go through all the different teams and see how passionate their supporters were.

Paris has its challenges when it comes to rugby. But even though the history with Racing and Stade Français goes back such a long time, you still know about the rugby down in the south, it's a way of life down there. In Paris with there being so many other competing sports, there was plenty to occupy people at weekends so it didn't quite feel the same.

But at Racing we had a very loyal supporter base that would always be there. We played in an environment at Stade Colombes that had so much history at the stadium. I'm sure teams didn't like going to play at Colombes under the old grandstand that felt almost like it was going to creak and fall down before the game. But I absolutely loved that.

When it came to cuisine, I'm happy to say, I tried it all from frogs' legs to snails! I had to give it a go to immerse myself in the culture – the foie gras, cheese, pastries; it was a very dangerous place. I had to make sure I did plenty of training to burn off the incredible food that I was able to experience.

The French take so much pride in their cuisine, the food is amazing. Just the number of different restaurants that you can go to that are world class, is incredible. It's not like you're trying to pick the top five or six world-class restaurants, they are all superb.

Just going down to the local *boulangerie*, the local bar or brasserie, just hanging out with the locals close to where I lived, was something I enjoyed doing as well.

I came to France wanting to immerse myself in the culture, and wine is a huge part of that. I wanted to learn about wine but I was a bit intimidated because there is so much history of wine in France, I didn't know where to start.

But looking at Paris, so close to the Champagne region, I focused on champagne. My wife and I love drinking champagne, so we'd spend quite a few of our free weekends heading out to the area and experiencing the cellars of the different *maisons* and just learning about the history.

It meant I gravitated towards champagne, but with Jacky Lorenzetti (Racing's president) owning several chateaux in Bordeaux, he steered us in the right direction to some good Bordeaux wine too. Obviously coming from New Zealand, where the major grape variety is pinot noir, it's hard to go past a good Burgundy as well. So you are spoiled for choice here in France.

My whole French adventure contained experiences that my wife and I will always look back on with pride and pleasure. To have experienced the French way of life is something we'll treasure forever.

Now, we just love coming back because we're not tourists

FOREWORD

any more. We have our favourite restaurants, our favourite bars that we love visiting again and again. And then there are the people and characters who feature so prominently in this book by Peter Bills.

I've known Peter for some years and I'm sure you will enjoy his personal journey to the heart of rugby in this superb country.

Prologue

In 2021, amid the Covid pandemic that had engulfed the world, a rugby match was played in France deep in the heart of the Basque country. Biarritz and Bayonne had long been rivals, the two pre-eminent clubs of the entire Pays Basque region since the diminishing of Saint-Jean-de-Luz as a playing power.

But this was no ordinary game, early as it was in the opening up of French sport to spectators after the long nights of self-isolation caused by the disease. Bayonne, clinging on to their prized Top 14 place all season, had to beat their fierce local rivals in the play-off to remain in the top flight. Biarritz, five-time champions of France and European Cup runners-up in 2006 and 2010, needed victory to return to the top level for the first time since 2014.

Given that this would be a match attended by spectators for the first time, just twenty-four days after the government announced a partial lifting of the restrictions that had closed stadium grounds, this was a delicate, significant occasion. Discussions with the authorities concluded with agreement that 5000 would be the maximum number permitted inside Biarritz's Stade Aguilera; 2500 tickets for the home club, 1500 for Bayonne with 1000 for assorted others.

Long before a ball was kicked on a hot, sunny and increasingly dramatic afternoon, it was obvious that the authorities, in attempting to keep a lid on Basque passion for rugby, had filled a large bottle with nitroglycerine and then given it a good shake.

Within fifteen or twenty minutes of the start, even those without tickets outside the ground had found the stadium's defences porous. So, in they poured. There are 9500 seats in the Stade Aguilera; 4950 in the Kampf stand, 4500 in the Blanco stand. The total capacity is 13,400.

For the play-off, not a spare seat was to be found. Add on another 4000 or so just milling around and finding whatever vantage point they could, and you had a crowd of about 13,000.

The local prefect, party to the agreement that no more than 5000 should attend, watched this invasion of the hordes with increasing dismay. A nervous club official offered a hurried explanation.

'It would appear,' he said with an air of solemnity, 'we have had a problem with the automatic ticketing system.'

Only problem was, Biarritz did not possess an automatic ticketing system.

The prefect, his face darkening by the moment, stood up theatrically at half-time and announced, 'I have been deceived.' At which point, he left the ground.

Alas, it got worse. Much worse.

A match wracked with tension throughout finished level at full time with the score 3-all. Then, an extra twenty minutes were played. At the end of which it was 6-6. Amid fever-pitch excitement, a hasty conflab ensued. A penalty-kick competition then began with the first ten kicks, five each side, successful from the 22-metre line in front of the posts. People were beside themselves with passion and tension, sharing bottles of champagne and wine, kissing each other, singing and waving their flags. Some just couldn't look, others were already crying. This outpouring of emotion spoke of the Basques' undiluted love for this game.

Alas for poor Bayonne, their sixth attempt failed. Up stepped an Englishman, Biarritz's Steffon Armitage, to land the kick that sent his club back to the Top 14 after eight years. Mayhem ensued.

Firecrackers exploded, smoke beacons lit, more bottles of champagne and wine plus cans of lager were opened and shared around. Thousands invaded the field. The Biarritz players were hugged and hoisted shoulder-high; their fans danced deliriously with delight. Not a soul gave a thought to social distancing, that novel phrase of those times, nor indeed even the wearing of a mask. Health considerations had vanished.

Nor did anyone imagine that just twelve months later, in June 2022, the roles would be reversed. Biarritz would tumble back down to Pro D2 league, a final day 80-7 thrashing at Toulouse confirming their inadequacy for the Top 14. But who should be sailing past them in the other direction at the end of the 2021/22 season? Bayonne, after hammering their rivals Mont-de-Marsan 49-20 in the play-offs. How times change.

Twelve months earlier, the authorities had spoken furiously of sanctions in the light of events at the Biarritz ground. But this surely was just another example of French flouting of laws and rules, allied to an intense passion for the sport.

Unbelievably, it got worse that night. A strict French government Covid curfew had been in place from December 2020. In June 2021, it had been stretched to 11 p.m., but it still applied throughout France. I happened to be at dinner at a small, delightful restaurant near the centre of Biarritz, and glanced at my watch. It was 10.30.

'I suppose then we'd better head back to the hotel,' I suggested to my French travelling companion. He looked bemused, as if I had ordered a bottle of English beer with the Chateaubriand. 'A curfew? In this town tonight? There isn't a policeman in the whole Pays Basque who would dare enforce a curfew tonight.'

The author can vouch for the veracity of that statement. Closer to half past one in the morning, with supporters still streaming through the town and drinking at the bars that remained open, there wasn't a single policeman in sight. Curfews might be for some but not Biarritz on the night of their promotion. The French make their own rules in such circumstances.

As French rugby legend Serge Blanco, a Biarritz man all his career, said afterwards, 'We beat Bayonne, a Basque match. It was fantastic, like we had won the World Championship.'

And speaking personally, it was fantastic to be back in the heartland of French rugby. That always induced a frisson of pleasure. Not to say excitement. Past games re-entered the mind, the soul and spirit lifted by thoughts of great rugby men encountered. On and off the field.

For me, it has been so throughout my life. I first went to Paris to see an international match in 1970 at Stade Colombes. But four years earlier, I had stood on the terraces at the old Cardiff Arms Park to witness the flair and innovation of a French team that included both Boniface brothers, Michel Crauste, Walter Spanghero, Jean Gachassin, Christian Darrouy and Lilian Camberabero. Among others!

I first encountered a French Rugby Championship final in 1973, Dax v Tarbes. The drama, colour and excitement made it like watching the game on another planet compared to the sober, sane games played at that time in English club rugby.

Just 22 miles separates England from France. But in almost every way, it could be tens of thousands of miles. Everything is different. Language, philosophy, mentality, cuisine, customs and attitude towards sport. Especially rugby...

* * *

Pierre-Auguste Renoir could paint an alluring scene of such beauty, viewers sometimes sat entranced for long periods, studying a single work.

Then there was Claude Debussy, who penned a musical line of such serenity that even fighting cats might stop and listen. As for Sacha Distel, well, let's just say he could croon with the best of them.

Each Frenchman illuminated his own genre, contributing richly to his nation's culture.

Others in myriad fields offered their own talents. Take the men of French rugby. With a glorious enthusiasm for the game and an often total disregard for its rules, skilful Gallic rugby men down the years have ensured that rugby has become as embedded in the French psyche as a plump clove of garlic. The game has contributed richly to French culture.

For rugby was, and remains, an endemic part of French life. Mind you, complex would be a wholly inadequate way of describing this association, this love affair with a game.

As someone once wrote, 'If you want to interest a Frenchman in a game, you tell him it's a war. But if you want to interest an Englishman in a war, you tell him it's a game.'

A game for gentlemen? Tell that to the victims of French brutality on the rugby field, those searching a muddied field in the after-match gloaming for a couple of uprooted teeth, lost amid the more fractious moments of a so-called game. Try telling that to the family of the now deceased Racing Club forward Armand Clerc, blinded in an eye for the remainder of his life by a punch thrown into his defenceless face amid the hurly burly of a line-out.

Then there were the fist fights where grown men squabbled like territorial geese.

Of course, you would never find such acts mentioned in rugby's rule book. But that was the key in understanding why France fell so passionately in love with a game introduced to them by the English. The obvious capacity to evade or simply ignore most of the rules struck a warming chord with the French mentality. It chimed with an inherent French trait.

In 2022, it was the 150th anniversary of the first rugby club establishing firm roots on French soil. The club, at Le Havre on the French north coast, was founded mostly by students living and working in the Channel port from Oxford and Cambridge universities.

With precision timing, the French national team marked the occasion by winning a rare Six Nations Championship Grand Slam, their first for twelve years. But what was of far greater significance was that it was achieved with a perfect mixture of traditional French style allied to the demands of the modern game: discipline, defensive security and concentration, plus kicking for strategic benefit. They were patient, too. In both attack and defence. So unlike the French. But this was the new France being created before our eyes.

The old style of French teams, cheerfully prepared to fling a risky high-percentage pass and see an entire movement consequently founder, had been replaced by a pragmatism demanded by the rigours of the modern game. Yet gloriously, France showed they could still craft thrilling, precise tries that lit up the stage, just as their most exciting players used to do. It was their hallmark, a spark residual in their souls.

But this new Gallic squad of players also demonstrated the progress they had made in coming to terms with rugby of this age. Gone, to a large degree, was the petulance, the emotional explosions that so often ruined any chance of continuity. Acts of wilful violence had likewise been largely discarded. This was radically different to days gone by.

In its place came dedication to a clear strategy. For example, only Italy kicked more times than France in that Six Nations season. The Italians booted the ball 169 times in five matches, France 151. Yet they kicked for territorial advantage and all the while retained that inbuilt ability to captivate an audience with a stunning moment of elan and style, most often executed at pace.

By clinching the coveted Grand Slam, these French players revived again all France's great love for this game. Their achievement fitted neatly into the intriguing overall story of how rugby union energised the entire French nation from the start.

Rugby spread at such a rapid rate across France because it offered activities so beloved of Frenchmen down the ages. Personal differences could be settled without recourse to the law. The *arbitre*, the referee, was no more than a token presence. Those wishing to sort out opponents for whatever reason could do so largely with impunity. Perhaps there might be a disapproving, wagging finger in response. But this was not serious retribution.

For breaking the rules was always a significant element of French culture. It is buried deep in their DNA. I have a friend who used to boast that he hadn't paid a single parking fine in over three years. By then, whilst living in Paris, he had amassed well over sixty tickets. Many lined his living-room wall, a kind

13

of constant taunt to the French traffic authorities. Frenchmen from all walks of life like to feel they have 'got one over' the authorities.

For the truth is, real power in France lies not in the hands of those in the National Assembly or the Senate. Still less, the Élysée Palace. It is in the grasp of those on the streets. If the French public announce themselves against a new law, a decree, then presidential wishes go up in smoke, like a pack of Gauloises.

People don't go to their representatives to complain about things. They take to the streets.

Late in the year of 2018, a new protest movement sprang up in France. It was called *les gilets jaunes*, the yellow vests movement. A populist grass roots protest movement for economic justice, it sought to remind French President Emmanuel Macron of the capacity of the people to cause mayhem on French streets. What is more, the protests that ensued were a mirror image of some of the violence often seen in French rugby. Certainly, in earlier days, if there wasn't violence on the streets on a particular day, the next likeliest place to find it would be the rugby ground.

All this struck a deep chord with those of a historical bent. Robespierre's day may have been long done, but the spirit of protest and resistance to authority flourishes to this day in France. As renowned ex-French President Charles de Gaulle once remarked sulkily, 'How can anyone govern a nation that has 246 different kinds of cheese?'

Of course, it has got much worse since De Gaulle's day. France now has more than 2000 cheesemakers in its midst.

Daft laws seem to bedevil the French. At a recent count it was found that there are around 10,500 laws and 127,000 decrees in France. Until recently, these included the right to marry a dead person (honestly, I am not joking), or your first cousin. I called up the guy in charge of the marrying the dead programme to find out more.

I mean, after all, how does that actually work? Do they exhume the skeleton from its grave and then call in a very good ventriloquist to speak the actual words of the marriage vow?

'Do you take this man to be your lawful wedded husband?'

'Well, I do but there was not much choice.'

But the bloke running that department, a guy by the name of Frank N. Stein, wasn't very communicative. And I got short shrift when I dropped it into the conversation with a cousin that maybe we should get hitched.

Until as recently as 2013, there was a law in France which banned women from wearing trousers in Paris. Even today, board shorts are still forbidden in public pools. Meanwhile, photos taken of the Eiffel Tower at night still violate French copyright law. Good luck with enforcing that one now the coachloads of tourists are returning to the French capital.

Mind you, it isn't just the French who have to live with stupid laws. For a long time, it was still legal for an Englishman to shoot someone from Wales with a longbow. I'm surprised no one thought of that when Gareth Edwards was torturing England's rugby men on an annual basis through the late 1960s and 1970s.

For years, the French were deemed unsuitable competitors in the Five Nations Championship.

The four Home Unions – England, Scotland, Wales and Ireland – gathered in 1931 in response to reports of French illegalities in their rugby and declared, 'Matches will not be resumed with the French until the control and conduct of the game in France has been placed on a satisfactory basis.' The ban lasted until 1947.

It was said that twelve French clubs were openly paying players, something abhorred by the Home Unions in a strictly

15

amateur game. Just as bad, player violence in French rugby was seen as endemic by the home nations. Although, for Welshmen familiar with robust, full-blooded (and bloodied) affairs within their own highly competitive club structure to sit in judgement on the French, surely risked accusations of the pot calling the kettle *noir*.

But the French rugby authorities could not stop or control their own clubs or players for a simple reason. No one could. The French had taken to this new game with such relish that they transferred that lingering delight for street protests, the flouncing of authority and punch-ups on to the rugby field.

Better still, the presence of thirty players on the same field offered wondrous opportunities for retribution. Hidden within the inner confines of a scrum, ruck, maul or even line-out, all kinds of nefarious activities were possible, from the sly kick to the sudden punch. Why, you could even hide the odd psychopath or two within the bowels of the scrummage. Several clubs did. All was seen as fair activity in love and war. The French were largely bemused by their ban from the Five Nations Championship.

What was a rogue boot here and there, a punch of passion amid the intensity of the game? It mystified Frenchmen then, and still does to this day, that such activities were tolerated in England, Scotland, Wales and Ireland with the traditional blind eye, but abhorred whenever they occurred in France. What if the occasional blind eye resulted?

As a French friend of mine said, 'For me, playing rugby was like playing truant from school, taking my role models from extraordinary characters in the game, and their attitude to life.'

In other words, being unconventional. But alas, the English didn't really understand such mentalities. Mutual suspicion and loathing, the long-held elements of the fractious Anglo-French relationship down the ages, again took root. These old foes regard each other with the snarling suspicion of cat and dog.

The French film actor Jean Gabin put the old, troubled relationship into context when arriving in New York during the Second World War. Asked about the French attitude towards the British, he responded, 'We are both pro-British and anti-British. Those who are pro-British say every night in their prayers, "Dear God, let the gallant British win quickly." Those who are anti-British pray, "Dear God, let the filthy British win very soon."'

Given that the game of rugby was first seen on French soil in the early 1870s, it might be reasonable to speculate that the English felt France may have been in need of some sporting distraction, after the tragedies of the 1871 Paris Commune. The short-lived Commune was ended by the intervention of the French Army during a bloody week in May 1871. Thousands of Communards who had rushed to defend democracy and their rights died either in battle or on the guillotine. Officially, authorities said six to seven thousand perished; others estimated it to be nearer 20,000.

Georges Darboy, the Archbishop of Paris, and others were taken hostage and shot in retaliation. The whole affair underlined French citizens' suspicion or hatred for the authorities. It is a flame that continues to burn to this day.

Yet against this unlikely backdrop, a simple game invented by the English was taken up with fervour by many Frenchmen. What is more, once it arrived, it spread like a forest fire. Quickly, great swathes of France were caught up in the excitement of the new game.

But then, as we shall see in these pages, it was not just the game itself which quickly captivated the French. As a contest and an element in social life, it represented many different things to different people. This new game appealed to many Frenchmen's sense of *joie de vivre*, their concept of fun. They

17

loved the social aspect of the game, the fact that when hostilities ended on the field, the tradition was for all, teammates and opponents, to gather and enjoy a drink together.

Uniquely, and unlike in England, it was a game that crossed all social classes and wasn't confined to elite schools. The local butcher might scrummage with a café owner and a fireman beside him. A young farm worker might deliver the ball into a scrum and a lawyer receive it when it was heeled. A dashing wing could be a medical student, with a builder playing inside him.

This intermingling of all French social classes was one of the triumphs of the young seedling inspired by the students of Oxford and Cambridge. It broke down barriers and brought complete strangers from all walks of life together. It was never like that in the UK, which may explain why rugby in Britain and Ireland has never become THE national sport.

Most of all, it was regarded as a game where what happened on the field, stayed on it. What was the odd missing tooth or bloodied eye? One well-known French rugby forward had his nose broken thirty-seven times during his career.

Another factor proved a strong element in the game's growth and popularity. Local pride and honour have always been imposing aspects of French life. It was true then and remains so to this day, albeit perhaps weakened somewhat by the tide of professionalism and pursuit of money.

Although, as we will see, money was changing hands in French rugby from comparatively early times. But with a few of those traditional Gallic shrugs, the French just kept on ignoring the rules.

If they didn't like them, they simply carried on regardless. Something of the sort still applies today in most walks of life in France. Changing that philosophy would be about as easy as moving the Eiffel Tower a bit to the left.

PROLOGUE

As the former Castres player, Stade Français coach and current coach of Argentina, Michael Cheika, says, 'I just think there is something much more tribal about French rugby than any other place. It applies at all age groups and all levels. It's so different. Over here, you are playing for your town or city and the town's evolution is all wrapped up in the development of its rugby club.

'That's one of the reasons why so many multinationals based all over France are associated with local clubs. The people who run those organisations grew up in a lot of these towns and understood the rugby association and what it meant. They knew how important rugby was in the landscape. They get involved because they see it's a great way of getting kudos in their local area. Because, in reality, these rugby clubs are very often the talk of the town. The president of the rugby club is the boss of the town in many ways.'

What of that tribalism which outsiders like Cheika attribute to local pride? In some of these regions, there have been local conflicts or battles going back centuries. When these local teams play each other, sometimes you can imagine what went on all those years before.

Cheika says, 'There is a lot more of that bravado in France, like "Don't cross my city's lines" sort of thing. The Anglo-Saxons are physical, but they will keep more within the laws of the game. The French are different. You have to put a lot of focus on the area around regions and towns such as Narbonne, Béziers, Perpignan, Castres. Perhaps it goes back to the history of such areas and the way they used to fight amongst each other.

'Every team thinks the other is worse but of course it's like the pot calling the kettle black. It is about bravado, about players thinking they don't want to be seen as weak and therefore they will impose themselves right from the start.

'But I think the French are quite good in the sense that they accept it for what it was in those times. Back in those days, the players who did those things like fighting, throwing punches, were lauded as heroes of the town.'

Finally, there was yet another intrinsic reason why the French took so readily to this Anglo-Saxon activity. To engage in this sport, particularly to catch a ball, seek open space and then run like the wind for the opposition line for the glory of scoring a try, represented one of the core elements of the French creed. Namely, *liberté, égalité, fraternité*.

This trait remains to the present day. Listen to France fly half Romain Ntamack after his brilliant attacking run from his own goal line, in a match against New Zealand in November 2021.

'I thought of nothing! It was so quick, I didn't have time to think at all. It was two seconds... in which time... I took the decision to try to get myself out [of his in-goal area] and from the moment when I broke the first tackle, I just accelerated downfield. But I had no time to reflect on what to do.'

It proved that spirit of adventurism, the innate pleasure of feeling ball in hand and the opportunity to run free, remains a critical element of the French rugby player's DNA. Welshmen, Irishmen, Englishmen, Scotsmen, South Africans, Australians and New Zealanders – we should all celebrate that. For the game is immeasurably richer for such talent.

To feel liberated within a game, running from those wishing to tackle and ensnare you, appealed to every participant. *Égalité* meant social and political equality, eminently suitable for a game played by all classes of people from every background.

Meanwhile a fraternity, strictly speaking, was an organisation, society, club or fraternal order traditionally of men closely linked to various religious or secular aims.

It was a short hop from there to adapt the so-called club or organisation to a rugby club. Thus, France's core elements of its society in the nineteenth century fitted rugby's requirements like a glove.

What the French brought to this new game was a cornucopia of creativity and invention. They are an inspirational, creative people. How else could they fill all those wonderful museums throughout their land with brilliant paintings, sculptures, etc?

On the rugby field, they created space and movement, offering scoring opportunities not just for themselves but those around them. As Australia's 1991 World Cup-winning coach Bob Dwyer says, 'The French are able to make space for those around them on a rugby field better than any other nationality I know. Most countries' players can make space for themselves. Few can make it for their colleagues, certainly not to the degree achieved by the French.'

In the artist's gallery or music room, men like Renoir, Debussy and Distel flourished in creating beautiful paintings or sounds. Others applied their great artistic bent to the kitchen, so much so that they established for their nation a traditional position of world leaders in the field of cuisine. All settled comfortably into the category of great creativity. It is only fair to say, rugby union the world over has benefited immeasurably from the application of that creative French talent.

There had to be other reasons for the French embracing this game so wholeheartedly, other than a basic desire to duff up some guy from the next village whom they didn't particularly like. These were some of them.

Yet too much tut-tutting from the other side of the English Channel and the Irish Sea bedevilled relationships with French rugby men for too long. Thus, it is appropriate, in telling the story of how France embraced an enduring love affair with this game, that we should celebrate the qualities brought to the sport by the French. They are many and varied and have contributed richly to the game's huge global following in contemporary times.

The French took up rugby union with all the zeal and freneticism of two lovers beginning a relationship. Of course, as with lovers, sparks have flown, but the passion of France for this game remains true to this day. To see and share that intrinsic love and support for the game is to experience a unique atmosphere and pleasure.

In this book I set out to retrace the original spread of rugby south from Paris to most of the regions. I wanted to discover the soul of French rugby and explore why it has become so integral a part of French culture.

I knew that the south-west represented the core of rugby in this land. But by no means only the south-west. And not only at the level of senior clubs, the likes of Toulouse, La Rochelle and Montpellier, the 2022 French champions. Junior clubs abound and flourish.

I wanted to meet some of the great living characters of the game and pay tribute to past greats now sadly departed. Above all, I wanted to see just how this game continues to capture the imagination of people at all clubs.

The journey was truly a trip to *la France profonde*.

CHAPTER 1

The Ruggers of HAC

Le Havre–Paris

September 1872. France is a nation in dire need of stimulus, a better tomorrow than today.

By May 1871, the Paris Commune has been brutally suppressed by the French national army. Spirits are low, times difficult. Yet certain elements will come together to raise hopes, expectations. Napoleon III's rebuilding of Paris, masterminded by Baron Haussmann from 1853 to 1870, is largely completed. Old medieval neighbourhoods have been demolished, the city has been beautified and doubled in size. Citizens stroll in popular locations like the Tuileries Garden as much to be seen as to see. For the better off, it is a world of music, books and lively debate.

Yet an odd time, you might just think, to launch a new sport. Its name is rugby.

It is launched in an even odder place. Yet with business and trade booming as the 1870s develop, a group of students from Oxford and Cambridge universities find themselves working in the Channel port of Le Havre. Together with some other expats, like railway worker F. F. Langstaff who is helping develop a rail system in that region, it is they who introduce the new game, rugby union, into the country.

Together with friends, Langstaff becomes the first president (1872–84) of the Havre Athletic Club (HAC), which he starts to organise. The early idea of a hybrid version of soccer and rugby is quietly dropped, leaving two sections, one for association football, the other for rugby.

They find an appropriate site in a nearby commune connected to Le Havre: Sanvic. Located in front of the church this land, rented for 600 francs a year, begins to be used from 1882. It is still used by the rugby section and was given the name Langstaff Stadium.

Around 430 miles away, something similar was happening on the Atlantic coast at Bordeaux, where young Britons were trading in the wine business. Here, too, the message was being spread about this new game. Before too long, a club formed at Bordeaux would become one of the best. Stade Bordelais would win seven French Championship titles between 1899 and 1911.

At Le Havre, they called their young players 'the ruggers of HAC'. They sought fun and frivolity in a social and sporting activity.

The first Le Havre club, founded on 14 September 1872, had the name 'Havre Football Club' until 1884 when it was rebranded as 'Havre Athletic Club'. Thereafter, Le Havre revelled in its reputation as the cradle of both sports in France.

Yet for all the optimism of its early founders, the new club on the French coast had a rude awakening at its first match, on the other side of the Channel at Southampton. It was a game of twelve-a-side and the expats got a hammering.

The *Hampshire Advertiser* newspaper dated 15–22 February 1873, announced it thus:

GRAND FOOTBALL CONTEST.

Havre v Portswood Park Football Club.

A match will be played at the Antelope ground (in Southampton) on Wednesday, the 19th instant, between the Havre and Portswood Park Football Clubs at 3 p.m. A dinner will be given at the Philharmonic Rooms at 6.30 p.m. the same evening. Tickets (including wine) 15s. To be had of Mr. Dartnall, High Street.

A large attendance is expected and those who are present may be sure of witnessing some good and spirited play on both sides.

So they set off, these brave pioneers of this new game, boarding the steamer *Fannie* at Le Havre docks. The irony was that Portswood had initially invited them over to play a *cricket* match, not rugby or football.

The result was:

Portswood Park: 1 goal, 11 touchdowns, 11 rouges (an undefined score).

Havre: 1 rouge.

So, twenty-three 'scores' to one. And lucky to get the one, as someone might have said.

The report went on: 'At the [after match] dinner, the viands [meats], dessert, wines being all that could be desired. Admirable catering by Mr. T. Dartnall. The room was decorated with flags and tables were decorated with some choice flowers and plants.'

One of the Havre players, George Washington who was Reverend of the Anglican church in Le Havre and a professor at the *lycée* in the town, said simply of his team's day, *'Battu, mais content'*, (beaten, but content).

The report concluded, after many toasts had been drunk to notable members of each club, Her Majesty Queen Victoria and the French President Adolphe Thiers: 'The Havre team returned to Havre in the *Fannie* at 12 o'clock (midnight), many who were present at the dinner accompanying them to the docks and bidding them good-bye.'

Few could have imagined that their exertions that day would pave the way for a sporting contest between English and French clubs that would last for 150 years and more. Truly, from small acorns grow mighty oaks.

For those involved in founding the first club on French soil, the likes of Frederick Field Langstaff (the club's first president), his son William Ramsay and other keen protagonists like C. E. Gabain, the day's outcome must have come as a rude shock.

The oldest image of these men surviving to this day shows a team photograph, the players seated or standing casually with Langstaff senior proudly seated in the middle of the front row. Among his young charges in their playing kit, he is wearing a dark coat, top hat and gloves. He sports a bushy white beard over much of his face.

Early in French rugby's days, probably in the late 1880s or 1890s, another intriguing photograph was taken.

The image, captured from behind one touchline at a match, shows a line of twenty-five men, all seemingly in suits. Most are wearing bowler hats; a couple have cloth caps. Some are seated on rough wooden benches, others lean against a metal rail. On the extreme right, there are two ladies in long dresses, wearing bonnets. Not a face is turned to the photographer; all are studying the play intently.

On the field, just about every visible player has a moustache.

The fashion of those times decreed that many players took to those early matches wearing black berets. Some had belts around their waists, too. Today, more than a century later, you look into their eyes as they face the camera for a team photograph, and you know their fate. The horrors of the First World War would ensnare far too many.

Unlike in England where it became a sport chiefly for the upper classes, nurtured in private schools, in France rugby was never going to remain exclusive to a small grouping for one reason. The French working class quickly took up the game.

This catapulted the game into the villages and towns of the land. Once there, it attracted all social classes and became emblematic of a contest that challenged local rivalries. A village or town could take on its nearest rivals for local bragging rights. It might sound trite or unsophisticated to twenty-first-century attitudes, but in an era when the focus of everyday life was on local areas, when universal travel had not yet become commonplace, it was the ideal activity to assert supremacy.

Yet there is a major uncertainty over all this. For the fact is, there may well have been a sporting precedent for this new game, buried deep in the archives of French history.

La Soule was a ball sport played in medieval times in France. It could often involve hundreds of players and spread over a vast terrain. The idea was to seize the 'ball' from any number of opponents and, with the help of your friends or teammates, take it back to a specified 'goal' in your home town or village.

The ball, named a *soule*, could be made of leather or even the odd pig's bladder. The leather variety was usually stuffed with horsehair or hay. It is said to have originated in the Normandy and Picardy regions of northern France.

What is fascinating is that in the mid-1800s, a Frenchman named J. L. Conde sat and sketched a scene from this very game. A large throng is seen as the central focus of the sketch. At the front, several characters appear to be scrapping for possession of some object, presumably the ball.

One man is on his knees with another splayed out below him on the ground, with the suggestion some blow is about to be struck against a rival. I looked closely and thought I could detect the assailant wearing a Pontypridd rugby shirt. But I may have been mistaken. No matter, hats are hurled into the air.

Meanwhile, from behind a large tree, two petrified-looking women observe the scene. They protect their youngsters carefully from the mob which is more than 100-strong.

In the background, there are some typical French nineteenth-century buildings.

The pencil sketch was published in a French newspaper, *L'Illustration*. Intriguingly, the caption reads *'La soule, en Basse-Normandie.'* It is dated February 1852 – almost exactly twenty years BEFORE it is widely believed rugby was introduced to France, in Normandy. Remember, Liverpool FC rugby club, the oldest in the world, was not founded until 1857.

So were the French, in fact, playing a larger, albeit more disorganised version of rugby football even before the English? It may be possible. Rather like a form of 'football' was played across Britain in the centuries before association football and rugby football was ever invented. Perhaps *La Soule* was only another version of this sort of traditional sport played out between communities and teams of many dozens of players.

What this medieval game or pursuit of local roots may also reveal is the origins of that near fanatical pride among Frenchmen in their home town or village, a trait that remains to this day. Whether it be engaged in *La Soule* or the coming game of rugby union, Frenchmen defended the reputation of their territory with a zeal that often spilled over into violence.

What is clear is that this was intrinsically a rough sporting challenge. If teeth got loosened or opponents knocked out, that was seen as no more than par for the course. Fair retribution was similarly a key ingredient.

At Le Havre, they had started playing on ground near the Avenue Foch and the Boulevard François 1er, but in 1882, after what was described as 'several misadventures', a ground was lent to them near the Église Sanvic.

Inevitably, the growing club attracted those visiting the town or sent there in pursuit of their business, like the Welshman, Basil G. Wood, said to be a trader in coal, and Julius Meyer, a cotton trader. As the club progressed, men such as W. H. Crichton and E. W. Lewis became French internationals. Crichton won two caps, against New Zealand and England, in 1906, Lewis a sole cap against England the same year.

So, Le Havre boasts a rich history. Yet I feel sorry for the place.

It's the big, ugly sister to two beautiful little siblings close by: Honfleur and Harfleur. I know it's going back a year or two, but the importance of the duo began to wane around 1517 when their harbours started silting up.

In medieval times, Honfleur and Harfleur were important fishing ports of the Normandy coast. Nevertheless, Francis I recognised the need for a bigger port and decided on Le Havre. That was where its problems began.

Back in the day, Le Havre might have seemed the ideal place to introduce a new sport into France.

It was an elegant, well-to-do town on the French coast in the early 1870s. Smart, genteel. Its citizens lived a calm, pleasing life. A port of growing size and importance, visitors from Britain and as far afield as the United States and the West Indies sailed into its large harbour.

Trouble was, Le Havre always had one distinct disadvantage. Just about everyone who went there, left. Quite soon after the new sport had been introduced into France, most of those Oxbridge young gentlemen moved on, many lured to Paris by the attractions, business and social, of the capital.

Then there were the passengers on the outgoing transatlantic liners that used the port. Naturally, they all waved goodbye to the town.

In 1914, many of Le Havre's young men also had to leave, for the trenches of the First World War. A horrific 6000 of them would never return.

In 1944, once Adolf Hitler had declared Le Havre a *Festung*, or fortress, which must be held to the last deluded soldier, the Americans and British decided there was only one way to get the Germans out of the place. Flatten it. The aerial bombardment, which lasted two days in September 1944, destroyed just about everything in sight. Then those Germans who were still alive retreated.

Once the Le Havre club had been established, the rugby men of Oxbridge argued passionately about the colour of the jerseys the new club should wear. 'Oxford blue,' said the Oxonians; 'Cambridge blue,' insisted the Cantabs. Of course, in the end they had to compromise. Oxford and Cambridge colours. It is the same today.

Le Havre might still be one of the top rugby clubs in France but for two considerable factors. One was the strong counter-attraction of Paris with its huge numbers of potential players and support. The second was its location.

I mean, can you imagine a well-travelled young man enticing his lady love to a weekend in France with the immortal words, 'Darling, we are going to Le Havre for the weekend.' It really doesn't quite have the cachet of Paris, does it?

Alas, what happened after the last of the Allied planes had bombed the hell out of the French coastal port in 1944 ensured Le Havre would never be on anyone's favourite weekend destination list again.

Five thousand people were killed, 12,500 buildings destroyed and the port wrecked (with some assistance from the retreating Germans) by the Allied planes. It became known as 'the storm of iron and fire'. Most traces of the original Le Havre were obliterated.

Unfortunately, what rose from the ruins was an aberration. UNESCO called the development at Le Havre 'An outstanding post-war example of urban planning and architecture based on the unity of methodology and the use of pre-fabrication, the systematic utilisation of a modular grid, and the innovative exploitation of the potential of concrete.'

I think that meant they liked it.

Presumably, UNESCO's men were attending, after the Second World War, the official opening of every lovely architecturally designed building all over countries like Bulgaria, Poland and Romania under the withering designer pencil of the Soviets. Perhaps the truth was better conveyed by someone who wrote 'New Le Havre would make a Cold War East German architect feel at home.'

When I last went there, I hurried as quickly as I could to the port to catch a ferry back to England. But I did notice a ghastly concrete block tapered down to a fine point at one end, the whole standing on ugly concrete stilts. It was a sort of nightmare creation of Legoland. Much of the city is like that.

Where once stood, in the 1870s, elegant, wide boulevards and classical nineteenth-century buildings, now exists a concrete jungle. The modern architects responsible for this abomination were a Frenchman, Auguste Perret, and the Brazilian architect and communist idealist, Oscar Niemeyer.

As for the rugby in those early days, who knows? Perhaps those early Englishmen working in the Normandy coastal port could already see the potential of this thrilling game to light up a nation. Whatever the reason, the birthplace of the sport on French soil proved to be only a starting point for the game as it rushed south. It wouldn't be here, on the Channel coast, where rugby union would explode, as it did in the south and south-west. After all, in the end the game bypassed most of Normandy and Brittany.

31

Of course, several junior clubs in those *départements* gradually emerged. And their enthusiasm for the game continues to this day.

But in recent times, only really at Rouen, near the mouth of the River Seine, and RC Vannes and Rennes in Brittany, are there clubs with ambitions of Top 14 rugby, albeit as Pro D2 (or lower) clubs at present. But perhaps we should beware dismissing rugby too soon in these regions.

In season 2020/21, the ambitious Bretons at Vannes missed promotion to the Top 14 by a whisker. The much-anticipated 2021/22 season was a failure with Vannes in mid-table mediocrity. Not that that diminished their ambition. Even before the last games, they were out recruiting several players, notable among them prop forward John Afoa, a former New Zealand All Black.

Afoa might have been thirty-eight by then, but he arrived from Bristol Bears in the English Premiership, fresh for the new challenge on the Brittany coast. His experience will be of incalculable value to the club at every level.

If RC Vannes, founded in 1950, are to succeed in climbing into the top flight, it would be a heady achievement, not to mention a landmark moment for the French Rugby Federation (FFR) and their attempts to spread the game from its traditional heartlands.

A Top 14 club on the Brittany coast? What's not to like? Bring it on.

Meanwhile, today, Le Havre Athletic play in Pool 8 of French League Fédérale 2. They're an amateur club, having fun, and there's nothing wrong with that.

They have a neat stadium, are enthusiastic rugby folk and love the game. You are never far from photographs of teams here, a testimony to their history. Long may they respect the game and that distinguished provenance.

But rugby was potentially too big a game, to an increasing extent too popular a sport, to be confined to a small region on the French coast. It was growing, mushrooming out of northern France.

Barely two hours away from Le Havre lay a city beloved of the world. Paris. But much more than that, Paris in the 1880s was a burgeoning city, the 'new Paris' as it became known. Haussmann's radical redesign of the centre of the city, with its splendid new wide boulevards and classical buildings, had heralded a new life for those living in or visiting the French capital.

Just as Parisian society embraced the considerable challenges of Impressionism in the art world, so it swept up the fascination of the new sport in its midst, one that created a fervour right from the start.

The dash south had begun...

CHAPTER 2

City of Mayhem

Paris

If arteries are the lifeblood of human beings, then railway systems represent the vibrancy of nations. For sure, the railway played a key role in the expansion of the new game of rugby in France.

Initially, the French had seemed well placed to lead Europe, if not the world, in railway development. A French engineer, Pierre Michel Moisson-Desroches, proposed building seven national lines as early as 1810, just two years before an inspired Napoleon awoke one morning in sunny Paris, threw open the windows of his Palais and exclaimed, 'I know what my troops would like most of all. A nice walk to Moscow.'

Only trouble was, when they got there, they found the natives distinctly unfriendly and had to walk back, too. Menaced by Cossacks part of the way.

Someone else who was destined to see his grand plans go up in smoke was Moisson-Desroches. Just think how useful it could have been if he'd managed to lay the tracks as far as

Moscow by 1812. Instead, his plan just evaporated.

Even as late as 1842, the French government was rejecting all major rail projects. Fear put off some investors. 'What will these metal beasts be that rush through tunnels at speed and asphyxiate every passenger?' one is said to have cried.

'Who said anything about going so fast people may die?' said a rather shrewder banker.

Even so, by 1842 Britain had almost 2000 miles of railways up and running. France had managed just 300.

But within a few decades, the French railways had received support from a very unexpected source. The Impressionist artists. Scorned at first in their own country, just like the railway system, the Impressionists began to turn the tide of public opinion. Painting trains in beautiful settings was a key part of that from the early 1870s onwards.

By 1877, steam trains were puffing, billowing, panting, straining and screeching their way from the Channel coast to the French capital. It is most likely that some of the young English students from Oxford and Cambridge who had lived in Le Havre took the service to Paris – with a few of those mysterious rugby balls in their luggage.

Claude Monet wasn't so much fascinated by rugby balls as the steam trains, dubbed the great iron monsters. So much so that in 1877 he took the train himself from his Giverny home in Normandy to Paris's Saint Lazare station. There, at the end of one of the platforms just inside the ticket barrier, he set up his easel and began to paint a series of works featuring the famous steam trains, some billowing smoke into the roof of the great station.

To this day, they capture the entire spirit of that age. After the tragedy of the Franco-Prussian War of 1870–71, society was eager to turn the page, to go forward. A new transport system was opening up which had a liberating effect. Now, too, a new sport was unfolding before their eyes. The two became enmeshed. Both offered a sense of fun, adventure and freedom, with the railways providing obvious advantages to rugby spectators by transporting them and their friends close to grounds.

Into this world neatly slotted the new game of rugby union. With astonishing speed, it completely captured the imagination of the people.

Just as the new style artists, whether you liked or loathed their work, were exciting considerable debate in French circles, the new sport of rugby was doing something remarkably similar. Some observers decried, even at that early stage, the sometimes overly robust style of the game. But the majority began to see an exciting, fast-flowing sport that could appeal in different ways to large and small, fat and slim, fast and not so fast.

At its birth, the new game had caught the imagination not only of the French. In 1877, for example, a club called 'The English Taylors RFC' had been formed by British businessmen in the capital.

* * *

The early French Championship match between two Paris-based clubs, Racing Club and Stade Français, in a one-off game in 1892, was refereed by Pierre de Coubertin, Baron Coubertin, who founded the International Olympic Committee and was its second president. He is known not only as the father of the modern Olympics but the possessor of a walrus moustache that looked so bushy you could probably have detached it, reattached it to the end of a pole and used it as a kind of mop to wash a floor.

Rugby teams needing players in those early days invited applications from all and sundry. Racing's 1892 team included two Englishmen and two Peruvians, who presumably turned up wearing bowler hats, still to this day a common sight throughout the South American country.

But already, rugby was quickly emerging as a game of international appeal. As early as 1892, Racing played a friendly match in Paris, at Levallois-Perret, against the Rosslyn Park club from London, followed by London Irish in 1899. By then, happily, the French could entertain their visiting rugby men in style. The Moulin Rouge had opened in 1889.

Racing won that first French Championship match in 1892 but Stade Français gained revenge the following year and dominated for the remainder of the decade. It wasn't until 1899 that provincial teams were allowed to compete.

*   *   *

Ever since those days, rugby men of all sizes, persuasions and nationalities have been dashing to, from or around Paris in suitably dramatic style. There must be something in the air.

After all, it's that kind of crazy place where a healthy bohemian disregard for rules and the authorities flourishes. Parisian life is fast and frantic, elegant and enigmatic. Revolutionary, too, at times.

You can sense it as you head south from the Channel coast and approach the capital. On the railway, the TGV train seems keen to smash its own speed records as it blasts past the muddied fields of the Somme valley. It's in a real rush to get you there.

On the roads, too, everyone seems to start speeding up as Paris looms. The race is on.

Arriving in the French capital is like stepping into a dodgem car at the fairground. Few regulations apply here, even for normally sane people. Exposure to Paris's frenetic pace and ways creates many raving lunatics.

Paris, you see. The city of sin. And mayhem.

But then, madcap scenarios involving rugby men have long since been commonplace in the French capital. Take 1910, for example, and the Frenchman who made a notable madcap dash out of the French capital on rugby matters.

Joé Anduran was busy minding his own business at the art dealer's shop where he worked somewhere on the Left Bank one afternoon, when three men burst in. A hold-up? A late bid for a Monet they were trying to sell? Not quite.

These gentlemen, it turned out, represented the French rugby authorities. Well, two of them did. The third was a reporter who had come along for the ride, sensing a story. He certainly got one.

Less than an hour before, the group had waved farewell to the French players chosen to travel to Wales for an international match at Swansea on New Year's Day 1910. Alarmingly, only fourteen players had assembled at the capital's Gare du Nord railway station to catch a train to Calais on the Channel coast. From there, they would sail to Dover and then head by train for London and, eventually, Swansea.

No one was boarding an Airbus A321 for the direct flight in those days.

But they travelled a man short. One of the French forwards had been detained at Bordeaux on military service. Which sent the French rugby officials into apoplexy.

Anduran, by the way, was a bit more than just an art dealer. He was a forward who played rugby for the Sporting Club Universitaire de France in his spare time. Even so, he was startled by these sudden arrivals and especially their message. 'Would you like to play for France tomorrow?'

Once he ascertained this wasn't some colossal prank, Joé announced he was most certainly up for the challenge. But when they reached his home to collect his kit, they faced an even more formidable hurdle. Madame Anduran.

'You want my husband to play rugby tomorrow?' she asked. 'Impossible. It will be New Year's Day and we have family engagements.'

Family visits on New Year's Day were then a ritual in France and still are. Madame Anduran stood firm. But Joé stepped in. 'What are family engagements when one has the chance to play rugby for one's country,' he retorted. The die was cast.

Old boots caked in dried mud and a sweat-smelling top – we had better not go any further down the descriptive road when it comes to an old jockstrap and shorts – were thrust into a *valise* and they rushed back to the Gare du Nord for a later train north.

The good news was, Anduran arrived at Swansea just in time to wear the famous French rugby jersey. He hooked for France that day. The bad news was, France lost 49-14, Anduran didn't get a mention in media reports and he certainly never played for France again.

More tragically, four years later, Joé Anduran again found himself away from home and his family. In the trenches of the First World War. He died at Bois-Bernard in the Pas-de-Calais on the second day of October 1914. The war had barely begun. When he perished, the memory of his one French rugby cap long gone, the rugby man who hailed from the Pays Basque was just thirty-two years old.

There were certainly some odd ways of getting into the French rugby team in those days.

Just twelve months after Anduran's solitary appearance in 1910, another Frenchman earned a first international cap in even more bizarre circumstances. On 2 January 1911, André Francquenelle went along to the Stade du Matin at Colombes (later named Yves-du-Manoir) intending to watch the international match against Scotland.

Aged twenty-two and hailing from Rochefort-sur-Mer, a port on the Charente estuary, Francquenelle played wing for his clubs, Vaugirard and Rochefort. He was squat, had a strong neck and wiry, clipped moustache. He wore his shorts almost down to the knee, as per the fashion in those times. He was also a renowned athlete in the French military.

He was astonished to be approached shortly before kick-off by a French official who recognised him. 'Quickly,' he said. 'One of our players has not turned up. Come into the changing room.'

Francquenelle borrowed some kit, was handed his first ever French national jersey and, when the originally chosen player finally arrived five minutes before the start, he was told his place had been given to another. Perhaps it was the very first example of that mysterious player often appearing on team sheets when no one quite knew who would finally make the team. A.N. Other.

Francquenelle did better than Anduran. France won 16-15 and their new recruit won two more caps, the last in 1913. He played at centre in all three internationals.

What is more, at the age of thirty he competed for France in the men's pole vault at the 1920 Summer Olympics, held at Antwerp, finishing tenth. He was later made a Knight of the Legion of Honour.

Francquenelle would have been just a boy, ten years old in 1900, when Paris staged the second Olympic Games.

Rugby was a part of it but there were some funny goings-on in all sports in those times. The Olympics was no exception. Some bright spark came up with the novel idea that live pigeons should be used in the shooting competition. A Belgian competitor is said to have shot twenty-one of them. Presumably he took them home and ate the lot for dinner for the rest of the week.

Perhaps not altogether surprisingly, it remains to this day the only Olympics where live animals or birds were slaughtered for the glory.

It is said they had to dissuade the organisers of the archery competition from hauling a few wild boar out of Versailles Forest to be used as target practice. Meanwhile, the marathon was a ramshackle affair. The course was poorly marked out and runners often got lost and had to double back on themselves before continuing.

Some doubtless popped into a café they were about to pass to ask directions.

'Excuse me, Monsieur, but am I going right for the Bois de Boulogne?'

'*Non*, Monsieur, you must go left for the Bois de Boulogne. But first, perhaps, Monsieur, *un petit cognac*?'

'*Ah oui, pourquoi pas.*'

And by the time the runner had emerged back on to the course, half a dozen French runners had slipped furtively past.

One American who finished fifth swore blind no one had passed him. Another Yank claimed he'd been run down by a cyclist as he made ground on some French runners. It all sounds like a sporting version of *Those Magnificent Men in Their Flying Machines*.

But French honour seemed to be satisfied when Michel Théato crossed the finish line and a band struck up with 'La Marseillaise'. However, later research revealed Théato was in fact a citizen of Luxembourg. Close but close enough?

Everything was all gloriously haphazard in those days, especially sporting contests. Take the 1900 Olympics rugby competition. Perhaps the Frenchman charged with refereeing the two games well knew the thin ice on which he was skating. Poor Monsieur Potter. He was on a hiding to nothing.

Only three teams participated: France, Germany and England. Alas, Germany against England was never played because the two teams could not stay in Paris for two whole weeks.

So the first game was vital: France v Germany. A replay of the 1870 encounter, maybe?

France won, 27-17, before 3500 spectators, because, it was alleged, Monsieur Potter kept on adding further time to allow France to catch up and pass the German score. On the website of the German Rugby Federation even an entire century later, the referee, long since dead and buried, was still being excoriated.

'France's match against Germany was, in the eyes of all the participants, and even of the French press and spectators, a scandal because of the incomprehensible decisions of the referee.

'While the Germans had reached half-time by demonstrating their superiority, the French referee whistled more and more incomprehensibly as the game progressed. The German team had indeed requested that an Englishman be appointed to referee this game, but their proposal was rejected. Thus the suspicion of bias never dissipated.'

Even the French had to concede that Monsieur Potter extended the game by about twenty minutes for whatever reasons.

No wonder the Germans enforced a rematch in 1914.

Two weeks later, the French met an England side that looked like robots. It turned out the Englishmen, who hailed from the Moseley Wanderers club, had played a match in Birmingham the previous day, travelled by coach through the night to reach Paris and arrived at six in the morning. France's 27-8 victory was not, therefore, the stuff of shocks.

It is said that 6000 spectators watched the match at the Vélodrome de Vincennes. Just imagine the fun, the colour and sense of occasion. Ladies in their long, flowing dresses, bonnets gently tied around the neck with silk ribbons, their soft skin sheltered from the sun by delicate umbrellas. The gentlemen in suits, starched collars, strong boots, top hats and boasting generous moustaches.

There were 594 people who paid two francs each for a seat, 3795 paid just fifty centimes and around 1600 got in for nothing. Shades of Biarritz and the 2021 Top 14 play-off decider just over a century later.

Monsieur Potter refereed the France v England game, too, prompting someone to observe caustically, 'Mr. Potter appears in the official photo of the French team... like virtually a friend of the family.'

But perhaps it just emphasised the point that Paris has always espoused a philosophy of fun and adventure.

They called it 'the most decadent city in the world'. Residents and visitors seemed to live on the edge. *Carpe diem* was most people's creed. It applies still to this day, albeit to a lesser degree. Whoever you are, you can find yourself caught up in madcap activities that would never occur elsewhere. Just ask legions of visiting rugby supporters who have spent weekends there.

For example, I once physically picked up a car in Paris. Well, it seemed the logical thing to do. It was in the way; my friends and I were late for a dinner booking and there was nowhere else to park on a busy Saturday night in the city. We spotted one of those old Citroën 2CVs in a space perfect for us. Of course, it helped that I had a couple of rugby pals with me, one a burly second-row forward from New Zealand.

He, along with an Australian mate from Sydney's famous Randwick club who was with us and myself lifted the car from the front, rolled it on its back wheels onto a piece of scrub ground – and parked ours. Then we went off to dinner.

I mean, I've never done that in London or Sydney. Why Paris?

Talking of cars, the Parisian traffic was either a nightmare or a challenge, depending upon your philosophy. I subscribed to the latter which meant all sorts of fun and games on the roads of the capital.

I remember once accepting a small bet from a working colleague that I couldn't make three complete circuits in my car of the Arc de Triomphe at some point of the evening rush hour inside ninety seconds. Now this was an unwise challenge on his part for three reasons. The first was that the car was a Renault 17 Gordini convertible, with a turbo system fitted at the old Gordini factory outside Paris.

It was a time when designers were instrumental in producing cars. Especially classic French cars, like the Alpine Renault, Renault Gordini and Citroën DS. Nowadays, accountants make cars the world over.

When the turbo was finely tuned, it went like the wind. When it was out of sync, stuck in heavy traffic, it spluttered like an old dog. On this occasion, it was hot, having just swept down from the Channel coast. Secondly, I was the driver. Strong men were known to have turned a sickly grey after being subjected to a normal journey at the hands of this pace addict. Especially with Fleetwood Mac's iconic anthem 'The Chain' blasting out of the German-made Becker music system on board in the late 1970s. It was liberation personified.

Thirdly, I had a pretty good idea of the best way of doing it. Namely, blast your horn at anyone within 10 metres, get into the centre and hug the kerb nearest to the famous arch. Then just put your foot down. I don't know about now, but in those days the majority of the traffic tended to be either just on the edges after joining the melee or in the middle.

There was no disputing it was a close-run thing. His shaking hands and unsteady stride when I eventually stopped the vehicle to let him out told you as much.

Contrast all this with the present day. In July 2021, the Socialist mayor of Paris, Anne Hidalgo, announced that she was imposing a speed limit for almost all of the Paris region of 30 kilometres per hour. A centre-right councillor called the new speed limit 'brutal'. I call it a passion killer.

Back in 1970, I had embarked upon my first madcap journey to the French capital, this time by train *pour le rugby weekend*. Truth be told, this was a trip with a combined intent. A first visit to the famous Stade Colombes for a France-England game and a first weekend in Europe with a new love.

L'affaire could not have been set for a better location. The trouble was, getting there.

A delayed boat meant a missed train from the Channel coast and a missed visit to the patisserie. Alas, in those days, the notion of buying food on French trains was about as fanciful an idea as, in contemporary times, expecting luxury service from Ryanair.

So as the train rumbled through northern France, two stomachs rumbled in concert. I resolved to my companion to do something about it the moment the train stopped. It screeched to a halt in Amiens and a door was flung open. A character could be seen sprinting up the platform to the barrier, and then exiting the station. I wasn't acting entirely on impulse: I had been told the train would stop for ten minutes.

In those days, some railway worker had to walk up and down the length of the train with a metal pole at the major stations, tapping and clunking the wheels, presumably to make sure they had not come loose on the low-speed journey from the coast.

My own task was straightforward. Buy two baguettes and a couple of pains au chocolat at a patisserie in the square close by the station and nip back to the platform inside ten minutes. Someone on one leg could surely manage that.

But then the problems started.

There was a patisserie but there were half a dozen people queueing for their bread. I hopped from one foot to the other as the queue gradually whittled down. In commanding schoolboy French, I ordered, and was astonished when the lady required a repeat. Was she deaf? Or just dim? Or totally unaware that the clock was ticking.

Relatively quickly, two bags were put on the till. Followed by calamity. I offered a 100 Franc note (that tells you how long ago this was) to which she responded with that time-honoured French expression, '*Ooh la-la.*'

She had no change, but next door would have. With that, and clutching my 100 franc note, she walked out of the shop.

By now, a hammering was going on inside my brain. It was a clock and every passing second felt like a crash. With nine minutes gone, she reappeared. Smiling. Honestly, I ask you. Who had time for smiles?

I snatched the two bags, clutched the fistful of notes and change and fled back to the station. A downward slope to the platforms catapulted a slow 100 yards runner into an Olympic sprinter. Alas, calamity appeared. The train was already on the move, on its way out of the station, and gradually picking up speed.

I looked up briefly and saw a figure wrestling with a door right at the back to try and keep it open. At least my girlfriend had not yet given up on me. But the forces of increasing speed and air made her task difficult. Nevertheless, I spied the gap and raced towards it. I made a head-first dive into it, crashing into a combination of the door frame, my girlfriend, two pains au chocolat and two baguettes. Ham and cheese. I ended up on the floor.

She helped haul me up and gave me a relieved hug as we departed for Paris.

Alas, some of the goods had clearly been damaged in my dive. I opened the bag to find two pains au chocolat looking like an elephant had sat on them.

* * *

Madcap men doing crazy things? Take the case of a certain Damian Cronin, Scottish rugby player par excellence from 1988 to 1998, but in the elite class entitled 'pranksters', a man without peer.

In 1995, Scotland won for the only time ever at the Parc des Princes, beating France with a pulsating last-minute try by their inspirational captain Gavin Hastings. Even Englishmen in the ground, emotions twisted like meat on a skewer, stood and roared their approval at this climax to a stirring international match. The night, the city belonged to Scotland. What a night it would be.

By glorious coincidence, Hastings had sought out Cronin earlier that week. He told him he wanted to deliver his post-match speech in French and Cronin, by then playing his rugby with the French club Bourges, was the ideal man to help.

To place such faith on any prankster may seem unwise. In the case of Cronin, it was downright perilous. After the usual niceties and pleasantries (of those days) at the official dinner, Scotland's smiling captain stood up, unfurled his notes and launched into an inspiring speech in the local tongue. Initially, the French beamed with delight. They love it when foreigners try to speak their language.

Alas, it wasn't so much the attempt at parleying with the natives which took the speech dramatically off course, but the actual content. What Cronin had written was an increasingly revealing portrayal of what his captain, in the privacy of his own bedroom, had got up to with his wife in the time between the match ending and the start of the dinner. A sort of blow-by-blow account, you might say.

Suddenly shocked female faces, with hands hastily covering up their mouths, ought to have conveyed instant alarm to the speaker, not to mention a few gasps here and there. But Hastings, a non-French speaker, smiled and ploughed on regardless, the intricate, intimate details delivered with a trademark grin. Cronin, meanwhile, sat at a table hardly able to hold himself together.

'Well,' he said twenty-five years later, 'it was his own fault, wasn't it? He must have been dead naive to say all that when he didn't have a clue what the words meant.'

Poor Gavin.

Another esteemed rugby man with French connections and a similarly devious sense of humour to Cronin was the late England lock forward Maurice Colclough. He, too, loved his rugby trips to Paris.

Dubbed the 'Marquis de Colclough' after he had joined the Angoulême club in south-west France, Colclough was notorious for his practical joke at a France v England dinner in 1982, when he emptied a miniature bottle of after shave (gifted to each player) into an ice bucket and refilled it with water.

By making something of a show to his England colleague Colin Smart, a prop forward, by downing the apparent original contents, he clearly invited Smart to do likewise. Alas, the prop had not emptied his bottle and replaced it with water. He downed the liquid and was immediately convulsed in pains and rushed to hospital where he spent the night. Colclough's humour hardly knew a finer day... unless you considered 1986 and England's visit to Paris.

England had a young No. 8 forward who had made a sensational start to his international career by scoring two tries in a victory over Ireland in the previous match. His name was Dean Richards and after what he called 'a dream debut' at Twickenham two weeks earlier, the young Leicester forward was excited to fly to Paris with the England team chasing the outright win which would give them that season's Five Nations Championship.

England didn't win; they got thrashed 29-10. But Richards admitted later he was just relieved to be alive when kick-off arrived. Why?

'Deano', as he was universally known, wrote later, 'I counted myself lucky just to get on the pitch for the game (at the Parc des Princes). We had arrived at the Trianon Palace hotel in Versailles and I was allocated a room with Maurice Colclough. He was a wily old bird. He and I were given a room right up in the attic. When we got there, Maurice opened the window and said, 'It's interesting here. They don't have guttering as such; it's like a walkway, a path. You can actually get along it from one room to another.'

'So, like a fool, the naive youngster from Leicester stepped out of the window and started to walk along this precarious ledge. The view when I looked over the parapet was a sight to behold. Louis the Sun King's famous Palace stretched away beneath me across the square, which was all very fine – until I suddenly twigged what was going on and looked back towards the window to see the Marquis closing it behind me.

'I was stuck out on some dodgy roof, 100 feet up in the air, and with not a thing to break my fall. I suppose I was out there for about ten minutes, nonchalantly admiring the magnificent view with trepidation in my heart, until one of the other lads let me in. When I got back, old Maurice was chuckling away to himself.'

* * *

Sharing fun with your friends. Well, the French would know about that from their long love affair with rugby.

Whatever its origins and wherever it was played, what has always appealed to them about this game was that it could be played together with friends. It was a team game and ensured that local pride would be won with victory. It would probably involve many or indeed most of the men of those places.

Thus, two burly farmers packing down in the front row might have the head of a gangly student thrust between their thighs at the scrummage. On matchday, *le patron* at the local café served not his customers but his outside half, from the scrum-half berth.

Nowhere epitomised this diversity of approach better than at the Racing Club de France, in Paris. The founders of this legendary club, rich in *joie de vivre* and style still to this day, established something that was a whole lot more than just a rugby club.

Today, the club has an estimated 20,000 members and offers seventeen different sports. Its golf course in the Bois de Boulogne is sumptuous. So, too, the full-sized swimming pools at the club. It has come a long, long way from its earliest incarnation. Yet there is a link between those earliest days and contemporary times. That link is wrapped up in the sporting philosophies that were at the heart of the game when it was first introduced into France.

Down the years, French teams at all levels have demonstrated that philosophy; one of fun, playing for pleasure as well as pride. And of all those who have graced this great game through the decades, two past players perhaps demonstrated better than most the importance of those qualities.

Jean-Pierre Rives and Franck Mesnel.

51

Both became renowned French internationals. But far more appropriate to this story, both typified a certain mentality concerning the sport that fitted perfectly the aspirations of its founders. Both played the game for the right reasons – pleasure, spirit, comradeship, pride and a sense of fun.

The French adored Rives, still do, for a certain *je ne sais quoi*. He was always humble, approachable. He listened to and cared for others. He was courteous, had a wry, ready smile and never seemed to take anything in life too seriously. Always he revelled in the company of his friends. These were some of the qualities that underpinned the game all the way back to its origins. His Corinthian spirit seemed to fit the sport he embraced so elegantly. Indeed, such values which still exist in the modern game, albeit mainly at the amateur level these days, remain ones to envy.

Two stories concerning both men from past times tell much of their character. One autumn afternoon in 1985, I found myself sitting in a chic apartment in the République area of Paris. Opposite me sat Rives, recently retired captain of the French national team. By then, Rives had become a legend in French sporting circles. Born in the Toulouse suburb of Saint Simon on New Year's Eve 1952, he had proved himself an inspirational leader at loose forward, renowned for the cuts which he so often incurred at the bottom of a ruck that sent blood streaming from his head into his long, blond hair. At 1.77m and 84kgs, Rives was hardly an imposing physical figure. But he had an energy, a nuggety determination and speed that made him superior to most opponents. Above all, he was utterly fearless.

He had enjoyed a spectacular career yet already his mind was straying to fresh fields far from rugby. Dredging up old tales from his rugby days had quickly become anathema to him, even for the biography of his career which he had asked me to write.

He yawned, yet the eyes twinkled as he suddenly announced, 'We must go. We have dinner tonight with a friend. In Geneva. We must catch the plane. Hurry. You drive.'

Of course, he had left it absurdly late to get to Charles de Gaulle airport. The late afternoon rush hour was nigh; streets were becoming clogged, queues forming. Extricating yourself from a Paris rush-hour traffic jam required the skills of Houdini, not an English sportswriter. But Rives urged me on.

A long queue at one set of lights was easily negotiated. I simply went up on the pavement and drove along it for about 50 metres to jump the queue. Rives sniffed. 'You are a crazy driver, just like the Parisians.'

I took it as a badge of honour.

Alas, a spectacularly ambitious shortcut took us not to the airport entrance but a farmer's field near the end of the runway. From where we watched our Air France jet to Geneva climb into the late afternoon sky.

In time, we reached the airport. All seemed lost. But when you travelled with the former captain of France, you soon came to understand that all things were possible. We once just walked into Roland Garros for an afternoon's tennis at the French Open. Literally, through the main entrance gate. Tickets? Passes? Please, be serious. Gate men were too busy genuflecting to concern themselves with such irrelevances.

Much the same happened now. With my help, Rives dragged not only an overnight bag but a huge golf bag with a full set of clubs up to the check-in desk. Under normal airline rules, even in those days, you had about as much chance of getting a golf bag full of clubs into the cabin as a barrel of real ale. But tiny details of that kind never bothered Jean-Pierre.

Having parked the clubs and our bags, I looked up to see a cosy scene unfolding at the check-in desk. Long blond hair (his) was brushed back into place as curly blonde locks (hers)

53

were shyly rearranged. This was like some pre-mating exercise and I knew the outcome. But it's not what you're thinking. She cooed and blushed and smiled as he shrugged and grinned. There could only be one outcome. Or rather two. Boarding passes for both of us on a new flight. Without charge. And the giant golf bag cleared as cabin baggage.

To general astonishment from fellow travellers, Jean-Pierre and I dragged two bags plus the golf clubs onto the next flight to Geneva.

The reason for it all? After an hour's drive into the hills, high above Lake Geneva, the lights twinkling below, our chauffeur pulled up beside *un petit auberge*. Inside we went to meet our dinner companion. Alain Prost, the then French F1 racing driver.

Rives once captained a French team that went to Bucharest to play Romania. On the day of their flight back to Paris, he was late. Nothing unusual in that. Except that when he finally appeared, his teammates were shocked. Rives turned up in a tattered T-shirt and pair of shorts. No shoes, jacket, tie or proper shirt in sight.

Mugged? Hung-over? No.

'Where are all your clothes?' asked a colleague.

'Oh, I gave them away. These people need clothes more than me.'

Which presumably means that, somewhere in Romania today, an old man is standing at his market stall, trying to sell a few tomatoes and bruised apples, wearing a French international rugby blazer. Not sure you could make that up.

He played most of his rugby for the great Stade Toulousain club. But when he became bored with too many predictable elements of life late in his playing days, he took himself off to Paris to play (briefly) for the Racing Club and share fun with his friends, especially his fellow French international Robert

Paparemborde. There, his elegance, in personality and style, fitted perfectly the Racing Club creed.

So, too, did Franck Mesnel's. Born at Neuilly-sur-Seine, just outside Paris, in 1961, Franck had a high IQ and a steely core. He could also play rugby football extremely well, whether it was at centre three-quarter or outside half where he often commanded a game with cool precision. He didn't have the quicksilver footwork of a Jo Maso or the searing pace of a Jean Gachassin. But a rugby team is a combination of skills and Mesnel brought a vision and control, both in the crucial number ten jersey and at number twelve. His efforts for the French national side at the first-ever Rugby World Cup, in Australia and New Zealand in 1987, very nearly took France to the title.

I knew well Franck's street-smart mentality from a single incident at an after-match dinner once in Bordeaux. Somehow, we found ourselves seated next to each other as the rugby men of France and Australia celebrated after the Test match earlier that day. I had flown from London to report the match and do a couple of interviews.

These being the days when alcohol was as essential to rugby men as a pair of boots and shorts, there was a minor stampede when the first wines were placed on the tables. Enormous hands grabbed the necks of the bottles, like farmers wringing their chickens' necks. I moved to secure a bottle for us to share but felt a cautioning hand on my sleeve.

'Not this one, Peter,' advised my expert oenologist.

Bewilderingly, he did the exact same thing when a new wine arrived with the next course. I sat back, puzzled. For by now, I was getting rather thirsty.

Then the third wine arrived. Like some grand chess master, Mesnel suddenly made his move, clinically and decisively. I noticed at once there were fewer of these, but Franck was not to be put off his task. Two bottles were secured in a single movement, one slipped adroitly under the table into his waiting bag. The other? He reached for two glasses and poured generously.

'I think you will like this one,' he smiled.

I did. Well, after all, it was a First Growth. And it was a French rugby dinner. They never stinted on those occasions.

In 1962, after France had beaten England 13-0 in that year's Five Nations Championship match at Colombes, the two captains, Michel Crauste and 'Budge' Rogers, resplendent in their black-tie ensemble, led their teams into the usual post-match banquet at a Central Paris hotel.

The menu was as follows:

Consommé Double Au Xérès

****

Paillettes Au Chester

****

Suprême de Sole Lutèce

****

Bas Rond De Pré Salé

Rôti à la Broche

Sa Garniture Bouquetière

****

Le Plateau de Fromages

****

Ananas Glace à l'Orientale

****

Petits Fours

And to wash it all down?

Riesling 1962

Château Batailley (Cru Classé de Pauillac 1962)

Champagne Taittinger Brut 1961

Café – Liqueurs

As for Franck Mesnel, well, he always had style written all over him. In 1990, at the French rugby final, Mesnel's Racing Club met Agen; chic Parisians against a cluster of toughened Agen farmers with noses as gnarly and bent as the branch of an old vine. Just to be sure they rubbed it in, Racing's backs wore pink bow ties and, at half-time, stayed on the pitch to be served champagne in crystal flutes from a silver tray, by a club official resplendent in shorts, rugby jersey and blazer, similarly with a pink bow tie at his throat.

Taking the proverbial?

The Agen farmers studied this act of derision and acted accordingly. As steam poured from their nostrils, the second half became one of the most brutal I ever witnessed. Faces were sometimes rearranged during the course of a single scrummage.

There were dramas aplenty in that final. On and off the field. Racing chose a South African-born prop, Murray Dawson, for the match, and by some strange coincidence, Dawson was engaged to Sylvie, sister of Agen front-row man Jean-Louis Tolot. You never expected harmony and goodwill among opposing front-row rugby men of those times. But what ensued was something else.

At some point, a scrum exploded into fighting, with Tolot nursing a smashed-up nose. Dawson was fingered as one of the possible miscreants, something not guaranteed to enhance family relations. That suspicion was confirmed at the end of

57

the match when Dawson walked out of the dressing room to meet up with Sylvie.

Now it was time for another kind of explosion. Blaming him for her brother's rearranged face, she screamed a special greeting for him. 'Go away, get lost. The marriage is off,' was the gist of it.

It took many months to restore family relations. But yes, they did eventually get married and have lived happily ever since. As has Tolot with his smashed-up nose.

As for Franck Mesnel, he triumphed on two fronts. Racing won the title, and his business, the Eden Park fashion company which he had founded with the pink bow tie as its emblem, received the attention intended.

Mesnel was clever because he was the first rugby man to launch so emblematic a clothing range allied to the sport, not just in France but worldwide. In time, it branched out to become a major fashion statement across France, Europe and the globe. It became hugely popular and, no doubt, profitable. After all, when Nike come calling to buy your business but you politely yet firmly decline, you have something going for you.

The clothing range remains innovative, beautifully designed and elegant. Somehow, Eden Park merged seamlessly with all the style of the Racing Club. Mesnel remained a source of inspiration, to those who played alongside him and others who worked for him.

Mesnel and his Racing colleague Jean-Baptiste Lafond once played a game for Racing in Bayonne wearing red berets as a tribute to the tradition of attacking play of the Basque club. Cute.

A single word is the key. Style. Somehow, men of rugby and Parisian life seem to exude that.

Yves Camdeborde is another example.

A former scrum half during his young days with a passion for rugby and good cooking, he left school at fourteen to pursue his dream of becoming a chef. In his youth, he trained in Paris at two of the most prestigious restaurants: the Ritz and the Hôtel de Crillon. The latter was so elegant, so upmarket that the Gestapo decided to live there during the Second World War. He also worked at restaurants like the famous La Marée and La Tour d'Argent.

In 1992, he acquired a restaurant called La Régalade in Paris's 14th arrondissement. It was almost out of the city, right at the end of one of the metro lines heading south, close by the Porte d'Orléans. Yet it hardly mattered. The hordes flocked as the master chef acquired a multitude of awards.

So transport your mind to a February night in the French capital. It is cold enough to snow and few passers-by loiter outside the cafés and restaurants. Along Avenue Jean Moulin, in the 14th arrondissement, outside La Régalade, a strange sight is to be seen.

Moving briskly from foot to foot in a vain attempt to repel the icy winds, four young men resplendent in blazers over fashionable rugby shirts are hanging around the restaurant. It is almost 10 p.m. yet they go nowhere. Alas, the restaurant interior is so crowded that they cannot even wait inside for a table.

Only the lights of the interior, splashed onto the wet pavement outside like dabs from an artist's canvas, offer some degree of comfort.

But Monsieur Camdeborde, a rugby devotee, and his staff are not oblivious to their plight. Amid the bustle at the bar, a silver salver appears. Four champagne flutes for the young men outside. Whatever you might think of French politicians, surly taxi drivers, market traders who can't add up when it comes to your change or ratty old men pushing in front of you at the bread queue, you simply have to concede one thing. The English don't do style like the French. On or off the rugby field.

One man very definitely blessed with style wasn't actually French. Pablo Picasso moved to France as early as 1904 and lived for a while in Paris before buying a base at Antibes, on the Mediterranean. Years later, Picasso was dining at a Parisian restaurant and used a white paper tablecloth to draw a sketch as he waited for his meal. The restaurant owner's eyes lit up.

'Can I keep it please?' he asked, adding that of course the meal was complimentary. Picasso finished the sketch and handed it to the owner. Alas, his expression changed.

'But you have not signed it,' he said to his famous guest. Picasso's reply was as *a point* as a perfectly cooked steak.

'But you promised me a meal, not the restaurant...'

* * *

William Shakespeare's slings and arrows of outrageous fortune found their target periodically against both the famous Paris-based rugby clubs, Racing Club and Stade Français, in the twentieth century.

Racing suffered relegation at the end of the 1995/96 season and, despite returning in 1998, were again relegated in 2000, no longer a member of the elite group in French rugby. How the mighty had fallen. As for Stade Français, their Parisian counterparts, the pain was worse. Champions of France eight times from 1893 to 1908, they then had to wait ninety years for their next title during which time they all but disappeared off the rugby map.

But both clubs found a saviour. Max Guazzini took charge at Stade in 1992 and saw the club become champions again in 1998, 2000, 2003, 2004, 2007 and 2015. It was an astonishing revival.

But Guazzini did so much more than just steer his club to French Championship titles. He transformed the entire thinking of rugby union per se. Once professionalism had arrived in 1995, hurriedly announced by a panicking International Rugby Board (IRB) at a hotel in Paris, the game sought to exploit new markets. It saw that it needed to become an attraction, a spectacle. That meant both on and off the field.

Of course, the old buffers who thought they ran the sport had long since been outmanoeuvred by some cunning players and dissenting countries. Like the French. They'd never had any time for the strict rules on amateurism. They saw all that as an outdated, devious approach of '*les Rosbifs*'.

For decades, they were not even paying lip service to them. In this so-called amateur game, players were being paid all over France, as we shall see. Throughout most of the southern hemisphere, too. There was nothing the crusty colonels who still thought they owned the game could do about it. Rugby's dinosaurs just had to die. The brandies hadn't run out but people's patience with a game that was living a lie certainly had.

So the old amateur game was officially dead, although the International Rugby Board (IRB) couldn't bring themselves to utter the dreaded word 'professional' when they made the announcement in August 1995 at the Ambassador Hotel on the Boulevard Haussmann in Paris. They simply said, 'We therefore announce that the game is now open.'

Open for business, they presumably meant. But most people were dumbstruck. What did it actually mean? What were the consequences? What had to happen?

One man knew. Max Guazzini. He had taken charge of Stade Français in 1992 and knew which way the wind was blowing. In no time at all, he would have his Stade team playing in garish pink shirts, some with images of Eleanor of Aquitaine all over them. Pink became the iconic colour of his club. Here was yet another Frenchman challenging convention.

In 2003, Guazzini's Stade Français beat Toulouse 32-18 in the French Championship final. Now these June nights normally had a rigidly structured schedule. Kick-off was never before 8.45 p.m., which meant the earliest the game concluded would be around 10.30. If there was extra time, add on half an hour. For those of us in the media seats, allow one hour afterwards for work and hope to catch a train before midnight from the Stade de France station, back to Gare du Nord.

Bed soon after? On nights like these? Don't be silly. With my young son, I found a taxi and directed the driver to the 11th arrondissement of the city. A superb restaurant, Le Vaudeville, awaited. We arrived at 12.20 to the astonishing sight of a restaurant completely full. God, I love that aspect of Paris life.

'*Un moment*,' advised the waiter. So I sipped a glass of champagne until a table became free. Eventually, we sat down to eat. At 0040. As you do.

Midway through the main course, my mobile rang. It was my French journalist pal, Serge, with an urgent message.

'Peter, where are you?'

'Eating dinner at Le Vaudeville with James.'

'But you must come to the Hotel de Ville. Stade Français are celebrating their victory and the media is invited.'

So sometime after 2 o'clock in the morning, we make our way across the city to the imposing, floodlit Hotel de Ville. This iconic Paris landmark is bathed in light. At the front, an enormous red carpet has been laid.

We ascend the huge stairway and wide-open double doors invite us into an enormous salon. There, on at least four long trestle tables, stand copious plates of *jambon*. It might have been a great night for the rugby men of Stade Français, but it's been a shocker for the pigs of the south-west, anywhere within the Jambon de Bayonne region.

When that lot is demolished, *confit de canard* with potatoes soaked in duck fat arrives, washed down with vats full of red wine. We depart sometime after 4 a.m. and manage about ninety minutes' sleep at the hotel before leaving for the Gare du Nord.

I can assure you, it wasn't a lively first Eurostar of the day that raced through northern France and under the sea to England...

Max Guazzini's generosity was matched by his innovation. One season, he selected an ordinary club home fixture against Toulouse and announced it would be staged at the Stade de France. Guazzini wanted to test the potential support of general Parisians for his project, people who were not hitherto rugby supporters. Stade Français's normal ground, the Stade Jean Bouin, held little more than 12,500; the Stade de France capacity was 80,000.

This was a bold gamble by Guazzini, ever the architect of enterprise. Hiring the Stade de France for a night is not cheap. But as ever, he had done his homework and pre-planned. He didn't just relocate a rugby match. He put on an enormous entertainment programme both before and after the game.

A great colourful spectacle unfolded prior to kick-off, with hundreds of children parading around the ground waving flags with lots of live music. It created a beautiful family atmosphere, for all over the stadium sat mums and dads, daughters and sons, entranced by the show.

Whether they were anticipating what happened next is doubtful. Into one corner of the field was wheeled an enormous wooden throne on a plinth. Standing beside the throne was a beautiful woman dressed head to toe in an exotic outfit. She was illuminated by a single spotlight, in a stadium of now total darkness.

As she was wheeled towards the centre of the pitch, a crescendo of music built. When the wooden structure reached the halfway line, the noise climaxed as both teams exploded on to the pitch to a background of flashing lights.

The lady in the centre of the field unfurled her outfit to reveal two curvaceous breasts not dissimilar in shape and size to well-inflated rugby balls. A most delightful spectacle for every red-blooded male anywhere in the place. Quite what the mums thought of it all is not recorded. But it proved one thing for sure. You now got a whole lot more than just a ham baguette at a French rugby game...

Immediately, she opened something else: a gold-coloured box from which she took the ball. Handing it to a player, she was wheeled back off the field and the game kicked off.

I think we can safely say that dear old Baron Coubertin's walrus moustache would have been on stilts by this stage.

When the game was over, we sat in the dark for ten minutes until a spectacular firework display lit up the night skies of northern Paris. Families simply loved it. A new kind of rugby had arrived in the French capital.

Max Guazzini never quite achieved his 80,000 capacity that night. The official crowd attendance was 79,779.

Jacky Lorenzetti would have nodded in approval at much of that. He didn't take charge at Racing Metro 92 until 2006. But the businessman of French-Swiss heritage, head of the multi-million-euro Foncia group, helped transform the fortunes of the Paris club.

Racing had not had to wait as long as Stade Français for another title. After their first successes which were repeated in 1900 and 1902, they won the coveted Bouclier de Brennus again in 1959 and 1990. But Lorenzetti soon made his elegant mark upon this famous old club.

His investment attracted some outstanding rugby players,

initially to the old crumbling Colombes stadium, but then to the 30,681 capacity Paris La Défense Arena which he built at a cost of €360 million. Chief among them was the New Zealand All Black Dan Carter who signed a three-year contract allegedly worth around €1 million per season. Lorenzetti's investment paid off when Carter helped Racing to the 2016 French Championship title.

It was an astonishing night. The match, against Toulon, was played at Barcelona Football Club's Camp Nou stadium because the Stade de France was hosting games for the soccer Euro 2016 competition.

Not that supporters were put off by having to travel to Spain. Toulon is much nearer to Barcelona than Paris. As for Racing, their fans hired planes, trains and anything else on wheels to get them to the Catalan capital. So, by the time kick-off arrived, 99,124 rugby fans had squeezed in. Even Barcelona soccer officials, well used to large crowds, were mightily impressed by this invasion. It was the highest attendance for any domestic rugby match anywhere in the entire history of the sport.

Racing were stunned when their scrum half Maxime Machenaud was sent off for a dangerous tackle, forcing them to play three-quarters of the game with only fourteen men. But masterminded by Carter, who directed the play superbly and also kicked five penalty goals, Racing somehow contained Toulon and then created scores of their own, winning 29-21. It was an astonishing success, on and off the field.

Irish rugby star Ronan O'Gara, by then an assistant coach of Racing, called it 'one of the greatest nights of my life'.

One of the delights of attending French matches such as these, and especially international games, is that you meet all manner of former players. They form an indelible part of the whole event.

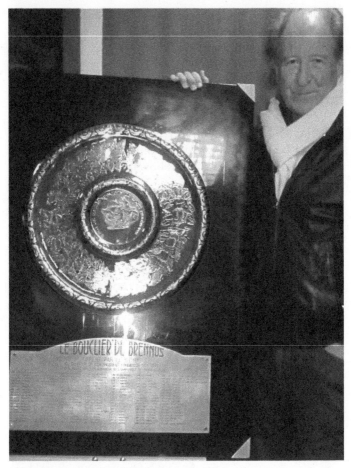

The author with the Bouclier de Brennus.

I long ago came to the conclusion that two particular categories of human beings enjoy primacy in the minds of most French people. One is former rugby players, the other is babies. When you can link the two for a specific purpose you hit the jackpot. The French simply love babies. They also revere their old rugby men.

Never was that so apparent as when Toulon hosted Stade Français early in the 2021/22 season. A trophy was contested, over both home and away games between the two, in memory of Christophe Dominici, the French World Cup wing who played for both clubs but died so tragically at the age of forty-eight.

The sensitivity with which French rugby remembers its lost ones is immensely touching. Before kick-off that night, Dominici was honoured, by family, friends and all rugby men and women. It was impossible not to be moved.

The connection between rugby football and family runs to the core of the French ethos. Both are quintessential elements of the culture of the nation.

I arrived with my family in Paris in February 1988 for a Five Nations match. Work to do, friends to see; favourite bars and restaurants to visit. Never enough time in the day with only twenty-four hours available. On matchday morning, we sought a spare ticket for my partner. Our ten-month-old daughter was making her first visit to the French capital.

A visit to Jean-Pierre Rives elicited the usual supreme hospitality. No ticket. But he had an idea.

No more than a fifteen-minute drive across the city was the restaurant of a friend. Ask him, he suggested.

Now Jean-Pierre Rives had, and doubtless still has, a great many friends in Paris. He knows some great restaurants, too. What he also knew was how to point you in the right direction. So we park the car, head inside and join a vast throng of people.

It definitely looks like the right place to be for an atmospheric pre-match meal. Maybe a ticket, too.

We explain who we are, who sent us and Madame smiles. Where no free tables seem to be, one appears for us. Madame has another plan, too. Sweeping up our baby daughter in her arms, she assures us they will feed the baby and we should relax and enjoy our lunch.

It turned out afterwards, in between flash frying vast entrecote steaks and doling out French fries on an industrial scale for the patrons, the chef found time to puree some vegetables and chicken. Just for Hannah, our ten-month old. Then, one of the waitresses was given the task of feeding her.

We sip a light wine, have lunch and are then reunited with our daughter. Seems like she didn't miss us at all.

Oh, and as we prepared to leave, Madame came up with another surprise. A ticket. My partner made it to the Parc des Princes, babe in arms.

* * *

They say the French love a party. Undeniably, Paris on a rugby weekend is a potpourri of action, colour, fun and excitement. The pace never slackens. You never know whom you will meet, what you will find. Like the night in 1989 when I arrived at the Champs-Élysées for a pre-dinner drinks reception, in the French team coach. To say this was unusual would be stretching credibility. Normally, it never happened.

But one man held the key to this bus, and it wasn't the driver. The following year, 1990, I would have a long weekend down in the Pyrenees in the home town of French coach Jacques Fouroux. He invited my wife and me to be his guests for the weekend, which took in the France v Romania match at Auch in the Gers region. Truly, a different man and a different world.

Jacques Fouroux could enrage, charm, delight and astonish you. All in the same day. Almost in the same conversation. Born in Auch in Gascony in 1947, the son of a fervent communist, Fouroux first played for Auch at seventeen. He was tiny, mini, at 1.63m and just 66kgs, but fiery. When he played, he was known as the 'little Corporal'. But his small frame hid a huge heart and zest for life. Fouroux won twenty-seven caps for France, twenty-two as captain. He led France to the 1977 Grand Slam and then coached them to the triumph in 1981 and 1987. He started his career at Auch, left for Cognac and La Voulte, but later returned to Auch. He simply loved the place and most of the locals loved him. A friend once said of him, 'He lived only for rugby. And he had one idea per minute. I remember him as an extremist, a passionate man.'

More of my weekend with him to come later in these pages. But that night, as I left the players' entrance at the Parc des Princes following interviews, a familiar voice called out.

'Peter, where do you go?'

I turned round to see Fouroux about to board the bus. The French players were already on board.

I told him I was heading for my hotel, but Jacques would have none of it. 'Come with us for drinks,' he said insistently. I'd finished work for the night and thought, 'Why not?'

So I clambered aboard. There were joyous players celebrating their win right down the coach, led in impromptu fashion by Fouroux. Outside, police outriders were blasting a path for us through the Paris Saturday evening rush-hour traffic. Sirens wailed as we roared down streets on the wrong side of the road. Parisians turned to stare at every junction.

I sat there bemused, observing this unique scene. It was like being caught up in a presidential cavalcade. But then, in a sense, Jacques Fouroux was presidential...

So now, here we are. The early evening lights of the elegant Champs-Élysées glow enticingly as the French team bus pulls up. Supporters crowd around; we file off the bus into a large entrance walkway beneath one of the buildings. I happen to cast a glance at the name on the brass plaque beside the door.

'Maison Moët & Chandon'.

So, I think to myself, this won't be too rough a do...

We take the elevator to the top floor and walk into an elegant, wood-panelled reception room. Any number of glasses are filled, on the table, waiting to be swept up and consumed. Through the French windows, we step out onto the terrace. There, laid before us, is night-time Paris, the Champs-Élysées directly below. To the left, we can see far down to the Place de la Concorde and beyond to the Louvre.

Waiters hover, all but desperate to top up our champagne flutes as we sip. Jacques Fouroux smiles like a crafty fox. But it is, above all else, an evening of elegance and vibrant French hospitality.

Former New Zealand All Blacks captain Graham Mourie discovered that world when he went to play in Paris back in the 1980s. He quickly learned about the extraordinary characters attached to the rugby scene. One was a rugby writer, a man apart from others. Jean Cormier lived in Paris but had a passion for rugby football and Cuba. Not necessarily in that order. He was a world authority on Che Guevara and he had a sense of humour as dry as a Chablis.

Mourie remembers, 'Jean had to go to Cuba once to do something about Guevara but before he left, he just said, "Stay at my house." So we did. It was on the Boulevard St Michel and we had a great time. He was a guy who would give you anything in the world if you wanted it.'

As with Jean-Pierre Rives and his clothes in Romania.

When Cormier finally retired, he put on the mother and father of all parties, to which his great friends were invited. They began at 5 o'clock in the afternoon, went through the evening and the night and arrived at breakfast time, ready for a reviving feed. That safely negotiated, they returned to the bar and drank their way through the day.

At 6 p.m. that evening, more food was called for and those still standing set off for another night's celebrations. It is said the last survivors finished at around midnight. Perhaps Che Guevara should have been among them.

Years earlier, Mourie had joined the Paris University Club (known universally as PUC, as in Puke). They were not playing the best teams in those days, still less today. These days, PUC like to style themselves one of the grand amateur clubs of the French capital. They even have a baby section for four- and five-year-olds. See what I mean about adoring babies?

But that notwithstanding, Mourie remembers one factor which burned deep into his soul. 'I don't think the passion for the game was any different, whatever the grade.'

He returned to Paris some while after his first trip and played for the Racing Club while working for Pernod in Paris. It was where he met Jean-Pierre Rives and the two became lifelong friends. 'We got on well and it was a real experience to spend time with him. We worked together for six months.'

The friends Mourie made in French rugby circles have lasted a lifetime. He still spends time with some of them whenever he is visiting Europe. They live all over France nowadays.

'The ability of rugby to introduce people and create friends is legendary, especially in France. My French friends have been amazingly loyal; they are wonderful people. The French culture is so different to our culture in New Zealand. There are so many unique experiences you can have in France.'

Former Australian World Cup-winning coach Bob Dwyer would subscribe to such sentiments after coaching Racing in 1995/96.

Dwyer was bemused by the laissez-faire attitude of some of the players in his squad. Not just the youngsters but some seasoned internationals, too.

Once, having sat down to select a team for a forthcoming match, he omitted one French international player because he had not turned up for training. Dwyer knew the player had an injury, a genuine one too. But he could not comprehend a senior player simply not turning up for an evening training session, even if he were injured. The Australian expected his players to attend. Whatever.

When Dwyer encountered his missing man twenty-four hours later, the tough Aussie coach put on an air of real concern for his player's welfare.

'How are you? Good to see you,' he exclaimed warmly.

The player smiled. *'Bon, bon – pas de problème.'*

Dwyer took one of the player's hands, gently examined it and said calmly, 'And how IS the hand? Is the injury better?'

The player was bewildered. *'Mais non*, Bob. It is my thigh that is injured.'

'Really?' shot back the coach. 'I thought it must be your hand. You were unable to call me last night to say you could not attend practice. It must be your hand that is injured...'

He made sure the player only got as far as the bench the following weekend.

* * *

Sadly, one experience no longer available to rugby men finding themselves in the French capital is to watch a match at the atmospheric Parc des Princes. The national team first played there in 1973 when the old Stade Colombes was finally consigned to history, in an international sense. By then, sections of the old terracing at Colombes were crumbling and unsafe, reducing the capacity to below 50,000. Weeds emerging everywhere from the cracked concrete mixed with the melancholy of the place.

Facilities for watching international sport at the ground in the second half of the twentieth century were, to put it bluntly, basic. The multitude of dressing rooms deep in the bowels of the old stadium (it had been built for the 1924 Olympics, thus the large number of different dressing areas) were an anachronism. They were dark, dingy and dirty.

Like watching an old friend confronting but failing that inevitable battle with age, it was sad to see it go. So many of the game's greatest names played here. And at times, France played rugby on this green sward to delight the gods. When the mood took them, most usually when a warm springtime Parisian sun shone on their backs, they played a version of this game beyond the imagination of most nations.

In that mood, there was a pizzazz, an intuitive step which captivated those who saw it. The flow in their game was more like a river in flood than a mere rugby team on manoeuvres. In two seasons, 1970 and 1972, the flying Frenchmen scored a collective seventy-two points to beat England, 35-13 in 1970 and 37-12 in 1972. They scored twelve tries against three in those two games alone.

But by the end of the 1972 season, a page had been turned in history. Colombes was silenced.

But they say every cloud has a silver lining. What replaced it was an extraordinary creation.

* * *

It is perfectly common, indeed even usual, for the living to visit battlegrounds from wars past. Or even just specific locations where blood has been spilled. This isn't being ghoulish, just respectful.

But it is rather more unusual to head for a sports stadium to commemorate such events. No matter, before we leave Paris and trace the footsteps south taken by those early rugby missionaries, there is one location in the capital where we should pay homage to battles fought.

In just 119 days, seventeen weeks to the day, from 19 October 1991 to 15 February 1992, France and England fought out two rugby matches that owed more to warfare than any sporting activity. Both were held at the iconic Parc des Princes ground in Paris's fashionable 16th arrondissement. They were two days when pugilists masquerading as rugby players hijacked the sport.

Agincourt, Crécy, Waterloo, Trafalgar? Mere Anglo-French skirmishes the lot of them compared to the two great battles of the famous Parc des Princes.

Should we have been surprised? Probably not. The French and the English have been snarling and snapping at each other since time immemorial.

They first staged sport (rugby, cycling and football) at what was initially called 'the Stade Vélodrome du Parc des Princes' way back in 1897. They used that stadium as the finish for cycling's Tour de France for decades.

It was called the 'Parc des Princes' because it was once a forested parkland where Louis XVI and his family used to hunt. Alas, come the revolution, the hunter became the hunted. The king lost his head in 1793. Even the wild boar in the forest, the *sanglier*, had less dramatic deaths than that.

A newer version of the Parc des Princes stadium was unveiled in 1932. But the one which captivated anyone who ever set foot in the place was opened in 1973. Some of the events that were to unfold in it were as dramatic as its design.

It cost up to 150 million francs and at those figures, you have to say it was worth every centime. I still cannot think of a stadium to match it anywhere in the world for atmosphere, even after a lifetime of sitting in such places. To the visiting player, it had almost a whiff of cordite, such was the hint of intimidation in the air.

To the visitor, it lifted the hairs on the back of the neck.

At France's rugby internationals, which were held there from 1973 to 1997, the innovative design helped create a unique atmosphere. It was the inspiration of the French architect Roger Taillibert and one of its proudest boasts was that no seat was more than 45 metres from the pitch.

Contrast that with the 'new' Twickenham where it's about a mile and a half from the playing arena to the top of the north stand. From up there, you can just about see people shopping in Richmond High Street. Players look more like figures from an L. S. Lowry painting, matchstick men more than rugby men.

The incomparable Parc, under which runs part of the Paris Périphérique, was described in French as a *caisse de resonnance*, which means a box of sound, due to the tight dimensions and the all-concrete enclosed area. It was also the first sports stadium to be built with a lighting system integrated into its roof. With its wrap-around seating on all four sides, it is regarded even today as an icon of French architecture.

Atmosphere? It had it pouring out of its gutters. There was more than a hint of the bullring about it and at full volume you couldn't hear yourself think. The sound rose and fell like an ocean wave even before kick-off. When a police band played a rousing 'La Marseillaise' and almost 48,000 voices joined in, it nearly brought the house down.

By this stage, with kick-off imminent, some of the French rugby forwards were in danger of a power overload. In true Gallic tradition to psych themselves up, they had bashed their heads against the dressing room walls or each other's nuts before even leaving the dressing room. This voltage surge of emotional stimulus sent some of them off their heads.

One of the delectations of the Parisian crowd was to let off firecrackers in the underground walkways of the stadium. In the narrow passageways with low ceilings, the concussive element was magnified. Analogies of battlegrounds did not seem so far-fetched at the instance of explosion.

Furthermore, it just so happened that France's national rugby team basked in a golden era most of the time whilst in residence at the famous Parc. With a team that had shrewdly amalgamated punishing forward power, physique and intimidation with Gallic dash, pace and invention behind the scrum, they won or shared the Five Nations title in 1981, 1983, 1986, 1987, 1988 and 1989.

There were three of the coveted *Grands Chelems*, the holy grail of the international game in the northern hemisphere, in 1977, 1981 and 1987.

They played a brand of rugby that took your breath away at times. Initially, flanker Jean-Pierre Rives led them with panache and considerable courage while full-back Serge Blanco ran such glittering, beautiful lines on the counterattack it seemed as if his boots barely kissed the turf as he glided on 50- or 60-metre runs downfield.

Others, the likes of Jean-Claude Skrela, Patrice Lagisquet, Jean-Baptiste Lafond, Franck Mesnel and Philippe Sella, complemented their leaders. Critically, they had a tight five set of forwards capable of mixing it in the darkest corners of any French port.

Later, 1.62m scrum half Jacques Fouroux drove his giant pack all over the field like a sheepdog pushing the flock.

This long record of supremacy did not go unnoticed across the Channel.

Which leads us on to arguably two of the most famous battles ever fought in the guise of rugby union. The Parc des Princes first hosted one of the quarter-finals in the 1991 Rugby World Cup which happened to be between France and England.

Tensions simmered every time an international match was played at the Parc. On this day, those tensions had been ramped up a few more notches by the prize of a World Cup semi-final place for the winners.

It was clear from the start a kind of Faustian pact had been sworn in the dressing rooms. Bodies would be willingly sacrificed. Physicality would know no bounds. Mayhem would inevitably ensue. The referee, Mr. David Bishop from New Zealand, hardly came from a rugby land of shrinking violets. Yet even he struggled to contain the violence.

England started it when their wing, Nigel Heslop – a serving police officer in everyday life, if you please – hit French full-back Serge Blanco long after he had caught a kick ahead. The outraged Blanco, having just had his lower teeth stuck back in and an arm reattached after being run over by the England forwards in another beasting, unleashed a volley of punches on Heslop, aided and abetted by abrasive French flanker Eric Champ.

Champ was a man who didn't so much breathe as smoulder. This set the scene perfectly for what was to follow.

Heslop, his lights punched out, was concussed but played on. It was that sort of game, those sorts of times. For sure, the blue touchpaper had been lit.

England's tactics were as plain as a roll-up cigarette paper. Wind up the French, get them excited. They did that and more. But then, these were not new tactics. After all, one Anglo-French squabble in the Middle Ages had lasted 100 years.

77

In one moment, Champ and England's mad barking dog of a forward, Mickey Skinner, squared up like boxers in a pre-fight press conference. Bristling, unshaven faces snarled less than a centimetre apart, eyeballs locked in like missiles. Skinner then smashed French No. 8 Marc Cécillon 10 metres backwards in a pounding tackle near the England line. Tackles of that magnitude deserved to be recorded on the Richter scale.

Skinner was the sort of fearless character who would face a field of bulls, round them up and barbecue the lot of them for dinner. Single-handed. He was a plain, uncomplicated northern lad who wasn't much good at minding his p's and q's. But if you wanted him to bring down a wall or dismantle an opposing rugby team, he was your man.

Fists flew, boots trod on delicate places. You felt bruised just sitting in the stand watching it.

England emerged, bashed, bruised yet unbowed. But to triumph, they'd almost had to match Henry V's brutality in slaughtering the French, up the road at Agincourt in northern France a few hundred years earlier.

Normally sane men can lose their minds in such moments. French coach Daniel Dubroca, by the end a human keg of dynamite just waiting to go off, greeted the final whistle and England's 19-10 victory by marching up to the referee in the dressing-room area and pinning him against the wall, snarling at his face and calling him a cheat.

It was a sad, ignominious end to his association with the national team. Dubroca had captained France at the 1987 Rugby World Cup, leading them to the final. He was a good man and he loved the game with a passion. But his wild, impetuous act four years later took him down resignation row. Even for an inherently decent man of rugby, there was no way back from that.

A wafer-thin seventeen weeks later, England returned to the Parc des Princes for the rematch in the Five Nations Championship. This was *Rocky II* on stilts. But if we thought the first bout was brutal, this one was even worse. The French looked so wound up when they emerged from the tunnel before the start it seemed like they'd been plugged into a mains socket for the last half hour.

Fists clenched, faces contorted, they were truly men psyched up and ready for war. Some appeared to have entered a parallel planet. But they'd learned nothing from the October encounter. England, meanwhile, just delivered more of the same.

Predictably, French indiscipline cascaded through the game like rainfall in a monsoon. This time it was an Irish referee, Stephen Hilditch, who was handed the gargantuan task of keeping the peace. Some chance. It would even have been beyond the powers of Henry Kissinger.

French prop Grégoire Lascubé was the first to go, sent off for stamping on the head of England lock Martin Bayfield. Soon after, volatile hooker Vincent Moscato followed him, for charging head-first into the scrum. Well, hookers do tend to put their heads first into a scrum. But having warned Moscato moments before for head-butting England prop Jeff Probyn, Hilditch had little alternative.

Mind you, Probyn had played a major role in the wind-up. Following the referee's warning to Moscato, Probyn allegedly smiled and winked at his adversary. It sent Moscato over the top.

The Parisian mob howled with injustice, baying for blood. It was the first time two players from the same team had been sent off in a Five Nations match. All the occasion had lacked was a boxing-type MC to introduce the combatants.

Lascubé and Moscato each received twenty-eight-week bans. Neither ever played for France again. But certain individual

England players, who had wound up the Frenchmen like devious horologists, were undoubtedly partly to blame. They escaped because they could, just about, control their emotions. Several French players, blinded by rage and frustration, could not.

But if the wily English felt this somehow enhanced the spectacle, they were misguided. It depended how you regarded rugby. France could play England off the park with the genius of the men in their backline. England knew that and understood that their best hopes lay up front with a big, cunning set of forwards. Plus their wind-up tactics. Nothing illegal in those of course. And you had to say, the French could only blame themselves for their over-reaction.

For those clad in the flag of St George, it might have been all that mattered. But some in English ranks were less than ecstatic. England might have won, handsomely at 31-13. But they put a size twelve boot into rugby's once-cherished values of fair play and sportsmanship.

As French coach Pierre Berbizier, a man with qualities fitted to the game he served in several capacities, reflected later, 'It adds nothing to their glory. In fact, it rather detracts from it. I can already picture the spitting and swearing the English have resorted to over the past few years.

'Surely they don't need that to prove they're better than the rest. They should be sufficiently confident by now not to have to abase themselves and the game of rugby like that.'

CHAPTER 3

The Journey South

Paris–Bourges–Vichy–Clermont-Ferrand

S o come with me now on the journey. The great journey south.

This will be a spectacular ride. As we head south, tracing the footsteps of the old rugby missionaries, those who spread the word of the great game in the early years of the twentieth century, we'll call in at some intriguing clubs. After visiting Bourges, Vichy and Clermont-Ferrand, we will track due south down the Rhône corridor, beside that mighty river, taking in a host of clubs of the region that were once household names in French rugby circles. The likes of Vienne, Grenoble, Carpentras, Romans, Valence and La Voulte.

Oh, and don't be misled into thinking the only clubs worth bothering with, or even watching, are solely in France's Top 14. A gold chest doling out riches that competition may be. But there is an increasing view in France that if you want to see real French rugby, the old-style stuff played with a passion and panache, albeit at a slightly lower level of technical excellence, then you head to the next level down, Pro D2. Or even lower than that.

In Pro D2 in the year 2022, you could find clubs with illustrious histories. The likes of Bayonne, Mont-de Marsan, Béziers, Grenoble, Narbonne, Agen and Carcassonne regularly used to supply players to the French international team. Many have won the coveted Bouclier de Brennus in their time: in one case, Béziers lifted the famous old trophy ten times in fourteen years, from 1971 to 1984.

Legends of the game. Then, even lower down than that, you will find clubs immortalised in the history of French rugby, such as Lourdes, Bagnères-de-Bigorre, Cahors, Dax, Tarbes, Nice, Nîmes and Graulhet.

The men of the Top 14, those crafty cockerels, would have you believe that the only serious rugby on show in France is their competition. It's true that the wealthy sponsors flock, fitness standards are exemplary, the contestants are built like brick outhouses, there is a glut of Pacific Island talent and any opponent getting hit by them will feel like he's lost an argument with a tank.

But is that the *real* rugby? Is that French rugby's true birthright? For make no mistake, at every single club, in each and every town, village or hamlet throughout this land, the flame of passion for this sport continues to burn brightly. The roots run as deep as those French plane trees (which can live to be 4000 years old) that line the old Route Nationale roads.

If watching enormous men flatten one another, seeing piles of bodies stacked up at every breakdown, and space so cruelly limited that you sometimes have the impression the game is being played on the back of a postage stamp, then take yourselves off to the likes of Bordeaux, Lyon, Clermont and Montpellier. For sure, you will find all these delectations for your pleasure.

Sometimes, whilst attending these games, I become a little confused. Is this French rugby or perhaps 'The Incredible Hulk' and his friends fighting their foes?

Pour moi? I confess, I am a rugby romanticist. Perhaps, these days, even a fantasist? The memory of such bejewelled occasions on French rugby grounds of the past stirs my soul. For to witness the kind of sublime skills over which you feel, at times, the French have exclusive ownership, is to know the joy of hearing a lark sing, perhaps a Sibelius symphony or the golden voice of a Gielgud or Burton. Simply incomparable.

I will tell you a small story on this theme. Back in 1985, when I came to understand that writing Jean-Pierre Rives's biography would be a nightmare if I had to rely solely on his memories – mentally, he had moved on from the game and was no longer really interested – I set off for a grand tour of France. To talk to all those who had known him so well, shared his ecstasies, suffered with him when defeat had all but broken him and his men.

One day on this trip, I drove into Perpignan on a Saturday morning. Headed, of course, for a local café.

On a wall close by was a poster – 'USAP (Perpignan) v. Stade Toulousain. 1500 hrs. Samedi'.

Its simplicity was rather like those rough posters they used to put up outside an athletics stadium in the 1920s or 1930s. 'England v Scotland. White City. Today, 1300 hrs'.

I queued outside the ground shortly before kick-off, bought a ticket and sat down. Within moments, it was clear that one player, a spindly youth with a shock of tousled hair in the Toulouse back line, was performing at a level quite beyond many of his older colleagues and opponents. His poise was balletic, his hands as delicate as a surgeon's. He simply caressed the ball, smoothly accommodated its arrival and timed its departure exquisitely from his hands.

Yet when he kept the ball, there was a surge of speed that destroyed his opponents. He seemed almost jet-heeled by comparison to others.

Even amidst the hurly burly of onrushing opponents and physical confrontation, he offered almost a languid approach. He had, it appeared, time allotted to no other player. Which is, of course, the quintessential definition of true class.

I turned to a spectator beside me.

'Who is the number twelve?'

'Ah, it is a good one, *oui*? His name is Denis Charvet.'

At eighteen years of age, it was probably the first time someone from outside France had seen Charvet's youthful genius. It sent a frisson of excitement down my spine. A gem, a sparkling jewel, had been glimpsed that day. He would go on to become one of French rugby's most dangerous, most exciting centre three-quarters, winning twenty-three caps. It should have been many, many more.

But where did young Charvet first embrace the great game? At Cahors, his birthplace, where the local club was, in those times, among France's most renowned. Like many others, it has produced some outstanding players for the national team.

So how many more gems of the future may be lurking in the relative anonymity of League Pro D2 or even lower?

Furthermore, how many grounds at the levels below the Top 14 offer a more intimate, perhaps old-fashioned view of the play? They may lack a few of the swish facilities afforded by the likes of Stade Toulousain and Clermont Auvergne. Perhaps you cannot find an entrecote perfectly cooked and a soft Bordeaux, rich in the taste of the *terroir*, for your pre-match meal in the humble grandstand.

But at the lower levels, you can find an earthiness that speaks of rugby in the grand old days. It is an experience that takes you back a few decades, with *merguez* sausages stuffed into a

French baguette outside the ground for a pre-game snack and that familiar whiff of Gauloises in the grandstand. At the Top 14 grounds nowadays, especially in Paris, you're more likely to sniff expensive after shave.

Perhaps, too, in humbler surroundings, there will be the local church spire visible behind a grassy knoll at the open end of the ground. Rudimentary? Perhaps. Atmospheric? Manifestly. Characterful? For sure.

Then, when hostilities have concluded, when the home team's cauliflower-eared old loose-head prop has fitted his false teeth back into his sore mouth, when the Jack the Lad half-back has showered and met up with his waiting girlfriend and slipped a promising arm around her waist to draw her close, then all can repair to the local bar, a short walk down the road from the ground.

There, the tales of derring-do back in the day acquire a sheen long forgotten. Old lock forwards, their skin a leathery texture from days working in the sun-drenched fields of the South of France, sup their beers or sip a pastis before a team dinner and recount days of glory gone. And as the autumn evening gathers, the lights inside the bar twinkle with an allure impossible to ignore.

The picture, the mental photo that emerges, is to be found the length and breadth of this land. For rugby is ingrained in the French culture, and culture is an endemic part of the French DNA. It is in their soul.

So, systems check this bright, sunny morning. Do we have: a) Espressos/cafés all round? b) Pains au chocolat? c) Or croissants? And d) a full tank? Right, let's do it. Hit the road. Fortified by a delicious mouthful of pain au chocolat – the light pastry making it superb – I fire the engine.

Pains au chocolat, croissants and beignets, by the way, are all a Frenchman's delight. The trick is avoiding the over-cooked ones that taste like lumps of cardboard. When you get one with the lightest of pastry that simply crumbles and melts in the mouth, it's like floating heavenward.

The best pains au chocolat I've ever known were at a small café at Place du Peyrou opposite Denis Pardies' restaurant and bar, named La Fabrique, in Toulouse, close by Saint-Sernin church in the old part of the city. But then, Denis and Valerie run one of the most convivial restaurants in the city. A secret from tourists.

But not the locals. For you can talk rugby endlessly with Denis. He is the son of Guy Pardies, the scrum half of Agen in the late 1960s/early 1970s. He played for France once, in a midweek game on their tour of South Africa in 1971.

Denis and his brother Pierre also played, mostly in Italy where Guy coached after finishing playing. Pierre said, 'Rugby sticks to our personality. It generates team spirit, pugnacity, valour and courage.'

But I digress. We'll get back on to the Périphérique at Porte de Saint-Cloud, close by the Parc des Princes. We need the eighth exit heading east. The exit road we want is the Porte d'Italie, and then the A6/E15 and A77 due south towards Montargis and Nevers.

Of course, we could have stayed on the motorway south, almost all the way from the Périphérique. But I want to go this way, I'm not interested in the motorway this morning. Yet it is something of a diversion.

Why? I want to visit Bourges, an old commune nestling in France's Cher department on the junction of the Auron and Yèvre rivers. Bourges is famous for its art and architecture, especially a magnificent thirteenth-century Gothic cathedral. As for the town's rugby club, it always enjoyed the support of passionate local followers. But few had pretensions of grandeur at their little club. Moreover, in recent years, like many others around France, it has felt the need to address the issue of a merger.

Yet in 1994 and completely out of nowhere, the Bourges club suddenly signed a Scotland international and 1993 British & Irish Lion. This was a bit like Stow-on-the-Wold Rugby Club in Gloucestershire or Blaenavon in Wales announcing the signing of Welsh legend Alun Wyn Jones after the Lions tour of South Africa in 2021.

So far as anyone could remember, Bourges had never had an international player before. They'd had a fireman, a café owner, a tax employee and a butcher or two in their ranks. Probably a couple of black market operators during the years of occupation in the 1940s, too. But a Scotland international and a British & Irish Lion? Never.

What they got with Damian Cronin was the complete package. Cronin was never going to die wondering in life. He did many things but seldom convention. He played the game as a lock forward rather like that, in the same totally unconventional manner. Authority and rules were never his exactly favourite. He played his own way and lived his life in a similar vein.

Why did he go there, to a club not even in the top two divisions of French rugby at the time? As a Scotland international and Lion on the 1993 tour of New Zealand, he could just about have had his pick of the top French clubs. So he chose Bourges. Just to be different?

He told me the story years later. 'They got in touch with me, I didn't choose them. We arranged a meeting at Heathrow airport and then I went over there to have a look.'

What he did NOT find was a cabal of wealthy French internationals as prospective teammates, a crock of gold waiting to be paid into his bank account or an apartment worth millions as a token gift. But Cronin wasn't looking for that. He wanted to meet genuine people, wanted to feel the place would welcome

87

him and give him a fresh perspective on life. It didn't put him off in the slightest that they weren't a top club.

Having seen the place and met the people, he made his decision. He signed. 'Off I went, on this big adventure,' he said. What fun he had.

In 1993, rugby was still officially an amateur sport. Well, the fairies at the bottom of the garden at least thought it was. In truth, France had never really recognised it as an amateur sport, and the Welsh players had been smiling at talk of brown envelopes stuffed with cash for decades. One Welsh international of the period I interviewed in the 1980s openly told me he got most of the car park fees from his club. Meanwhile, the elderly gentlemen of the IRB continued to insist 'their' game was amateur. Of course it was...

Cronin quickly understood how it worked. 'There was a flat involved and a car and expenses. But I didn't care about the money.'

If he had, he'd have grabbed an offer from Pierre Berbizier, then coach of the Racing Club in Paris, who phoned him one day and asked if he would join the esteemed Paris club. Cronin's answer must have astonished the former French captain. 'I told him I didn't want to live in Paris. The life I had in Bourges was fantastic; it was just a very nice place to be.'

But what about the Scottish Rugby Union, doughty defenders to the last of the amateur faith who continued to select Cronin for their national side? 'No one ever asked me questions,' he smiled. No wonder the whole house soon collapsed on top of itself. Amateur rugby union was, by then, rotten to its core. The walls were cracking, the roof stoved in.

Living in France enabled Cronin to learn the language. He'd hated the subject at school but, in Bourges, it quickly became 'locked in my brain'. It took him eight months to master conversational French. But in the meantime, the wily Cronin would use it judiciously. If he didn't want to understand something he quickly had an excuse.

What he did understand was an opportunity. It came when Scotland asked him to attend a series of training weekends for the national squad up in Edinburgh. By then, he was starting to build a business in reclamation and his new life at Bourges meant he didn't have to go and borrow money from the bank. A big bonus.

'It wasn't like winning the lottery. The expenses were quite modest. But I met people from whom I could buy and sell and it enabled me to build the business.' With delicious irony, one of his most lucrative business arrangements of the time came courtesy of the dear old Scottish Rugby Union.

He'd had an agreement inserted in his contract with Bourges that he could return to Scotland for national training sessions whenever he was required. Bourges didn't mind; they were proud to see 'their' player called up by his national team.

Meanwhile, Cronin had found an outlet in the UK for quarry floor tiles, which were cheap to acquire in France. 'I used to load up the sponsored car in Bourges on a Friday with 600 tiles, drive north to Le Havre and catch the ferry to the English coast. I'd be there by 6 a.m. Saturday.'

His contact had a business in Devizes, Wiltshire, and Cronin headed off on the, er, slight diversion to the west. Having paid 10 pence per tile in France, he unloaded 600 of them, at £1 each. God knows what state the sponsored car's springs were in by then. No matter.

He collected the money, drove to Heathrow airport, parked the car and flew to Edinburgh ready for training on the Sunday morning. Monday, he would make the return trip.

At some point over the weekend, he presented his 'expenses' to the Scottish Rugby Union. Mileage from Bourges, France, to Heathrow airport and back (no one ever specified which route he should take so he assumed the Devizes diversion was OK), all at 41 pence per mile. The tile man was happy, the SRU seemed happy, Cronin was happy. What's not to like?

He achieved legendary status at Bourges following one Scotland international match of the era. Cronin knew his club was playing an important game twenty-four hours after the international at Murrayfield. So he finished the international, dashed off to get changed and rushed to Edinburgh airport. He caught the last flight to Paris, overnighted there and was in a car headed south for Bourges by early the next morning. Bruised and battered, for sure, but far from deterred.

He made it to Bourges by mid-morning, had a shower and changed, nursed a few bruises from the day before... and ran out among his teammates for the game that afternoon. They appreciated that at Bourges. Deeply appreciated it.

Mind you, he well knew what the toughest part of the international weekend would be. The Bourges game against some local rivals.

His first ever game for the club had been a local derby against Vierzon, the club 38 kilometres up the road. 'It was the biggest game we played because they were the nearest town. The whole game was just a fight. That is what French rugby was like in those times. A guy had his jaw broken in a fight. I think we had scored a try and were running back to our half when a guy from the opposition punched our try scorer from behind. It broke his jaw and cheekbone.'

Which triggered the bejaysus of a fight. 'A massive scrap,' Cronin called it. 'There was a lot of thuggery in those days. Why? That is the way they work. Rugby was always a proper working man's game. It wasn't like a gentleman's game which you had in the UK.

'I personally don't think the violence was generated in most cases by the players, but by the crowds. They could be vicious and there was a lot more fervour then.'

But he looks back these years later and smiles. 'The whole thing was such an enjoyable experience. I was young and stupid, but I met some special people. When I went back a year or so ago and found some of them, they hadn't changed at all. Still wonderful people. Great times, great friends. They offered amazing hospitality and friendship. It's people like that who make rugby what it is. There is nothing bad I could say about the whole experience.

'It was a little bit of the Wild West at the time. But then someone has got to be a pioneer.'

*   *   *

About 150 to 170 kilometres to the south-east from Bourges as the French cockerel flies (or at least, if it could) lies a town whose name once stained French honour. Vichy.

Now, just excuse me for a few minutes while I don suitable apparel for this task. Heavy duty outer protective coat, anti-explosive head protection and large, padded boots. You can't be too careful when you stray into a minefield such as this.

'Vichy' continues to evoke strong emotions throughout the land. It is now eighty-three years since Marshal Pétain did his grubby little deal with Adolf Hitler to administer what was laughingly called a 'Free Zone' in central southern France. 'Free' wasn't quite the feeling those brave resistants had when they operated anywhere in Vichy. 'Free' was definitely the last sensation the Jews felt inside the Vichy region as Pétain's violently anti-Semitic Milice hunted them down. French policemen working there completed the grisly task by driving them into cattle trucks for the nightmare journey to places like Ravensbrück and Auschwitz.

The memories are like an open wound that refuses to heal.

Take Vichy rugby club. Foremost on the introductory page of their modern-looking website in 2022 was a proud boast: 'Racing Club Vichy Rugby is living its 116th season.' Well, I am glad they told us that. Because you wouldn't be able to work it out from the website.

When I last checked, a variety of categories were offered near the top of that first page.

Reception/Club/Our teams/Partners/Shop.

It's terrific. You can shop online to your heart's content. You can buy an RC Vichy rugby bonnet, pompon cap, backpack, mug as well as T-shirts, polo shirts and rugby jerseys. You can also visit the rogues' gallery with mug shots of almost all the first team players.

But one thing you manifestly cannot do is learn anything about Vichy's history. It's like it has been entirely airbrushed out. I find that odd.

If the club is 'living its 116th season' then there's a fair chance it was around in the 1930s and 1940s. So what happened to the club in those painful decades? What were the club's links to Pétain's regime? Was it used by the authorities to pursue their agenda? If so, were there some in the club's ranks who resisted and paid the price of imprisonment or even death?

You can trawl through the archives of most French rugby clubs and you'll find extensive coverage of their past. I looked up the site of CS Vienne, champions of France in 1937 but these days very much a junior club. They had team pictures from 1900, details of every season and a superb all-round package documenting the successes and failures of their years.

At Vichy, it's like the club has no history. In 2022, they were in the Fédérale 2 league and they have a strong youth section doubtless aimed at feeding useful talent into the club's ranks for the future. But try and get on to their 'Archives' section and you're met with a blank page.

There IS a website with all the history you would expect of Vichy rugby club. After all, they've had some notable players in their ranks down the years, particularly Amédée Domenech, who was one of France's greatest ever players, winning fifty-two caps between 1954 and 1963, although many of them with Brive, his second club. But the name of that website is a familiar one. Wikipedia. Vichy's own website had next to nothing – apart from a mug and pompon cap.

But then, if this is a deliberate attempt to airbrush the past as if it never happened, the rugby club would not be the first organisation in Vichy to decide the past is best forgotten. You see, the Vichy government under Pétain saw rugby union as a political weapon. They were even playing rugby in the war years, when people were dying thanks in part to the role of the collaborationist regime.

What happened and how rugby union was used as a political weapon is an extraordinary story. By the start of 1931, France had met England twenty times in international matches and won just once, in 1927. By the time England journeyed to Stade Colombes in April 1931, a meeting of the Four Home Unions (England, Scotland, Wales and Ireland) had been held back in February, deciding that matches would no longer be played against France.

This related to two issues – the ongoing allegations of payment to players and violence in the French game. Their ire doubtless stirred by the realisation that this would be their last appearance in the Five Nations tournament for an unknown number of years, the French fought nobly at Colombes that day, winning 14-13. In fact, it would be their last match against England until 1947. In the intervening years, a great deal

93

happened and not just the obvious of the Second World War.

Rugby league began in France in 1934 and it made some startling early progress as union's fortunes declined, partly due to its isolation by the Home Unions. By 1939, the number of rugby union clubs in France had fallen from 891 in 1924, to 471. By then, too, clubs like Narbonne, Brive and Carcassonne had become league clubs.

Rugby league said of itself, 'This game is more open, quicker and more attractive.' They had a point.

In just five years, as union declined, rugby league grew from virtually nothing to 434 associations. The writing was on the wall for rugby union in France.

Also, by 1939, the French rugby league team had beaten England. Many of those who had played rugby union including some internationals watched league and became attracted by its preponderance of handling and running. There was altogether less kicking than in union. It soon became an alluring image.

What compounded the attraction of league was the ban on France's rugby union side. Thus, what began as a trickle of players changing codes became something of a floodtide. The rugby union authorities in France became alarmed.

So, too, once they had taken power in Vichy in 1940, did Pétain's regime. They brought an austere controlling conservatism to their region and part of that was wrapped up in something called 'morals and values'. Pétain and his associates regarded the Armistice with Germany of 22 June 1940 as a calamity brought about by a lack of morals and values in French society of that time. They bemoaned what they saw as a lack of moral fibre among young men, distracted by the years of excess between the wars.

Not for the first time, Pétain saw sport as a solution, believing that it was for moral as well as sporting development. Fitness, training and discipline were key ingredients of the activity, qualities Pétain revered and believed France would require to rebuild its shattered nation. Whenever the time came.

In fact, Pétain had been among the leading military men propounding the use of sport, rugby especially, as an antidote to what they saw as France's pusillanimity back in 1915. Word filtered down from the generals that, to fight most effectively in the First World War, France's young men needed toughening up, mentally and physically. The new game of rugby union was regarded as an ideal recruiting ground for young men with such qualities.

If you take time to ponder the figures from the Battle of Verdun in 1916, arguably France's most courageous fight in its history, you could surmise that the need to bolster French physicality and mental fortitude had paid off. In 303 days or just under forty-four weeks, French casualties amounted to almost 400,000 men. It was a grotesque slaughter. Yet the Germans suffered equally. Technically, historians say, it was a French victory. But at what cost?

Yet in 1940, Pétain's mantra went way deeper than that. The Vichy government announced that it was nationalising sport. Because it saw professional sport as a corruption, it decided to ban rugby league. Sport, it reasoned, was a powerful cultural force but it needed to be amateur to be useful to the government.

Pétain's regime did not want star players. It did not want to focus on the individual; rather, it wished to promote the values of teamwork, togetherness and unity. It wanted players to embody the state's agenda. In its eyes, amateur sport created a self-discipline which made for better people in their youth. It was felt they were less likely to be disgruntled, rebellious citizens.

Vichy was, quintessentially, a group of Frenchmen who wanted to live in the past. They wanted to go back to a rural-based society, a kind of agricultural utopia. The trouble was, they believed professional rugby stood for everything that was contrary to their own beliefs.

League was seen as more of a spectacle than union. But the Vichy government said it was impure because of its open payments. They said that rugby union had the purity of its origins.

Which, of course, completely overlooked the fact that union had apparently been paying its best players increasing sums of money. After all, it was those types of allegations that had led the Home Unions to ban France from the Five Nations. As for the violence which was becoming rampant in the French union game, Vichy said little.

It didn't bother the Vichy officials, many of whom coincidentally were men from the South in leading positions in rugby union, that their logic was warped. They believed the fate of France and rugby union were bound up together. Restoring the unity of rugby, ending the era of two versions of the game, was akin to restoring the unity of France. 'You cannot have two games in one sport,' was their creed.

As for moulding their young people in a particular physical and mental manner, this smacked more of the Hitler Youth and a 'Be strong to better serve' philosophy, than anything thought up by Frenchmen.

Nevertheless, rugby league was the only sport banned by the Vichy authorities. It was seen as a challenge to hierarchy, a challenge to deference. Vichy, forever insecure betwixt and between the Germans and the French, had a fear of the masses for they were seen as mainly rugby league types. In Vichy's eyes, rugby league had become too popular too quickly, there were too many crowds and too much money was involved. It needed shutting down.

Thus, a cluster of rugby union diehards persuaded the old Marshal to ban it. But he did even more than that. Rugby league's grounds were closed, assets stripped and the sport left empty. The owners of grounds asked by rugby league men to stage games of their version were warned by the rugby union diehards in Vichy that they would boycott that ground evermore if they agreed. Unsurprisingly, the threats worked.

Rugby league in France took a blow that still has consequences to this day. Meanwhile, rugby union was handed league's assets, both structurally and financially, which enabled it to grow rapidly as a game thereafter.

In parts of France and especially the South to this day, some continue to espouse the cause of rugby league. It's known now as *rugby à treize*. And although Vichy ended, swallowed by the Germans in August 1944 following the Allies' invasion of France, none of the money or assets seized from rugby league clubs was ever returned.

It hardly qualifies as France's finest hour.

* * *

Vichy rugby union club was never going to rule the roost in its region for one simple reason. Barely an hour's drive away, straight down the A71 road, lies Clermont-Ferrand, home to one of France's top clubs.

Sandwiched between two regional national parks, Livradois-Forez to the east and Millevaches en Limousin to the west on a chain of eighty ancient volcanoes and high up in the mountainous Auvergne, the city is famous for its Gothic cathedral of black lava stone. The building is so black it looks as though it has been ravaged by fire. Or left to withstand the damage of pollution down the centuries.

You can stand in the city's main square, the Place de Jaude and the mountains are close by. You can also study a very grand and famous statue of Vercingetorix, chieftain of the

Arverni, sitting astride a splendid warhorse and brandishing his sword. Just to make the great warrior feel he was truly at home, in 2010 when Clermont became champions of France for the first time in their 99-year history, some nut climbed the mighty statue and attached a supporter's flag to the very top. It must have been a perilous ascent.

But that's how closely integrated rugby union is to the history, heart and soul of this city.

Somehow, you sense at once a feeling of history in Clermont-Ferrand. There is too a feeling of distance and isolation, both from Paris and the Mediterranean, when you get there. But there is plenty of compensation to be found in the region's rich foods.

Milk, cream, cheese, dairy cattle, lots of meat – add on a plethora of wines and you get the picture. The people of Auvergne don't go hungry or thirsty. Wines were grown in the region from 50 BC and in the nineteenth century it was the third-largest wine-producing area in all of France. The wine plague of phylloxera wiped out countless numbers of its vineyards in the early twentieth century but times have improved once more.

The region's most famous cheese is Cantal which has been produced since the time of the Gauls. It was served to Louis XIV and was widely enjoyed at court. It is one of the oldest cheeses in France. Cantal Vieux, aged for up to twelve months, is the grandest Cantal of all. It is a delicious hard cheese, a little reminiscent of cheddar, which is made of raw cows' milk and contains a fat content of almost 50 per cent.

The French hack off chunks of it and eat it with their baguette, or put it into soups and salads, or a creamy cheese fondue.

Thus, we have two key cultural ingredients of great roots in French life – history plus cuisine. But there is another, especially pertinent to this region.

Soon after the turn of the century, as the new game of rugby union burst out across most of France, clubs were being set up in rapid succession. Stade Toulousain was founded in 1907, a club at Toulon just a year later, in 1908. A little earlier, in 1888, a new company had been established with its base at Clermont-Ferrand. It was called the Michelin tyre factory and was run by two brothers, André and Édouard, who had taken over a failing, ramshackle business of agricultural goods and farm equipment, upon the death of their grandfather. It was a propitious act.

Cycling was becoming increasingly popular in France and revolutionary tyres produced by Michelin saw the business boom. Then came the motoring age.

In 1900, the company produced the first Michelin Guide, designed to promote tourism in France on wheels (car and bike) and thereby grow the business further. Then, in 1911, Michelin decided to set up a sports club for its company employees. Its founder was Marcel Michelin, André's son, and was called AS Michelin. The name changed to AS Montferrandaise in 1919 and in 2004 it became Clermont Auvergne.

The Michelin business has been ploughing money into the town's famous rugby club ever since.

French rugby clubs have long since had their roots embedded deep among the local region or towns. Their life and times reflect the social swings and changes of fortune among the general society and population. Marcel Michelin, after whom the stadium was named, was a member of the resistance in Clermont during the Second World War.

Caught by the Gestapo, he was deported to Buchenwald concentration camp, together with his son, and died there in January 1945. He had been a passionate supporter of the Montferrand rugby team, and a player too. Two of his sons, Philippe and Hubert, served in the RAF during the war while another son, Jean-Pierre, was killed in Corsica during the liberation of the island in 1943. He was only twenty-five.

Tragedy has often seemed to stalk many great families of business success. It struck once again in 2006 when Édouard Michelin, great grandson of the original Édouard Michelin, was drowned off the Île de Sein, in Finistère. He was forty-two and had six children.

Before that, in 1976, another pall had fallen upon Montferrand when Jean-François Phliponeau, one of their players, was struck by lightning and killed on the pitch at the Marcel Michelin stadium. He was twenty-five and had played twice for the French national team, against Ireland and Wales, in 1973.

Clermont Auvergne and Stade Toulousain are the only clubs that have never lost their place in the top rank of French rugby. Yet Clermont's agony of near misses in pursuit of the French Championship title became notorious for almost seventy-five years. At times, it seemed doubtful whether even the country's greatest literary detective, Maigret, could unravel the mystery of why.

From 1936 to the start of 2010, AS Montferrand (and, from 2004, Clermont Auvergne) contested the final of the French Championship ten times. They lost every single one.

For so proud a rugby city, a club where passion is a byword for the game, this series of setbacks was hard to take. Imagine the scenes, then, when on 29 May 2010, Clermont returned to the Stade de France in Paris for a repeat of the 2009 final in which they had lost to Perpignan. This time, the gods smiled on Clermont. They lifted the elusive Bouclier de Brennus with a 19-6 win that sent the entire Auvergne region into raptures of joy.

Just to be sure it was for real, they returned in 2017 and beat Toulon 22-16. But they did lose further finals in 2015 and 2019.

I made a call across the world, to a home beside the beautiful Lake Taupo on New Zealand's north island, to speak to someone who knew better than most the emotional wringer the people of Auvergne went through in their pursuit of the holy grail.

Joe Schmidt, a professional rugby coach of significant talents who later went on to coach the Ireland national team and become a selector and then assistant coach for the New Zealand All Blacks, was captivated by the challenge of what he saw as 'a real rugby city'. The New Zealander became assistant coach to Vern Cotter at the French club in 2007 and helped take them to Paris for the final in 2008, against Toulouse, and 2009, against Perpignan.

They lost both matches and, as Schmidt said, there was no hiding when you failed at the final hurdle. 'You couldn't be anonymous there. There were approximately 300,000 people in the wider vicinity and although Clermont might have a small town feel to it, wherever you went you kept running into people you knew.'

Even when he went back, years later, and was sitting outside having a coffee in the town, people whom he knew ten years earlier would come up to him and want to talk rugby. In that regard, Clermont is that quintessential French rugby city; peopled with those who love the game and are desperate for their home club to succeed. Rugby is their culture. It is in their genes. A proper rugby city.

You will find this throughout France's great rugby towns and cities, the likes of Toulon, Toulouse, La Rochelle, Biarritz, Pau, Brive and so many others. The roots run deep into the soil. But perhaps Clermont Auvergne somehow leads them all for fortitude and passion for a club. Isolation, high up in the hills of the Massif Central, probably plays a role.

Australian Tim Lane saw it all at first hand. Today, Lane can look back and reflect on coaching stints at several French clubs: Lyon, Clermont, Toulon and Brive. But Clermont holds a special place in his heart. What was it that made the support for the club so special, I asked him?

'I think the Michelin tie-in is what makes it special. They told us that in days gone by, the workers at the Michelin factory would knock off when there was a game, walk across the road and watch the match. When the game was over they would go back to work. The town was built around that.'

In 2001, Lane came within a touch of becoming the first coach in the club's history to lead AS Montferrand to the glory of a French title. 'We beat Toulouse home and away that season but lost the final to them, 34-22. I think the weight of not winning a final was probably a factor at that time.'

Lane also has likely explanations for the intense focus of a club like Clermont for winning at home. 'Winning at home is all that matters in French rugby. It is the spirit it generates. The home crowd gives the team a lot of legs. They grow 2 metres tall from that.

'It is all about the pride of representing the town or city and the area.'

One day during his stay, Lane sensed a chance to do a deal with senior club officials. The players and coaching staff were worn out by excessively long coach journeys for away games. Sometimes, he said, the bus would arrive back in Clermont at 0400 or 0500 the morning after a game. That would kill them.

So Lane asked senior club officials if they would fund flights to the furthest away games. 'Win three games away from home and we'll give you a plane,' was the reply. When the wins were achieved, the club was as good as its word. 'We would fly on the morning of the game and fly home that night. It made an incredible difference,' said Lane.

He left after a year, lured away to join Harry Viljoen as an assistant coach of the Springboks. But even by then, the emotional ties to Clermont were strong. 'It was a hard thing to do and hindsight is a great thing. You sometimes make decisions but if you could change them, you would.'

He had a spell at Toulon as a consultant. It didn't quite work for him, or at Brive even though they beat Toulouse away while he was there. 'The night we won at Toulouse, they told me I was gone. The trouble is, most clubs don't have patience. Everyone wants success, especially from foreign coaches. It's a tough ask.'

Yet he still gets sent messages occasionally from Clermont people.

Even across the seas in Ireland, one distinguished player of yesteryear speaks warmly of Clermont and rugby's role in its strong local community. Tony Ward was an Ireland international, a British & Irish Lion in 1980 in South Africa and the outside half who drove his fellow Munster men to their famous victory over the 1982 New Zealand All Blacks in Limerick. Ward, now an acute observer of the rugby scene, admits a soft spot for a particular French club.

'I would dearly like to see Clermont win a European Cup because of the passion they bring with them. Also the way they play the game. They have an attacking intent and seek space on the field. They like to keep the ball alive.

'When they play like that in their Stade Michelin, the atmosphere in that ground is like Thomond Park in Limerick. It might seem impossible for a rugby club to come to prominence when they are so geographically isolated. Yet look what they have achieved. Furthermore, they are the type of club that looks to play rugby. Proper rugby.'

Victory at the ultimate hurdle, the final of European rugby's Champions Cup, has three times been cruelly dashed from Clermont's grasp. They finished runners-up in 2013, 2015 and 2017. It was their golden decade from 2010. But clubs like

Clermont attract widespread support in their region because they offer many varied attractions. It is not just the winning of tin cups that lures people. Comradeship, spirit, a shared sense of fun and excitement, the pleasure of vibrancy in their community and pride in their town or city. These are the elements, the values that draw people to clubs like Clermont with their strong community.

It certainly suited Joe Schmidt being there. 'I love that feel of community, I have always enjoyed that. Even as a coach, it was never them and us. Just all of us seeking the same outcome, success for the club. Within the rugby community there were really good relationships.'

He was astonished at what he saw from day one. 'I couldn't believe it when I first arrived. It was a bit like concert tickets. People would queue way down the street to get their tickets for the next match.'

Mind you, the wily Auvergnois are shrewd investors in their team. At one stage, in May 2014, Clermont had gone seventy-seven matches unbeaten at their Marcel Michelin stadium. Opposition players looked forward to a match there as much as a shocking hangover. The place had become a fortress, ended only when Castres beat them in the 2014 Championship knockout.

Yet here is the dichotomy about French clubs. Former South African wing Breyton Paulse joined Clermont Auvergne for the 2005/06 season. The Springbok thoroughly enjoyed his time with them but was mystified by a single aspect of life with a French club. It pertains, not just to Clermont, but almost all French clubs. It is an intriguing element of their DNA; almost, a defective gene, if you like.

Paulse explained, 'When we played at home, morale was always high. You saw a confidence in the players that was unshakeable. No one was going to come to our ground and beat us, they seemed to believe. Very few people did.

'But when we went away, the attitude was completely different. Sometimes, the players would seem to accept they wouldn't win that match. Worse still, they would go out on the field with that approach. It was bizarre. Because the next week when we had a home game, it was the same group of players but with a totally different attitude. There wasn't any doubt in their minds we'd win the home game.'

That attitude has almost been handed down through the decades in French rugby. It is weird. Quite often, some clubs virtually write off an away match, silently acknowledging they have no chance by picking a weakened team.

Paulse was always puzzled by this approach. But he learned to accommodate the ways and means of French rugby life. The long, sometimes eight-hour bus journeys to a town far away from Clermont could take their toll. But the Springbok remained philosophical. It was an experience, and one he wanted to savour.

Likewise Joe Schmidt. The New Zealander confirmed that team selection was often influenced by whether a match was home or away. 'It is a long season in France. So you did pick and choose when to play certain people.

'How do you win... or at least draw... seventy-seven consecutive games at home? That speaks of the *need* to win at home and the *want* to win away.'

The difference is subtle.

Besides, he said, it didn't happen all the time. 'The first year I was there we got ninety-six competition points and we had some special wins away from home. But I think at home there is a belief you *will* win.'

It returns to the issue of tribalism. Whatever might happen when you go away, at home you defend your territory (and by inference, local honour) like tigers.

Schmidt is a Kiwi so don't expect bleating about the

Clermont climate. Still, it does get very cold during the long winters high up in the mountains. 'It could get to minus 10 in the middle of winter. The first two years I was there were very cold. At one stage, we had snow on the ground for three weeks and had to train inside every day.'

Yet the quest for the holy grail, the French Championship title, continued. It was a dream they had been chasing since 1911. And although the workforce at the Michelin factory, close by the stadium, had declined from twenty to thirty thousand in its heyday to twelve to fifteen thousand today, the almost Messianic belief in Clermont's right to hold the famous Bouclier de Brennus never diluted.

Schmidt went on, 'That close link between the Michelin staff and the rugby team has very much stayed alive. They have a rugby museum now which is a fantastic experience. The town exudes rugby. People would put aside the whole day for everything around the game. It was like a series of rituals. They would meet for coffee, chat and have a drink. Then they would have lunch followed by the game.

'All this just for a humble club game. It was about so much more than just what went on on the pitch.'

Yet still, in 2009 after a second successive defeat in the final in Paris and a tenth overall final defeat, the hurt continued. They had recruited all manner of players, scouring the world for the men to drag the dreaded monkey off their backs. In 2007/08 it was the South African World Cup-winning captain, John Smit. Still, they couldn't do it.

Yet the support never wavered. As they returned in sadness from another failed night in Paris, this time in 2009, Schmidt was astonished to glimpse a sea of yellow awaiting the team's return. They estimated 30,000 had turned up to share the team's sadness, simply to say, 'We know the pain, we share it. Please, just keep going.'

Schmidt remembers turning to his fellow coach Vern Cotter and saying, 'Just imagine what it would be like, how many would turn out if we actually won it.'

Twelve months later, they got their answer. Victory in the 2010 final over Perpignan ended what so many supporters had come to regard as a curse. It led, said Schmidt, to one of the greatest nights of his life. He called it 'a seismic event'.

In Paris, the victorious players, coaches and officials repaired to a nightclub on the Champs-Élysées, emerging much later into the growing light of dawn. 'We got back to the hotel and managed about thirty minutes' sleep,' he remembered. 'We had to be up and away by 7.30 and caught the first train back to Clermont.'

Halfway home, the smiles and jokes suddenly stalled. The exhausted players had finally run out of steam. Except that, as they stumbled from the train in Clermont and made their way to an open-top bus for a tour of their city, the enormity of what they had done hit them.

Over 60,000 people lined the streets to welcome them home, most of them chanting and singing. Old men, unshaven at the early hour, their berets tilted to a favoured side on their heads, stood as proudly and erect as the years would allow, tears pouring down their cheeks. Children ran about excitedly; adults exuded the pride of conquerors.

For this wasn't just the rugby club's triumph, it was theirs collectively. Everyone knew the history, had shared the sadness and longed for the elixir of victory to touch their lips. Now it had and Clermont Auvergne wore its heart on its sleeve for many days and weeks to come. It is the way French rugby clubs become part of their entire communities.

Schmidt soon departed to take over at Leinster in Ireland. But he would never forget Clermont and the club of the Auvergne would never forget him. 'It was a special time in my life,' he said with a simplicity that went deep. 'When I first arrived, I didn't speak a word of French. By the time I left, both myself and my whole family were fluent. We made friends then who will stay friends for the rest of our lives. I just know that. These were special people.'

CHAPTER 4

The Lost Corridor

Strasbourg–Lille–Besançon–Dijon–Mâcon–La Voulte-sur-Rhône–Cavaillon–Nice

A Six Nations Rugby Grand Slam decider on a crisp, cold March afternoon...

Most of the UK, Europe and rugby followers around the globe wait with bated breath for the explosion of sound, colour and physicality.

Does it get any better than this?

Well, it's not strictly true to say everyone's interested. My friend is on the French motorway this sunny March morning, en route from the UK to a chalet near Megève, in the French Alps. His journey takes him close by Alsace. A region rich in restaurants, cafés and bars. The perfect place to settle down and watch the rugby.

A meal is perfectly possible. But the rugby?

'What rugby is thees,' says one bar owner, the TV dark and silent in the corner.

'*Non*, Monsieur, we have no rugby 'ere.'

It is the same everywhere he goes. My friend shrugs, pays for his *café* and gets back in the car. They don't know about rugby in this region. How strange.

For France's Alsace-Lorraine region has more than 13,000 square kilometres of territory. It has a population approaching 2 million and is more religious, more conservative than most other parts of France. You can do all sorts of things in this region: hiking, biking, walking, skiing, climbing, swimming, fishing. But manifestly what you cannot do, it seems, is go and watch a rugby match on TV in your local café or bar. Insufficient interest, presumably.

Mind you, there are compensating cultures in this part of France. Find a small town named Rethel in the French Ardennes region close to Épernay and you will be at the origin of one of France's most delicious dishes: *boudin blanc de Rethel*.

This is a white pudding sausage made from prime cuts of pork, pork fat, fresh eggs, milk and a blend of seasonings. Its origins go back to the seventeenth century. Typically, it is grilled and served with roasted or mashed potatoes and a glass of champagne. For added piquancy of flavour, cut up a couple of Granny Smith's apples, core and peel them and cook gently in a little cider, until soft.

Together with some lightly fried, cubed potatoes and a few sticks of broccoli, what better dish to taste for dinner after an afternoon's exertions on the rugby field...?

For rugby and cuisine go hand in hand in most regions of France. (Apart from Alsace, apparently.) They are fundamental struts of the life and culture of this country.

In the Ardèche, a club called RC Plats, on the Rhône near Valence, offered a 'Matinée Boudin' one Saturday in winter, featuring sausages, fricassee and *boudin* as a special event meal at lunchtime on matchday. It was hugely popular.

Such dishes might not appeal to everyone. But for the

adventurous rugby supporter finding him or herself anywhere in France, the choices are many and varied, whether you're watching the likes of Toulouse, La Rochelle or Pau or, from the lower levels, Mâcon, Bourges or Stade Niçois.

On the face of it, perhaps to outsiders, the game might not appear to exist to any serious extent in this eastern part of France. OK, maybe that's a bit of a generalisation. There are rugby clubs in Strasbourg, Épernay and Metz, to name just three centres. But you'd have to drive either 500 kilometres back to Paris or 500 kilometres south to Lyon to find a Top 14 professional club.

Take Rugby Club Strasbourg. In 1990, they were champions of France in Nationale 3 league, the first ever club from eastern France to win that title. Optimism abounded. A largely amateur club still, for sure. But hopes rose for the future.

In 2015 they were in Fédérale 1 with expectations of further upward progress. Season 2017/18 saw them in what was called the antechamber of Pro D2 league. Then it all fell apart.

The club was relegated to Fédérale 2 for 'administrative problems' and in 2019 it vanished, after a judicial liquidation.

A new club, Strasbourg Alsace Rugby, then emerged. But these events tell of the difficulties of rugby at a lower level in several parts of France.

The rise of Lille Rugby Club in the 2010s was seen as propitious for those in the French Fédération de Rugby (FFR) keen to expand their sport into north-eastern France. International matches had occasionally been awarded to Lille, an important industrial city with a population of just over 1 million in 2021. Indeed, in recent times, the semi-finals of the French Club Championship had been played in the city, another exercise in spreading the gospel.

Meanwhile, the club had made significant progress. Former Lourdes and France prop forward Michel Cremaschi, by then retired from playing, had joined the club to help coach. 'I went there because I like discovery. We went up several times – Fédérale 3, Fédérale 2, Fédérale 1, Pro D2.'

In season 2014/15 Lille seemed to have earned the right to prepare for a new season in Pro D2 league, one below the coveted Top 14.

But hope collapsed, like a pricked balloon. Allegations were made of financial improprieties at Lille involving as much as €1 million. Cremaschi explained, 'There was a financial problem with the president and the club just disappeared. It was a pity because at Lille there was potential and real public interest.

'It is a town which loves rugby. But they lacked a president who could take them forward. If one day they get a franchise, it could be a great team.'

The club appealed against its suspension. But their case was dismissed by French rugby's financial controllers. Quickly, the club filed for bankruptcy in March 2016 and less than a month later was liquidated.

Of course, it would be fatuous to say that rugby union has no presence, no roots or tradition, in eastern France. Olympique de Besançon Rugby, established partly by soldiers who were garrisoned in the town, were playing their first external match, against Dijon, as early as December 1904, the year of the club's creation.

They gathered to lay down the structures of this new club in a new sport, at the Café de la Bourse, in the Place de la Révolution. A splendid photo exists from the time, taken outside the café with a butcher's boy in serving apron, boldly looking at the photographer, among many men in the street, resplendent in jackets and boaters.

The words 'G. Chelon, Proprietaire' are on the bottom of the photo. It is of another day, another time.

Indeed, further south before you reach Lyon, you will find vibrant, ambitious junior rugby clubs, like Dijon, Mâcon and their ilk. By now, you have reached a region famous for one of the great glories of France. The Burgundy wine region.

For a real rugby and cultural experience, drive down the Rhône corridor headed for Mâcon, the town created capital of the Saône-et-Loire *départmente* in 1790, during the Revolution. The town derived its name from the wine grown in the vineyards close by.

AS Mâcon Rugby Club, 60 kilometres north of Lyon, was founded as early as 1909. Today, it plays in Fédérale 1, but has formulated a project entitled 'Horizon 2024' which aims to develop the club and its infrastructure with the target of reaching Pro D2 league, the stepping stone to the Top 14.

Now why would the visitor stop at a club like Mâcon? The answer is to see and feel *le vrai rugby français*. You can experience the real heartbeat of the game at a club like this. A visit is an experience. Of course, being in Burgundy, you're not likely to struggle for a decent meal or quality glass of wine after the game.

But before the match begins, drive less than 10 kilometres out of the town to the Domaine Perraud in the small hamlet of La Roche-Vineuse, where they make fabulous Burgundy wines, such as the Montagny Premier Cru, le Vieux Clocher. You can find vineyards off almost every junction of this part of France. But Domaine Perraud offers that alluring mix of friendship, knowledge, approachability and great wines. Properly chilled, their Montagny, rich and buttery, is exceptional.

Burgundy and its culture at its best.

* * *

Where on earth is Renoir when you need him?

Or maybe Manet or Monet. It's just that this iconic scene is so exquisite it deserves to be immortalised on canvas. Right here and now.

I've driven from Nice after an early morning start, wound along the Mediterranean and then struck due north up the A7 autoroute.

I'm heading for a little town called La Voulte-sur-Rhône. There, we will hear a wonderful rugby tale from a man at the heart of the triumph.

But the approach to little La Voulte is enchanting. A deep blue sky is reflected on to the mighty Rhône River as it flows south past the town. A long commercial barge chugs upstream, the bow creating little splashes of white like an Impressionist artist dabbing his canvas.

It is a September morning yet the sun is strong and warm here in the south. Like so many places, global warming is having a profound effect. Since 2003, the highest temperatures ever recorded have risen alarmingly: April 30.6°C, May 33.8°C, June 38.1°C, July 40°C, August 41.1°C and September 36.2°C.

The townspeople sip their mid-morning espressos or Ricard, the men digest the news from *Midi Olympique*, that unique, yellow-paged newspaper which is a twice-weekly bible for rugby men throughout this land. For it was here, in this town, where a quite extraordinary event occurred.

Only the old men can now remember the details. For it was more than half a century ago when little La Voulte became the toast of France. In 1970, they were crowned champions of France, an astonishing achievement for so small a town. No town of anything like a similar size in France has ever achieved anything like it in the half-century since. None ever will.

La Voulte is a town that time forgot. Geographically, it is virtually isolated. If you want to take an overseas flight somewhere prepare for a long drive. The nearest main airports are Lyon–Saint-Exupéry, 135 kilometres away to the north, or Marseille, 179 kilometres distant to the south.

As for a train, therein lies an oddity. I see the track with railway arches, rebuilt in pre-stressed concrete, after being destroyed by the retreating Germans in 1944. There is even a station. What's more, you can buy tickets at it. But you can't get a train because there are no passenger trains here in the Ardèche. There haven't been since 1973. Loriol-sur-Drôme, 5 kilometres away, is the nearest passenger line to La Voulte. Ardèche has been the only regional area of France to lack a passenger train service.

It struck me that the guy who sits in the ticket office at the station, selling the occasional ticket for a line that runs 5 kilometres away, has something of an interesting job. And if you have a train station ticket office with no passing trains for passengers in La Voulte, don't tell me that's the only one of its kind in the whole of France. There could be loads of them.

Imagine this man's working day. If he wants to have an extra half hour in bed in the morning, well, what's to stop him? 'Oh, hold on a minute. I've got that goods train coming through at 12 noon. Need to be there for that, to wave to the driver.'

What about lunchtimes? I mean, you could spend half the afternoon in the local restaurant. 'Another cognac, Monsieur?'

'*Ah oui, pourquoi-pas*. It is not so busy at work today.'

If you got a job like this, you could retire at forty. Or fifty. Who would know when you had permanently knocked off, I mean retired, rather than just going for a long, long lunch break. Or siesta.

My word, you've got to hand it to the French. They do know how to play the system.

In 2015, there was talk of reopening the line from Valence down to Avignon and therefore stopping at La Voulte. But the idea was postponed... until 2023 when SNCF revealed it was considering such a move.

For the last forty-nine years, only goods trains or trains engaged in maintenance on the line have rumbled through the town. There is even an automatic level crossing. But you have not been able to find any passenger trains, no matter how long you waited.

Sophistication? La Voulte wouldn't know it if it saw it. Style? Not in this part of France. Vibrancy? No. The gently flowing waters of the nearby Rhône would offer more movement and turbulence.

Yet those old enough to remember, recall a time when sleepy La Voulte rocked with excitement. In 2018, the population of this small hamlet set beside the river was 4918. Back in 1970, it was just under 6000. Hence the incredulity that spread across this nation when La Voulte lifted the famous Bouclier de Brennus of 1970 after squeezing out a 3-0 victory over AS Montferrand in the French Championship final.

Grown men shook with emotion that day at the conclusion of the final in Toulouse's Municipal Stadium. Thirty-five thousand people had attended, a thousand or two from La Voulte itself. They'd clambered on board a few hired buses that morning for the near 450-kilometre journey to the famous city known as 'La Ville Rose'. Few motorways in those days; they would have gone through some of the great rugby towns on the way, like Narbonne and Béziers. Clubs much bigger and grander than La Voulte. But they had failed to make the final that year.

La Voulte had built their success on two ingredients. One was a strong pack of forwards, always a basic requirement for success in the French game. The other was a pair of brothers, Lilian and Guy Camberabero. They called them the 'imps' of La Voulte.

La Voulte's 1970 French Championship winning team.

If you just glanced at them, there wasn't much to see of either man. Guy, the outside half, was 1.7m tall; Lilian stood 1.62m in his cotton socks. Each weighed 64kgs, which is about the weight of a modern-day player's arms and legs. But each possessed an attribute that was priceless. Scrum half Lilian had a pass so fast, flat and long that his brother on the other end of it could have taken a sip of his *café*, carefully put it down and still be ready to catch the ball. Meanwhile, the only way to imagine how so slight a figure as Guy was so powerful a kicker of a ball, both in general play but especially to goal, was to believe that he must have had steel cables instead of tendons inside his legs.

When the pair tried to lift the heavy, solid wood Bouclier de Brennus shield, it threatened to crash down on their heads.

Together, the tiny twosome drove La Voulte to the 1970 final, eliminating along the way some of the great clubs of the day: Bayonne, Graulhet, Brive, Agen and, in the final, Montferrand. The greatest irony was the only score of the final was a try by centre Renaud Vialar. Guy Camberabero, their points scoring machine, missed the conversion and did not land a single penalty. Still, it was enough.

117

LE COQ

As one English sportswriter, Michael Melford of London's *Daily Telegraph* said of Guy, 'Unlike most French fly halves, he appears to pass the ball only as a last resort, when he doesn't have time to kick.'

In La Voulte, the men who gained sporting immortality for their tiny town are revered to this day. On a wall inside the *mairie*, in the office of Jean Alcalde, president of an association of the sporting life of La Voulte, is a simple photograph. It was taken in 2020 and shows a group, perhaps nine in all, of old men. These were the survivors of La Voulte's champion team from half a century earlier.

They had come together to celebrate the 50th anniversary of their triumph. Sadly, Covid had wrecked plans for a grand celebration. So there they stand, some a little stooped by the passing years, others, how do you say, follicly challenged. Yet there was, too, almost a discernible light in the faces of these survivors, a glow of pride and pleasure at their lifelong memories.

Lilian Camberabero sadly passed away in 2015 at the age of seventy-eight. But his brother lives on, his mind and memory as sharp as the morning sunlight that dapples the town square.

To find him, we need a guide. Monsieur Alcalde. He's no spring chicken, but hanging on to his back wheels as he swings his car around the lanes and up the hills behind the town, takes some doing. There are more twists along this road than at Spaghetti Junction. The road meanders through little villages, up and down and around sharp bends, until we lose sight of the flowers in the back gardens and see open fields.

In time, we go through a gate and climb a steep approach path to a solid brick-and-timber house of good proportions.

Flanked by his daughter's two collie dogs, he comes to meet me and shake my hand, a smile lighting up his whole face.

118

Monsieur Guy Camberabero. Eighty-five years young yet still nimble and upstanding. And ready to offer his memories of those times so, so long ago.

I notice first the eyes. They're not the eyes of an old man, tired of life. They're bright, they broaden with expression, they dart here and there, taking in his inquisitors at one moment and then casting around the room. His rugby mementoes adorn the walls, stand proud on a table and close by the fireplace. Here is a real man of rugby, a rugby man to behold.

Monsieur and Madame Camberabero, with the author, at their home near La Voulte-sur-Rhône.

His era, from the 1960s through to 1970 when La Voulte were champions, was unique. By then, the brothers had helped France to her first Grand Slam, in 1968. The nation had waited more than half a century for that honour to be bestowed.

But which, I asked him, was the triumph he most revered: the 1968 French Grand Slam or the 1970 French club title? He puffed out his cheeks in temporary bemusement at such a notion. The question was absurd, his expression seemed to say. 'Playing for France?' he repeated dismissively. 'It never bothered me. If they called, I played. If they didn't call, I didn't play.

'Playing for La Voulte meant much more. To play for France was personal. But to win the Championship with La Voulte was extraordinary.'

Well, you could understand players being philosophical in those days. The autocratic French selectors played ducks and drakes with the players of that time and their careers. They were selected and then dropped, like bruised pears on a market stall. The selectors, those gods who sat in the stand and metaphorically raised or lowered a thumb at an individual French player's performance, decreed all.

In those days, French selectors changed their teams like they changed their shoes.

Sometimes, even after a victory, four, five or six players of the winning team would be dropped. It was fascinating and fun to watch from the other side of the English Channel, a sort of contemporary cull along the lines of the Revolution. For the French players, it was the height of frustration.

Which perhaps explains Guy's frankness on the topic. In the 1960s and early 1970s, France had the Koh-i-Noor diamond of all rugby players, Jo Maso. He came from the south-west and was a free spirit, perhaps from his early times in rugby league which he played at junior level, winning a French XIII title with his club, XIII Catalan.

Maso then moved into rugby union, playing centre or fly half for Toulon, Narbonne and Perpignan. He had hands as soft as silk, and his timing was exquisite. With his pace and vision, he found space where others could not. As Bob Dwyer said of the French, they are the best in the world at sensing and creating space for colleagues. He had Maso very much in mind when he made that statement.

Maso was different; he had rarely gone with tradition. It was the Western world of the sixties and early seventies and he wore his hair long. Certain members of the French selection committee, almost certainly with the opinions of austere FFR president Albert Ferrasse in their ear, acquired a clear distaste for this individual genius. Maso would win just twenty-five caps in his entire French rugby union career. It was an absolute scandal, an outrage. He should have won more than double that and would have done but for petty bureaucrats meddling in the sport.

Guy Camberabero remembers vividly the club's homecoming after their triumph in the final, the famous Bouclier stored in the team bus. Monday, the day they got home, was Pentecost and there was a big celebration. 'Everything was closed in the town but there were about 15,000 people out in the streets. For us, it was incredible. We had never seen anything like it.

'I was very proud to play for La Voulte. My father had played rugby for twenty years, at Tyrosse near Bayonne. I am from the south-west. But I arrived at La Voulte in 1955/56 and stayed.'

But the morning after the celebrations, he quietly went back to his job in the textile industry, for which the town was known. Later, he would run a small *tabac*. A simple life of quiet and calm after the excitement of the rugby.

Today, most of the locals who cheered and sang in joy at their team's triumph have gone, imaginatively side-stepping their way into the endless horizon beyond the sun. At the simple

121

stadium on the outskirts of the town, there is a melancholic mood of times past. The old man shrugs at such talk.

'Matchday in La Voulte has changed completely. When I first played for them, they were in the second division. Then they went up and stayed in the first division.

'But now the team is low down and there is hardly anyone at the stadium. Maybe a dozen or so. We used to get 10,000 sometimes for the big games. It was mad.

'But now the club is amalgamated with two others, Valence and Romans. They are in the fourth division. It is a question of money now. Money leads everything.'

What's more, the distances preclude any sense of regional loyalty or support. Valence is 20 kilometres away, Romans 43 kilometres. It's like La Voulte has suffered a takeover, not an amalgamation.

They only play a few matches in a season at La Voulte's quiet, slumbering ground. For the most part, the ghosts of 1970, when the little stadium became one of the most famous in all France, can be left undisturbed. Much is as it was: the small stand with concrete steps on the western side of the ground has had a coat of paint. But as for modern-day comfort and facilities, well, they slipped past on the river.

In the afternoon, after a little lunch at the Restaurant au Petit Creux, a typical Ardèche *hostellerie* offering the midday *formule* at €14.50 (including wine and coffee), I take the car and drive down to the ground. It is not five minutes from the centre. There, on a wall beside the main road, are the proud letters 'Champion de France 1970'.

Le stade is named the Battandier-Lukowiak sports complex in memory of two resistance fighters from La Voulte. They were shot together by the Germans in the Second World War.

Behind the goal line at the southern end of the ground stands a line of trees, some of their leaves fluttering down

122

in the gentle autumn breeze. I smile at one of Guy's abiding memories of playing here. The Rhône valley where La Voulte is situated creates a funnelling effect for the Mistral which blows through this part of France, down to the shores of the Mediterranean and out to sea. It is strongest in winter and springtime and, while it is more normal to blow for a day or two, it can last for a week or more.

Guy's eyes sparkled at the memory. He rose from his chair and bent his frame into an imaginary heavy wind so that he was close to being bent over. 'That wind! It was a big problem for someone small like me. Especially kicking into it. It could be very difficult.'

But what of the game these days. What are the differences he has seen take over his sport since professionalism arrived in 1995?

He leans forward in his chair, almost conspiratorially. 'I will tell you. The clubs have all changed. I try to explain but it is just so different. The players now are so big compared with me. But that's just how it is. I'm not against that, I'm OK with it. I am not a spoilsport. But to me, the game has changed a lot.'

There is an understandable bewilderment with this octogenarian at some of the modern ways. 'In my time, the game was violent sometimes, but we always respected the referee. I saw a match on TV the other day with two French clubs and the referee was speaking English! Why? There were four or five English-speaking players but they must learn French. I agree with French people learning English because that helps with communication. But not referees in a French game! It has all changed.'

You'd wonder how a man of just 64kgs and 1.7m survived some of those times in the French game. The violence of that era could be shuddering. Was Camberabero ever concerned for his own safety on the field? After all, the Béziers club of that time came with a fearsome reputation.

'Yes, they were hard. But today, the tackles are hard and fast. And it always existed... that side of the game. But no, I was never scared on the field. You must love rugby to play, not be scared. It's not worth playing rugby if you don't love it.'

* * *

Across south-eastern France, you can run your finger due south on a map and trace a whole host of small-town rugby clubs or even lesser-known cities that have contributed internationals to the French national team. These were once the breeding grounds of the international players of the future.

La Voulte would be one of the smallest, but a whole host of others fit the category: Vienne, Nîmes, Chalon, Roanne, Grenoble, Bourgoin, Valence, Romans, Carpentras, Chambéry, Le Creusot, Carmaux (who were champions of France in 1951) and Mazamet.

Some have fallen upon perilous times. Mazamet, French Club Championship runners-up to Lourdes in 1958 and club of the great old French captain Lucien Mias, found themselves in Nationale 2 in 2022. Their season, moderate in truth, ended in catastrophe when they lost in the round of the 'Barrages' to La Seyne-sur-Mer. To say they lost was putting it kindly. La Seyne, the club near Toulon on the Mediterranean, won the match 88-17, scoring thirteen tries to two. It was a humiliation for Mazamet. Mias, by then ninety-one years old, would have been horrified.

Mias, a lock forward, led France to the 1959 Five Nations Championship, their first ever title. The year before, he played so outstandingly well on the French tour of South Africa that the local press called him 'the best international forward ever to be seen in South Africa'. Many of these old French rugby towns are places which the new, sleek TGV professional rugby train overtook. In fact, it swept past so fast the old-style clubs never knew their fate until it was sealed.

These great old clubs like Mazamet helped form the entire bedrock of the rugby union game in France. Le Creusot was founded way back in 1901; Chambéry, in Savoie, even earlier, in 1898. Some of the names who excelled with them became legendary in French rugby circles.

Sébastien Chabal, he of the wild flying hair and beard as thick as a mountain hunter's, played for Bourgoin when they were a top-flight club. Great French international lock Élie Cester was a stalwart of the Valence club. Michel Vannier was an elegant full-back and captain of Chalon, a player who suffered a grievous knee injury in South Africa on the 1958 French tour. Vannier ruptured both cruciate ligaments and dislocated a knee joint. The damage was so serious it was feared he would lose a leg.

Yet it was saved, together with his career. Sadly, he was to die at just fifty-nine from a heart attack.

In just about every case, rugby's revolution caught out these clubs. But it is undeniable that the process of money defining the success of a French club began way, way before the game officially became professional in 1995.

Clubs like these declined because they couldn't compete financially with the big boys. Later in this story we will come to a couple of clubs that were THE biggest of their day in France. Yet in the end, time caught up with them.

As former French captain and later national coach Pierre Berbizier said, 'We have lost the culture of the small and big town club in French rugby. Now we have big city owners. Today, it is finished for many clubs. For example, Lourdes fell to the fifth division.

'It is a big revolution and I am afraid for the future. Before, the new players, players of the future, were in these areas.'

Others of his era speak even damningly of contemporary times. Former Biarritz and France prop Pascal Ondarts says, 'The French have completely lost their identity and culture. That is partly because there have been too many foreigners in the French clubs. Nowadays, the few French players in a French club have to learn English to speak with most of the players.

'If they carry on like this, it will be the end of French rugby. Besides, it is impossible to have a collective team when you have some players getting €80,000 a month and some getting €5,000. It is impossible to have unity in a real sense and it doesn't correspond to the values of rugby.

'When you have to naturalise foreigners to play for France, as we have done, then I am against this system. But the businessman is very strong in France now and especially in rugby.'

So that's the glass half empty syndrome. It's all but 100 per cent true to say we'll never see the likes of La Voulte or Carmaux in another French final. We won't see the renaissance of the Bourgoin-Jallieu club. One hundred and seventeen years old in 2023, Bourgoin were French Championship runners up in 1997 and the same year won the European Challenge Cup, European rugby's number two tournament. Even as recently as 2009 they were runners-up in the European Challenge Cup.

Yet where did this proud heritage get them when the financial pressures mounted? Catapulting through the trapdoor, firstly into the second division of the French game and then the league below that. In season 2020/21 they slumbered just below halfway in the Nationale league. Anonymity had descended, like mist on an autumn morning.

Why? Bourgoin epitomise the plight of so many once powerful French clubs. Life moved on, from the small

French country towns to the major cities. The money flowed unerringly in that direction, the people in its wake. Where once were proud, successful clubs in towns like Valence and Bourgoin, nowadays the money is tight. Or, in some cases, non-existent.

Meanwhile, Lyon, the 2022 European Challenge Cup winners, are a major attraction for the ambitious players from that region.

But even those rugby followers with a modest income can rejoice in the cuisine of such regions. Savoie is a *département* in the Auvergne-Rhône-Alpes region. Grenoble is a city in that region, famous for its cheeses, such as Reblochon which is made in the Haute Savoie from raw cow's milk, and which can be used in the making of the Savoyarde pizza. It is one of the best you will ever taste.

First, make the dough. Use 400 grams of fine flour, one sachet of yeast, one teaspoon of sea salt, one teaspoon of caster sugar, two tablespoons of olive oil and one tablespoon of polenta granules. Mix the flour, yeast, salt and sugar, make a well in the centre, then add the oil and about 225 ml of warm water and bring together.

Tip out onto a floured surface and knead for one minute. Leave under an upturned bowl for about an hour, during which time it will increase in size. Roll out on a floured surface, sprinkle a large square of baking paper with polenta and lift the dough onto the paper. Stretch and press out with fingers, and cover with around three tablespoons of half-fat crème fraiche, leaving a small gap around the edge. Then add the topping of the already cooked onions, lardon and potatoes. Top with slices of reblochon cheese and cook for about fifteen minutes in a very hot oven.

Délicieux, as the French say. It is also known as Pizza Tartiflette or Pizza Raclette.

127

As for Lyon, it has become the major centre of the south-east, a large city where a host of companies, many with international outlets, base their business. These companies become natural sponsorship targets for the Lyon Olympique club. Either collectively, or through wealthy individuals, the rugby club receives considerable financial support.

Then there are the multi-millionaires, the likes of Mourad Boudjellal who lifted Toulon from beckoning anonymity to the pinnacle of French champions and champions of Europe. He did it by splashing enormous amounts of money on many of the world's best players.

How to put this kindly? Well, the local garage owner and small insurance company back in towns like Valence, La Voulte and Bourgoin simply cannot compete. They never will, ever again.

You could say that a club like Clermont Auvergne, back up in the Massif Central, ought to have been vulnerable to this trend. Geographically isolated, Clermont is a reasonably sized but not enormous city. But they were lucky. On their doorstep is an international business worth billions worldwide. The Michelin tyre company. Their links to the local rugby club are as strong as their steel core tyres, as we have seen.

But for Michelin, Clermont could have gone the same way. But they won't because the company's strong financial support for the club is unlikely to waver. Until it does, Clermont can count themselves in the fortunate few.

But then there is the glass half full syndrome. It is apparent at a club like Cavaillon in the Vaucluse *départmente* at the foot of the Luberon mountains. It's true that the British author Peter Mayle sold so many copies of his *A Year in Provence* book (based in the Luberon) that he could have bought up the whole Cavaillon rugby club and probably made them champions of France AND Europe by now. But perhaps Cavaillon wouldn't have wanted that.

Today, Cavaillon know and accept their place in French rugby. They're a lower league club but are official partners of Castres Olympique, the Top 14 club. But maybe more importantly than that, they run thirteen teams, have 120 school players (in general, youngsters in France don't play much organised rugby in their schools, they join their local clubs as youngsters and rise through the grades) as well as seventy senior players.

So if you want to find the quintessential definition of a healthy junior club, maybe Cavaillon is one of the best examples. It just depends on whether your criteria for a club's success is providing a few players for the French international team or offering a facility for young people in their local community.

Of course, the first is important for the national scene. But I'd be tempted to say that the junior club offering years of physical exercise and inculcating the need for discipline in young people through the demands of this sport, is providing the greater service to its town or community. Take away clubs like these and you're going to have an awful lot of young people hanging about on street corners or in the local park. Doing nothing for themselves, their local rugby club or the community.

It is a totally different system in the UK where young people at rugby-playing schools are involved in the game in each year. In France, the clubs mostly fulfil that task and a highly valuable piece in the jigsaw it is for their society. Clubs such as Cavaillon emphasise how deep rugby's roots go in French culture and society.

* * *

The old bells in the fourteenth-century church tower in our village chime eight times. It is early on Easter Sunday morning. Around the area of the old Grimaldi-built castle, once called 'the Montmartre of the French Riviera', the first customers sip

The medieval hilltop village of Haut-de-Cagnes, where rugby men from Nice once headed for the nightclubs on the Place du Château.

a *café* at the *tabac*. Shafts of early sunlight are thrown across the town square. Far away in the distance are the snow-capped peaks of the Italian Alps.

Many from the creative world came to Haut-de-Cagnes, this old medieval hilltop town, rugby men among them. At its zenith, it was a haven for artists. Pierre-Auguste Renoir lived in the town from 1903 to 1919 while others included Amedeo Modigliani, Yves Klein and Chaim Soutine. The writer Georges Simenon, creator of 'Maigret', also lived here.

Modigliani, now regarded as one of the most important Italian painters of the twentieth century, was the quintessential tragic genius of the art world. He caught TB early in his life and suffered constant ill health. When he moved to the village, the smell of hashish and strong drink like absinthe was omnipresent around his home. He plunged into a world of excess, abuse and depression, yet at times vividly illuminated by his genius on the canvas. He painted many of his finest works whilst in the old town.

He died, in Paris, at the early age of thirty-six. His young, common-law wife, Jeanne Hébuterne, shattered with grief at his death, threw herself out of a fifth-floor window the day after, destroying her own life together with that of their unborn child. A young daughter was left orphaned.

Many years later, the village of old houses and narrow, twisting little streets and alleyways acquired an unlikely reputation of a different kind. As many as ten nightclubs began to operate in and around the Place du Château, at the top of the old town. Among the customers were the rugby men of the Nice club who would arrive on a Saturday night, often with some of their opponents from a match that day.

Racing Rugby Nice was founded as far back as 1912, just four years after Toulon, along the Mediterranean. Nice's golden era was the 1980s when they contested a French Championship final with Béziers in 1983 (losing 14-6) and winning the 'Challenge Yves du Manoir' in 1985, beating Montferrand 21-16 in the final.

Nice, with five-time French capped international back-row forward Éric Buchet their captain, and Jean-Charles Orso, who played eleven times for France at lock, were a strong side in that era. Little did they know it in the 1980s but decline would thereafter follow. In 2012, with cruel irony in the 100th year of their story, they went into liquidation.

But the rugby experience has been reborn on the Côte d'Azur. Stade Niçois play in the Nationale league, the third division if you like, of French rugby. This rebirth may be a propitious act for Nice. The city has become one of the most favoured destinations in all France, not just for the French but overseas visitors, too. Weekend trips from the UK and Ireland, not to mention many other countries on the European mainland, are becoming ever more popular. Businesses of growing importance and wealth are establishing themselves in the city.

The local rugby club can only benefit from this scenario. So, on this Easter Sunday, I make the short trip along the coast to the Stade des Arboras, a little to the north-west of the city centre near the Var River. Here is a spacious stadium, not that old, with plentiful capacity and a family atmosphere, with youngsters running free and their parents socialising.

Beloved of all rugby clubs is the clubhouse, and Stade Niçois have their own. But in this Mediterranean climate, most sit outside soaking up the warm sunshine. A boutique selling club replica shirts, jerseys and plenty of junior and baby kit, does a steady trade, serenaded by the twelve-strong Stade Niçois band which belts out the old numbers with great gusto.

Dax are the visitors this day and a lively, open, attacking match ensues. True, the kids cannot quite wait until half-time for sustenance, badgering *Maman et Papa* for a carton of *frites*. But with everyone served, we settle back for the second half, either under the shade of the 2600-seat main stand or standing out in the open to catch the rays.

This might not be Toulon against Toulouse and there may not be 20,000 people in the stadium. But there is a strong, loyal core of keen rugby men and women here, working devotedly to put building blocks in place for a successful future for the rugby club of Nice.

They end their day happy, too, Stade Niçois just edging home, 19-14. As the final whistle sounds, we repair to the tables and chairs outside the clubhouse, to share rugby talk.

Nice won't be in the Top 14 next season nor the season after that. But something is being regenerated beside the Mediterranean and for sure, you could hardly find a better location in which to build a thriving rugby club of the future.

CHAPTER 5

A Day at The Lake

Sète

One of the great glories of France is the sheer variety of its landscapes.

It's true, the Côte d'Azur, with its multi-million-pound homeowners and their luxury yachts to match, the earthiness of the many restaurants in the Pays Basque and the great oyster beds on the coast at Marennes in the Charente are all in the same country. But it's difficult to reconcile.

You could hardly find greater differences. In philosophy, aesthetics, food and cultural ways.

Likewise, rugby football in France. As we have seen, it knows many homes.

You can find yourself in the company of rugby men at the hugely atmospheric (and oldest bar in Toulouse), Bar Concorde, in the Rue de la Concorde; beside the port at Toulon overlooking France's great naval base or in the town square of La Voulte beside the Rhône in the country's east.

Or, like me on this soft, mild, sunny late autumn morning,

you can stand bemused at the beauty of the scene in front of you in a quite different setting.

We're in the *départmente* of l'Hérault, close by the Mediter-ranean, a short distance between Montpellier to the north and Béziers to the south. Familiar landmarks to the motorists who pour south down the great A9 'La Languedocienne' autoroute towards Perpignan and the Spanish border.

For years, this was one of the great core regions of French rugby. Within a few dozen kilometres on the motorways, you could stop at Béziers, Narbonne, Montpellier, Perpignan, Nîmes. Each one, in their time, a rugby club of considerable standing. Sète is renowned as a port, a boating haven with a series of canals '*à la* Venice' which offer year-round mooring. But it has a strong and growing enthusiasm for rugby, too. In season 2021/22, Sète, playing in Fédérale League 3 pool 8 with other clubs of the region such as Alès, Uzès, Sigean, Avignon le Pontet and Arles, reached the final of the Championnat de France Honneur. They had won every game of their league season and played Sévignacq in the final. They were the pride of the town.

Alas, Sète lost, 19-6 in the final. Yet they still finished champions of Occitanie and vice champions of France at their level. A Bouclier sits proudly in their club offices.

Why was this special? Because Sète Rugby Club was only established in 2012.

The local mayor gave a reception to honour the club for what he called their 'exceptional season'. The players lined the balcony of the Hotel de Ville with their supporters cheering, celebrating and waving French flags below in the *place* (village square). And the local traders hurried to sign up for sponsorship for season 2022/23. It was another example of a small-town club thriving in the French rugby world.

It just so happens that our host for lunch this day, Christian Trallero, is a rugby man who scored a very famous try for

Narbonne, one hour away from here to the south, in the 1979 French Championship final. His touchdown helped Narbonne beat Bagnères-de-Bigorre to secure the famous Bouclier de Brennus. The small matter of forty-three years ago.

Trallero owns a holiday home here in a location for which just a single word will suffice. Idyllic.

You drive out of Sète evading, if you can, the dodgem-car-like antics of the locals, and take the road to Le Barrou. It is misleading; the minor road eventually ends in a boat yard. Bizarre. But we park up and investigate.

In a moment, a gate swings open and we find our friend. He leads us along a narrow, sandy towpath. On the left, stand a line of properties; on the right, the vast Étang de Thau, or Bassin de Thau. It is the second largest lake in all France and the largest of a string of lagoons that stretch all the way along the southern French coast from the River Rhône in the east to the foothills of the Pyrenees, by the Spanish border. It is called a lake yet has a direct outlet to the sea.

On this inland stretch of water, there are almost 2500 oyster beds and as many as 600 locals, families and commercial companies make a living from them.

A yacht and then a small passing rubber dinghy with an outboard motor chug past. A little later, a canoeist paddles by. They send some light, gentle waves onto the foreshore. Soft whispers of wind above the water create tiny patterns of movement. Although it will be November in a few days' time, it is 21°C. We pass a man fresh out of the water, just in his swimming trunks, chatting to a friend.

There is a calmness to this setting you might need to drive thousands of miles to better.

On a table in our friend's front garden, a delicious sight awaits us. To start lunch, slices of quiche Lorraine, followed by seven dozen oysters for the seven of us, all freshly shucked

Freshly shucked oysters beside the Étang de Thau at Sète.

with generous-sized cuts of fresh lemon, on a large plate, ready to devour. They are as fresh as the air on an autumn morning.

The rugby men have gathered, ready for the feast. They look at the plate of oysters like an egret studying its prey.

There is Alain Lorieux, whose distinguished performances at lock forward for France in the inaugural 1987 Rugby World Cup helped the French reach the final. Lorieux did not take up rugby until he was twenty-two years old, a remarkably late starter. Yet he won thirty-one caps, his last ones despite moving from FC Grenoble to the lower division club Aix-les-Bains.

Jean-Pierre Garuet was a prop forward of immense power and technique. Anyone who followed the legendary Robert Paparemborde into the French number three jersey had to be some player. Garuet was not only that but also a hugely loyal rugby man, representing FC Lourdes for twenty-two years from 1969 to 1991. He won forty-two caps for France. When

136

he retired, he became a deputy Mayor of Lourdes. Just to put something back into his community...

His fellow *Lourdais* has travelled with him. Fellow prop Michel Cremaschi was another outstanding forward who won eleven caps for France between 1982 and 1984.

Also joining us is one of France's best rugby journalists of recent times, Serge Manificat, who wrote for *Midi Olympique*, the great Toulouse-based rugby newspaper. He worked for the paper in Paris for years and his knowledge of the scene – the latest rugby news, the important rugby men to know, the best wines, most atmospheric cafés and top restaurants – is legendary. Besides his knowledge of the game.

We are in distinguished company. Two of these great rugby men were in the same forward pack that took apart New Zealand in that epic Test match of 1986, known ever after as 'The Battle of Nantes'. Jean-Pierre Garuet and Alain Lorieux. I imagine their bruises from that ferocious game have just about healed by now. But the scars will remain...

For it was one of the most brutal Test matches ever played. France had been beaten the previous week in the first Test at Toulouse. Coach Jacques Fouroux demanded revenge. The injuries some sustained were gruesome. After the match, as we waited in the corridor to enter the French dressing room to talk with the players, the door of the medical room opened. There, laying on the treatment bench, was New Zealand No. 8 Wayne Shelford. Having his torn scrotum stitched up...

But here, the wounds of sporting battle have long since eased. The pile of oysters gradually declines on the plate, together with a bottle of Auxerrois white and much of a bottle of Muscat. So we adjourn upstairs to a table overlooking the lake. And there begins what we might call *un vrai après-midi de rugby*.

Of course, says Alain Lorieux, it was very different back in the day. Players of his era had their 'expenses', shall we say.

But they also had jobs. In Lorieux's case, many of them. And that led to a considerable experience of life, rather than just rugby, as contemporary players know it.

'From sixteen to eighteen years old, I did all sorts of jobs such as working in restaurants. From eighteen to twenty-two, I was a fireman in Paris. After that, a fireman in Grenoble. Then I was director of a campsite and when I finished playing, I was regional director of the Taittinger champagne house. I did that for thirty years.'

Was he a fisherman? 'No, I prefer to cook the fish. Sometimes in a crust of salt.'

Cremaschi was more the fisherman, originating from Urrugne in the Pays Basque, 6 kilometres from the frontier with Spain. But he was proud to become a player for the great Lourdes club. 'Rugby has given me everything in my life. At eighteen, I left a small village for Lourdes which had its past history. For example, the story of [probably France's greatest ever captain] Jean Prat, Mr. Rugby. My passion was always for rugby and at Lourdes, I was always in the cradle of rugby.

'I met Jean-Pierre [Garuet] at Lourdes. He arrived young from the army; I, too, from the military. [National service in France was not completely phased out until 1996 to 2001.] Lourdes' glory days may have seemed gone, their last title won in 1968. It was their eighth title in twenty years. But at the end of the 1970s and start of the 1980s, they found a new generation of players, like Pierre Berbizier, Jean-Pierre Garuet, Alain Caussade and me. Berbizier was like Antoine Dupont now. Then Louis Armary arrived. And from 1980–82, Manuel Carpentier, who won eight caps for France, was there too.

'For a time, we came back to that level [of 1968]. Then, briefly, it was about Lourdes, Agen and Béziers.'

All Lourdes celebrated the return of what they called 'The Lourdes Way'. It was a game based on movement and fluidity, one of passing of the ball by both backs and forwards, keeping it alive and fracturing defences (not to mention exhausting the opposition) by the timing of the pass and taking out of opponents by making the ball do the work. It was the mantra of French rugby in the 1960s and early 1970s.

Almost exactly fifty years later, at the end of the 2020/21 season in England, the Harlequins club was receiving plaudits for the enterprise and vibrancy of its attacking play in winning the English Premiership title. But the French had been doing the exact same thing half a century earlier. Ingenuity with ball in hand, searching for space, offloading before going to ground and always seeking support for the ball carrier at every turn, to maintain continuity.

The French hallmarked these qualities in that early era, through the attacking instincts, enterprising desire and judgement of men like Jean Prat, Michel Crauste, André and Guy Boniface, Pierre Villepreux, Christian Darrouy and François Moncla. It has just taken many other countries far too long to appreciate the simple yet essential requirements for success, both aesthetic and practical, in this game.

Plus ça change and all that...

At the start of our lunch, seven bottles of wine stand sentinel on the dining table, one a magnum of red, a wine made by the great Paul Jaboulet Aîné. Alas, it would be an untruth to say that every bottle is left untouched as the rugby discussion roams far and wide. Deep, penetrative assessment and intriguing analysis of this great game, with its myriad qualities and traditions, is indeed a thirsty business.

Alain Lorieux picks up a bottle and pours himself a good glass of red, settles himself on a comfortable chair and stretches out his large frame. He is a man with four children (three daughters and a son) plus four grandchildren, three of them boys. 'My passions now in life?' he repeats my question.

139

'Very simple. Family, friends and rugby.'

It is a towering combination. It was always thus.

Our chef this day, Christian Trallero, nods in agreement. Trallero understands as well as any that, as the Roman conqueror was always told, all glory is fleeting. The former Narbonne centre, scorer of the only try in their 10-0 victory over Bagnères-de-Bigorre in the 1979 French Championship final at the Parc des Princes, announced he would play no more in the top flight the day after his greatest playing achievement.

Instead, he went back to his home village, Bédarieux, which had a lower league team. And with some friends from the area, like former French internationals François Sangalli and Jacques Cantoni, they took the little club almost to the gates of glory. How? 'I had a good business which enabled me to have the *means* to enjoy it,' he smiled, enigmatically. Ah, long live the great days of amateurism...

Of course, he still remembers the fun when Narbonne finally got back to the town twenty-four hours after their success in that 1979 final. 'We flew from Paris to Toulouse, took a bus to the outskirts of Narbonne, then changed onto an open-top bus. There was a parade and reception (with an orchestra) at the town hall. People still remember it after forty years.

'There were 10,000 people in the streets, it was mad. But then, that was rugby in France in those days. In the towns and villages it was very, very important.

'Today, rugby is about lots of money. Narbonne is only a small town with 50,000 inhabitants. Therefore financially, it doesn't have the means to have a good team. There is a culture of rugby, the children and everything. But after that, it is finished. It will never exist again. That is why our title from 1979 is so important. It will never happen again.'

Our main dish of the day is Macaronade, a typical dish of the region. Beef and pork cheeks plus sausages have been cooked slowly for several hours in a rich tomato sauce, with a bed of pasta and Parmesan sprinkled on top. It is rich and delicious.

The omnipresent cheese course follows, Roquefort with chunks of fresh baguette. And in hot pursuit come two desserts, not one. Citrus sorbet in limoncello followed by rum baba, with a little extra pouring of rum.

We talk until the warm sun begins to weaken, until that golden, glowing late afternoon light emerges to captivate all who see it. It has been a wonderful day, a testament to rugby's enduring qualities and attributes.

Four rugby men on a boat in Sète harbour. From left: Christian Trallero (ex-Narbonne), Jean Pierre Garuet (ex-Lourdes), Alain Lorieux (ex-Grenoble) and Michel Cremaschi (ex-Lourdes).

Later, in my hotel room, I reflect on it. Two things especially intrigue me about this day.

The first is the remarkable fact that three former French international players who have never set eyes on me in their lives are prepared to travel for hours on end to make this meeting for my benefit. Lorieux lives not far from Geneva but scorned the suggestion that we could chat on the telephone.

'No, no, we must meet. I want to talk face to face,' he said. The cost of the long drive and the time donated? All on his account.

Michel Cremaschi is another I never knew when he played, apart from sitting in the press box writing about matches and players. Yet he is willing to drive three and a half hours from Lourdes, deep in the Pyrenees, stopping off near Perpignan to pick up Garuet, and then head north up to Sète, to meet a rugby writer they have never seen and probably never heard of.

At a lavish lunch provided by a former Narbonne player under the simple banner of 'French hospitality'...

Alain Lorieux seemed genuinely surprised to be thanked for going to so much trouble. *'Sachez que cela était pour moi un plaisir partagé'* he wrote. ('Please know that for me it was a shared pleasure.')

'La fraternité et l'amitié sont les piliers de notre sport.' ('The friendship and brotherhood are the props of our sport.')

Different mentality. Oh, and one other difference. Different class to some others outside France.

It becomes increasingly apparent when I think of all those associated with French rugby who were only too keen to help with this project. And others like it. The new captain of France, Antoine Dupont, together with his exciting half-back partner at Stade Toulousain, Romain Ntamack, sat down for separate, exclusive interviews at the Toulouse club one winter afternoon. Likewise, the retired ex-All Black, Jerome Kaino who is now to be found coaching junior sides at the club.

'How can we help? What would you like to know?' was their response. Humble and helpful. So refreshing a difference. And they give you as much time as you want. These are the people who uphold rugby's values.

There were countless others; really, a multitude of people who have understood what makes the French game so special and wish to nurture its principles, strengthen its key values. Even under the auspices of professionalism.

As Bob Dwyer says, 'This is undeniably true. The French leave an ever-growing legacy to all of us who have had the chance to experience the fraternity of which they are a part.

'We are forever in their debt.'

It is my belief that the true spirit of rugby shines stronger these days in France than in Britain or Ireland. What I mean by that is that the French, even now the sport is professional, have a deeper respect for rugby and its traditions. This was apparent many times during the process of writing this book.

People went out of their way to help. Then, when you thanked them for their time, most looked puzzled. 'Why wouldn't we?' seemed to be their reaction. It is part of rugby. But it isn't necessarily like that in the UK and Ireland.

I suspect, too, that a reason for this is that most French rugby players are less focused on finances and dredging the last pound or euro from the sport. Mammon is not their only concern. The game and its reputation counts more for them than their counterparts in many countries. Naturally, they take commercial opportunities like any other professional sportsmen around the world. Of course, the top players are paid handsomely for their talents. As they always have been.

But here is the critical difference. A large number of French rugby men have been used to earning money from the game. It was always part of rugby in France and they grew up against such a background. It wasn't a great drama. They received financial benefits going way back.

It wasn't like that in Britain and Ireland. Thus, there is perhaps less of a focus on money in former and present French players' minds than you would find the other side of the Channel.

In the towns of the South of France, where rugby is a life and almost a religion, the health, prosperity and reputation of the game is still of great importance. Everyone, past and present, who has had an association with the sport, is keen to see its health enhanced. Any small thing they can do to assist that process, like reminiscing about the old times with people from the media or just ordinary supporters, is accepted.

Those who have played or coached this game at a high level in France have indeed formed, collectively and perhaps almost unknowingly, a unique rugby family. It is a large family that spans all of France, where the roots run deep and where people are regularly in touch. They look out for their rugby family members, watch their backs. They help, wherever and whenever they can, when help is needed.

Their links are close and carefully preserved. This 'family' shares mutual respect. They make time for each other. If you want to contact someone, they can help with a number. They love to talk rugby, their beloved sport, and warmly welcome those outsiders with no agenda, just others who share their love of the game. Trust is a key element in this 'family'.

It is an endearing cluster of people with key values at their core. To me, they epitomise much for which this great game once stood. It is hugely encouraging to see that such values among rugby men have not died, have not been trampled underfoot by the modern-day mania for money under the guise of professionalism.

Of course, it would be fatuous to suggest that many of

the older rugby men of Ireland, Australia, Wales, Scotland or wherever do not mirror these values. Of course, they come together for special times, to enjoy others' company and share their memories. To give their time in helping others less fortunate, too. Look at the Scottish rugby community and its help for the motor-neurone-stricken Doddie Weir. They have done more than their fair share.

But the French rugby 'family' is uniquely strong and vibrant. It is proud and willing to welcome outsiders, whatever their standing or cause.

Rugby union, the sport per se, might do well to ensure these qualities, these great values do not die out when the time comes for the passing of this generation.

Others beyond France have also come to know these bonds of friendship up close. It has been thirty-four years since Gareth Edwards experienced one example of what he continues to call 'exceptional and memorable French hospitality and friendship' from some of his former opponents.

When Edwards was in his prime as a player, French rugby men like the massive Castres and France international prop Gérard Cholley did their level best to knock his head off his shoulders. Wales and France dominated European rugby at that time and the contests, although highly skilled, were also huge physical battles.

But nine years after his retirement and at the age of forty, Edwards took a call from the former Castres player, asking him if he would participate in a charity match at his former club. Cholley's shopping list for players represented the cream of the crop: Edwards, JPR Williams and Phil Bennett from Wales; Mike Gibson, Ken Kennedy and Fergus Slattery from Ireland. To name but a few.

What no one knew when the event was planned, was what would happen late in the week before the game. A clue. It was

1987 and a British meteorologist made a very bold promise live on television, saying, 'A lady just called to say there's a hurricane coming. Well, don't worry, there isn't, although there's going to be a lot of wind in Spain.'

Windy? Just a little. Eighteen people were killed in the UK, homes torn to shreds and millions of trees uprooted. It was carnage. And the next day, Gareth Edwards and his buddies arrived at Heathrow airport to fly to Toulouse for their rugby weekend.

Edwards remembers that Cholley had sent an envoy to London to make all the arrangements and take the players and their partners down to France. But when the flight was delayed by the weather and aftermath of the storm, they adjourned to the lounge at Heathrow for a meal. Preceded by champagne.

So the legendary French hospitality began. In this case, wined and dined, they eventually took off hours late. A coach was waiting at Toulouse to take them on the sixty-minute journey to Castres.

They stumbled out into the darkness outside a clubhouse around midnight. Ostensibly, to have a quick drink and thank the remaining staff for preparing the food, before retiring to the hotel. What they didn't realise was that hundreds of people had waited for hours for their meal, refusing to eat until the players arrived from London and joined them.

The trouble was, as Edwards said: 'We had eaten so much at Heathrow, we were practically stuffed like turkeys.'

Alas, an alarming spectacle greeted them. Plates of steak, lobster and foie gras were brought into the room, along with industrial quantities of chips. It looked like whole fields of potatoes had been harvested for the occasion. Ready and waiting on the tables were more bottles of champagne, followed by bottle after bottle of red and white wine.

Bulging stomachs were called upon to accommodate this

146

latest culinary feast. The torture ended sometime after 2 a.m. Tired players were taken to their hotel to sleep... but only until 11 a.m. the next morning, when the bus pulled up outside.

'We were driven to this wonderful medieval castle for a welcoming lunch. But we were still full from the night before. It was like death by gastronomic torture. As for the wine, it was the absolute best,' remembered Edwards.

Eyelids slumped among the British and Irish contingent as this version of forced feeding, like the ducks that produce foie gras, continued into the evening. They eventually escaped to the hotel to sleep at 4 p.m. Alas, the 'worst' was yet to come.

At 7.30 p.m., the bus arrived to take them to the official banquet. 'They wanted to thank us officially for coming,' Edwards said faintly. This time, duck breast was the main course. With potatoes cooked in duck fat. Naturally. With more bottles of red wine to wash it down.

Even the next day, on the day of the game, there was another shock. They met the French players who had been chosen and both teams sat down together – for a good lunch of huge steaks, fries and more glasses of red wine. 'I couldn't believe it when we sat down for this lunch. We were going to play two hours later.'

Edwards, God bless him, then made an almost fatal mistake. 'At one point in the game, I picked up the ball and threw a huge dummy. Everyone bought it, a big gap opened and instinct took over. I went through it and ran as hard as I could for the line.'

At some club matches in Wales, Edwards had remembered hearing Maureen, his wife, shout, 'Run, run, Gareth.'

This time, Maureen was seriously alarmed. 'Stop, Gareth, stop, stop,' he clearly remembers hearing her scream. No wonder. It was invading the territory of the heart attack. But he got there in the end. Well, Gareth always did, didn't he?

But it wasn't his abiding memory of an extraordinary weekend.

'The welcome we had there was amazing, something never to forget,' he said, thirty-four years later.

CHAPTER 6

A Litany of Tragedies

Sète–Béziers

It's a short hop, forty minutes by car, to reach Béziers from Sète.

You take the road along the causeway with the Étang on your right, the sea out to the left. It's 36 miles, everything flat, largely uninteresting and deserted, apart from a few large amusement parks. Nothing beauteous here in keeping with the South of France legend.

Then, when you reach the outskirts of Béziers, you crawl through the modern-day scourge of most French towns. The industrial estates which represent an impersonal forest of commerce and seem to surround almost every one.

But when you actually get to Béziers, you wonder at this place…

So much drama has gone on here, and too many violent deaths associated with the town have occurred, especially with a rugby connection, that a single word comes into your head. A 'curse'? Perhaps it is not such a far-fetched notion at all when you consider the facts.

Violence has been going on in Béziers for a hell of a lot longer than just during the local rugby club's days of yore. Take 22 July 1209. Not a good day for the world peace movement.

Béziers was a stronghold of the Cathars, seen as heretics by the Pope, Innocent III. (Can a man ever have been so misnamed?)

He launched a crusade against them, his army led by the papal delegate, the Abbot of Cîteaux, Arnaud Amalric.

What ensued was beyond human comprehension, even for those times. When the slaughter by the Catholics was over, Amalric sent a message to the Pope, proudly boasting, 'Our men spared no one irrespective of rank, sex or age and put to the sword almost 20,000 people.' The town was then burnt.

He called it 'divine vengeance'. Amalric, apparently not exactly a shy, quiet, retiring man, is said to have roared at his flock, 'Kill them all. God will recognise his own.'

(PS Why is God always dragged into these ghastly happenings? After all, there are no records that suggest God descended upon earth, called the locals of Béziers together and said, 'Right, lads, follow me. And don't forget to bring your Kalashnikovs with you. We're going to make mincemeat of these damned Cathars.')

In somewhat happier times, the building of the famous Canal du Midi in the seventeenth century, which linked the Atlantic with the Mediterranean, brought great business and no little prosperity to the town. It was engineered by a son of Béziers, Pierre-Paul Riquet, and it became known as 'Riquet's ditch'.

Work began on it in 1666 but alas, Riquet died in 1680, just six months before it was opened. Most of his money had gone by then, spent on bringing his dream to reality.

Béziers derived much of its prosperity from the wines it grows in great profusion all around the town. The reds are the most popular and there are several grape varieties: Carignan, Cinsault, Grenache Noir, Syrah, Mourvèdre, Cabernet Franc and some Merlot.

Some of the Corbières wines they made nearby used to be pretty violent too, on the palate. Château l'Assault was widely harvested and bottled.

But no more. They have long since become so much smoother, almost bordering on the sophisticated. For that, the region must thank local growers such as the Bertrand family, *père et fils*, whose wines are a triumph of bouquet and flavour.

But on the issue of violence, surely too many famous men of Béziers have experienced it for us to accept at first hand the notion of mere coincidence. This is a region of often violent extremes in many senses. Take the climate. The fierce wind of *Le Mistral* on the Occitan side is called the 'tramontane', while the searing heat of midsummer triggering storms and the penetrating cold of winter nights can wreak havoc in the vineyards. Then there is the 'feria', including the traditional bullfights that dominate the town each August. Locals claim the feria is to Béziers what carnival is to Rio or Venice.

It has been going since the last years of the nineteenth century. Those into violent endings have seldom been disappointed.

France's Second World War resistance hero, Jean Moulin, was born in Béziers on 20 June 1899. During the war, Moulin reached London in 1941, after the German invasion and establishment of Vichy France, to meet General de Gaulle, the self-titled leader of the Free French.

Moulin trained in London but was asked by de Gaulle to return to France in 1943 to unify the various resistance factions that had formed. It was at a meeting he called on 21 June 1943 of the seven heads of resistance movements, in a house in a Lyon suburb, where he was betrayed and arrested.

Moulin was brutally tortured by the German Gestapo chief of the region, Klaus Barbie, a pitiless man dubbed 'Barbie the butcher'. When Barbie had sufficiently sated his barbaric lust, Moulin was sent to the Gestapo HQ in Paris where he was subjected to more torture until being thrown, barely alive, into a cattle truck for the train journey to Germany. He died on the train, somewhere near Metz in eastern France on 8 July 1943 without leaving French soil. He was forty-four.

Violence and the Béziers region have for so long walked hand in hand. The local rugby club has suffered more than most. The rugby seed took root in the first years of the twentieth century, as fever for the game spread across the south of this country, like a forest fire in the heat of high summer. Two men of Béziers, Louis Viennet and Jules Cadenat, bought land on a site near the outskirts of the town, in the early 1900s. The stadium opened in 1911 but the dark shadow of war was already building. Several young men of Béziers would be lost in the Armageddon that followed.

But then, rugby men associated with Béziers have continued to lose their lives, not just in wartime but especially in recent years, with a disturbing regularity. On 30 September 1985, the Béziers rugby captain Pierre Lacans had just led his team to victory in a Championship match at local rivals Narbonne. Lacans was a superb flanker – 'very like the New Zealand captain Graham Mourie. Had he lived he would have become captain of France,' said one of his friends, the French 1987 World Cup final lock, Alain Lorieux.

Lacans had also won nine caps for France and played for them in their 1981 Grand Slam triumph.

He was in the Béziers teams that won the French Championship title in 1978, 1980, 1981, 1983 and 1984. His last final for the club, 1984, was an extraordinary affair in front of 44,076 supporters at the Parc des Princes, Paris.

Béziers led Agen 9-3 at half-time in that final but were pulled back to 12-12 by the end of normal time. They played half an hour of extra time, by which time the score was 21-21. Each side had scored a try, converted it and kicked four penalties and a drop goal.

A hasty discussion ensued among the harassed officials. Nothing could separate the two sides. But, they agreed, there would be no 'extra' extra time.

Thus, as the clock ticked long past 11 o'clock at night, the two teams set out on a penalty-kicking competition in a desperate search for a winner. Several were taken successfully until, *quelle calamité*, an Agen player missed his kick from the 22-metre line. Béziers were champions again, albeit in remarkable circumstances. I remember it well. It was a strange night.

But just sixteen months later, titles and glory collapsed into the irrelevant category. Making his way home by car from Narbonne, through the Corbières vineyards and close by the small rural commune of Conilhac-Corbières, Lacans saw a car stopped on the road ahead. Too late, he tried to avoid it but swerved and his vehicle crashed head-first into one of the plane trees along the road.

Béziers' captain was dead, at twenty-eight. *Midi Olympique* newspaper called it 'Nightmare in the Night'. The whole town of Béziers fell into mourning.

More extreme deaths were to follow. Strangely, fifty years to the day after Jean Moulin's violent death, barring just forty-eight hours in fact, one of Béziers rugby club's most renowned players was also killed in violent circumstances. In the early hours of the morning on 10 July 1993, a single shot rang out from a bar, Le Bar des Amis in the Avenue Gambetta in Béziers town centre.

Armand Vaquerin, the club's famous loose head prop forward and twenty-six times capped French international, slumped to the floor with a bullet wound to the head. He was forty-two years old, just two years younger than Moulin when he met his violent death.

By then, Béziers had dominated French club rugby for a decade, winning eleven titles. Vaquerin had played in ten of them, a record that still stands to this day and will surely never be matched. But at his bar in the town, there had been a surprising late customer in the small hours of Saturday night/ Sunday morning. Furthermore, the stranger carried a weapon, a pistol. Vaquerin was challenged to a deadly game.

Russian roulette.

Much later, long after Vaquerin had been buried in the town's new cemetery, strange stories began to emerge. Allegations were made that the player had long been involved in the world of cocaine. There was talk too of his alleged involvement with certain figures in the Mafia Toulonnaise. There were also murmurs of strange meetings between Vaquerin and unknown men in the middle of the night.

Whatever the truth, as a shocked town was forced to come to terms with his death that summer, strong winds sent many stories and unproven accusations swirling around the town, together with the falling leaves of late summer.

Alain Lorieux shed some light on the incident and circumstances that surrounded it. He knew Vaquerin well.

'I played with him and against him. I was at his Jubilee, it was a great event. He was a good man but he had troubles now and again and that led to his accident. It wasn't suicide as some said, just an accident. In fact, he was tired, he had played cards all night. He had a coffee.

'He had a guy next to him who said, "Do you know Russian roulette?" He went to find the gun and then it happened. It was absolute madness.'

Yet still the violent deaths with a Béziers link continued.

On 5 June 2015, the New Zealand rugby international Jerry Collins, who had been playing rugby in the South of France for a few seasons, was in a car being driven by his partner Alana Madill on the A9 autoroute just outside Béziers. It was 4.30 in the morning when, it is alleged, Alana fell asleep at the wheel. The car, which also contained their three-month old baby daughter Ayla, was hit at high speed by a following coach and the car was destroyed.

Collins, who was thirty-four, and Alana were both killed. But subsequent examination of the wreckage found that Collins, clearly aware of what was about to happen, had dived into the back of the car and put his body between the baby and likely point of impact. By doing so, he saved her life. Ayla was rushed to hospital in Montpellier and spent two weeks in a coma and a month in a critical condition. But she survived.

Days later, as his New Zealand friends performed a haka beside the motorway in tribute to their dead colleague, the people of Béziers were left to reflect on another appalling tragedy to befall a rugby man in their region. The grief of the entire New Zealand nation was palpable.

One day a few years later, far, far away from Béziers and the Hérault region of the south, in the Paris suburbs where Top 14 club Stade Français train, they held a simple ceremony. The club's training ground was officially renamed in honour of one of their former players, Christophe Dominici, a sixty-seven-time capped French international who had played for France in four Six Nations winning teams, two of them Grand Slams, as well as starring in the 1999 Rugby World Cup.

Throwing out numerous names and dubbing them legends is the stuff of the popular press. But in this case, it was justified. But equally importantly, the link with Béziers and yet another violent death was harrowingly unmistakable.

155

In early 2020, Dominici was the key figure in a consortium, backed by investors from the United Arab Emirates (UAE), intent on taking over the financially troubled Béziers rugby club. It was said the consortium had expressed major hopes for the club's future, wanting to take Béziers back to the summit of French rugby. They had the backing of Béziers' Mayor Robert Ménard who publicly espoused the project.

The plan was for Dominici to become future president of the club. He spent long weeks and months working on the project, lining up backroom staff and many members of a new playing squad ready for the 2020/21 season.

Alas, in early summer, it started to become clear the bid was in trouble. The DNACG, financial regulator of French rugby and its interests, announced that the guarantees of the Emirates group were unconvincing. The world was about to fall in on Christophe Dominici's project.

On 23 June, he held an emotional press conference at the Raoul-Barrière stadium (named after Béziers' hugely successful coach from their glory years). Dominici told the media, 'I put all my heart and all my soul into this project. We have been faced with injustice, cheap blows, backbiting.'

The deal officially collapsed in July 2020.

But by then some of his erstwhile supporters had made their excuses and bailed out, notably Mayor Ménard. But did what he said of Dominici play a part in contributing to a heartbreaking outcome? Certainly, his words aimed at the famous former French wing could not have been more lacerating.

'By making believe things of which he did not have the beginnings of proof, Mr Dominici did a terrible harm to this club and to this city. He is no longer welcome in this town hall. He was a huge rugby player but he should have stuck to that reputation.'

Dominici was said by his friends to have taken the failure very badly. But one of his closest friends, fellow Stade Français and French international wing Thomas Lombard, went further, saying, 'He was deeply marked by the various comments and judgements pronounced against him on this subject.'

Just a few months later, on the afternoon of 24 November 2020, a witness saw a solitary figure climb the roof of a derelict building at the old Sully military barracks overlooking the Seine, not far from Stade Français's training ground in western Paris. Soon after the figure reached the top, it was seen to fall to the ground. They found Christophe Dominici's shattered body shortly before his wife arrived, desperately searching for him. He was forty-eight.

You might think that was more than enough sorrow for one town. But Béziers had not finished with tragedy. It crept up on it again, like a silent assassin, as recently as August 2021.

It should have been a happy night. A group of young rugby men headed out to Béziers Plage and the local bars for a night out together beside the Mediterranean. One of them went along as the nominated driver with the other four pledging not to go near their cars.

Alas, hours later, an eighteen-year-old from the Béziers club's training centre, decided to drive home. It was 2 o'clock in the morning. When challenged about driving, he allegedly became aggressive. The maximum permitted level of alcohol for a driver in France is 0.5 mg/ml. But for drivers with fewer than three years' experience, which applied in this case, it is 0.2mg/ml.

The driver of the car was later found to have a reading of 1.4mg/ml. Seven times over the limit.

Adam Lassaux was said to be the young driver's best friend. They were like brothers, it was claimed. Lassaux, a passenger in the car, was later found to have an alcohol reading of 0.77 mg. By now it was 2.30 in the morning and, apparently going too fast, the driver lost control of the vehicle and hit two plane trees, the type that had killed Pierre Lacans.

157

Lassaux suffered grievous injuries and died within a day or so. Like the young driver, he was eighteen and had twice won the title of 'French Cadet Champion' with Béziers in 2018 and 2019. Before that, he had played for ten years at Bédarieux where his parents were stalwarts of the junior club.

When the driver was prosecuted seven weeks later, he claimed not to remember anything about the evening including the accident. He was found guilty on a charge of involuntarily killing Lassaux and received a four-year jail sentence, with one year suspended.

All this grief, all this pain. Of course, the easy solution is to call it just a series of unconnected tragedies. But might it just have been the consequence of an ancient curse, perhaps by an old Cathar being slaughtered, together with his family?

After Adam Lassaux's death, a tribute ceremony was held at the spiritual home of Béziers rugby club, the Stade de Sauclières, on the edge of the old town. Here, they knew their great days, times of glory. The ground is now a forlorn site, with the team having moved in 1989 to the then-named Stade de la Méditerranée, a vast, soulless slab of concrete in the shape of a shell, up on a hill outside the town. Lassaux's tribute ceremony must have been a desperately sad sight.

Not too long after that ceremony, I walked around the old Béziers ground. The French call folk from Béziers *'Les Biterrois'*, and the day of Lassaux's funeral was another bitter occasion for the men and women of this town. Too many young rugby men have died in France down the years in car crashes. But Béziers seems to have hallmarked the connection between violent deaths, lethal assaults and the town or region.

In 1978, the Béziers lock forward Michel Palmié was banned from ever representing France again (he had won twenty-three caps) for punching an opponent, the Racing Club lock forward Armand Clerc, in a French Championship semi-final match.

The back of the main stand at Beziers' old, famous ground, the Stade de Sauclières.

But this was no ordinary punch. Clerc was smashed so hard in the face by the Béziers man that he was partially blinded in one eye. The reason? Clerc won a Béziers line-out throw.

Violence and Béziers rugby were like blood brothers. The club's glory (or gory, perhaps?) years were built on the foundations of a massive, intimidating forward pack. It was easily the most feared in Europe. Other forwards, big men playing the game in France, had a scintilla of dread when they set out to meet Béziers in that era.

Alain Lorieux was certainly no shrinking violet. But he shivered when I asked him about those days. 'I did not enjoy those moments. There was violence in every match and I did not understand why. I enjoyed playing good rugby, winning the ball and running with it. But the violence was everywhere then.'

159

Were Béziers just a hard team or was it too violent?

'Yes,' was Lorieux's response. He meant in both senses. 'They were very naughty, very hard. Alain Estève was monstrous.

'In international rugby, I always found the English were massive, hard. I played against Steve Bainbridge, Paul Ackford, Wade Dooley. The Béziers players were like that. Massive. They walked all over you like a machine.

'But as for French rugby at that time, everything was violent, every game. Perpignan, Narbonne, Graulhet, Lavelanet. It was the culture. On the ground they were killers.'

It certainly was when Béziers were involved. I walked around the back of the old Béziers stadium. It is now used by the AS Béziers soccer club. Young, fresh-faced footballers, their clean training kit hardly stained by a single drop of sweat, worked out in the solitary stand, running up and down the steep steps.

But somehow, this image before my eyes simply didn't fit with the history of the site. This ground will always be remembered as the place where a dream of glory was built, albeit on brutal philosophies. The weather-beaten, craggy, beaten-up faces of so many of the old Béziers tough men will always be the abiding image of this place. Palmié, Martin, Estève, Paco, Vaquerin, Wolff... they were tough men in the toughest of eras.

Behind the old stand, the River Orb meanders past, silently as if not to disturb the ghosts of that past. But I don't have a problem with those ghosts. There was a time when this place throbbed with rugby passion. The list of clubs who came here to challenge the mighty Béziers represented the cream of the crop as far as French rugby was concerned.

But few ever left victorious. One way or another Béziers and its fearsome reputation ensured that. Béziers were the dominant force in French rugby throughout the decade of the 1970s and up to 1984. Their power, domination and success sickened rugby men in the traditional French rugby lands of the Côte Basque, Toulouse, Stade Montois and Agen.

The statistics tell you that Béziers' record will almost certainly never be equalled, never mind beaten. From 1961 to 1984, they were crowned champions of France eleven times. They also won the Challenge Yves-du-Manoir four times. This ascendancy spanned a generation.

Through those years, France saw its society begin to change. Leadership started to be questioned, the dictates of traditional rule makers, like parents, teachers and priests, was challenged. Old ways and customs began to fade. Some of the pillars of traditional society were beginning to crumble. It was the shock of the new.

The habits of the past, strictly adhered to by the older generation, were increasingly under threat from the new generation. France was becoming a different country, to the optimism of its youth but despair of its elders and traditionalists. It was a veritable changing of the guard.

When the 1970s unfolded, violence was still endemic in rugby union. But by the mid-1980s, when Béziers had won the last of her crowns, life and attitudes were fast beginning to alter. An era was starting to slip away.

Already, there was more than a suspicion of a trend emerging concerning a transfer of economic power in rugby union, from the country towns like Béziers, to the metropolitan hubs, the likes of Lyon, Bordeaux, Toulouse and, most of all, Paris. It didn't mean a club outside those cities could never again win the coveted Bouclier de Brennus, the famous old log. Clubs like Agen, Perpignan, Biarritz and Castres would still win the crown occasionally. But crucially, they would only do it with significant financial backing from wealthy investors. All four clubs enjoyed that largesse at important times. But none lasted forever and for sure, Béziers never got a sniff of the money tree.

LE COQ

Pierre Villepreux remembers the day in the mid-1980s when the entire Béziers supremacy unravelled against his Stade Toulousain team. How does Villepreux, coach of Toulouse at that time, reflect on what Béziers did in French rugby?

'In France, I always said that you had three different schools... of rugby. A long time ago it was Lourdes with Jean Prat. Lourdes, where the game was give the ball to the backs and after we will see. After that, you had the Béziers school where you gave the ball to the forwards and the backs could go to the bar!

'After that, you had the Toulouse school, where continuity, fluidity and movement were the arch principles. We had a match, Toulouse against Béziers in the quarter-final of the Championship one year and I was (Toulouse) coach with my young team.

'Béziers had all their team playing but we beat them easily. It was 21-0 in the quarter-final. After that, Béziers were finished. Since then, the Toulouse game has been the school... teaching others, showing the way.'

Thus, the die was cast. Driven on by professionalism, which arrived in 1995, power in French rugby was shifting irrevocably away from the smaller towns. The old game in which the French had invested years, or rather decades of an intense passion that somehow intermingled all the violence with a great love for the game, would never quite be the same. Somehow, the future would be different. A new game was emerging.

But as French rugby changed, so the Béziers era died away. When you consider some of those who featured most prominently in that era and their philosophies, perhaps you'd conclude that it might not have been a bad thing.

Béziers built the foundations of their dominance of French rugby on hard men like Alain Estève. If some day someone doesn't make a film about Estève's life, then there's something

162

remiss. As if to remind us of how deeply ingrained rugby issues of the past are embedded in most French people's minds even to this day, in September 2021, *Midi Olympique* newspaper launched an inquiry into an incident that had occurred fifty years before at the Toulon v Béziers 1971 French Championship final.

Toulon's key forward André Herrero, their talismanic figurehead, was brutally assaulted in that match. He suffered four broken ribs in an incident French rugby has never forgotten or satisfactorily explained. *Midi Olympique* described it as 'a filthy blow'. A mystery remains, wrote the paper. 'Who hit the captain of Toulon and gave Béziers a decisive advantage?'

What followed was an interview with Béziers forward Alain Estève, by Jean-Luc Gonzalez, which raised your eyebrows. At seventy-five years of age, the old second row/No. 8 player who stood 2 metres tall reflected on a life few of us could understand.

By then, in September 2021, Estève had been diagnosed with throat cancer. Five years before that, he'd had an illness which prevented him standing up. He lost 10kgs in weight around that time. But as he ruminated on his past, you had the feeling those illnesses from more contemporary times were the least of his troubles.

His life, he confessed, had not been easy. From the age of eight until he was eighteen, he was incarcerated in a correctional facility at Trèbes, a small, almost anonymous town lost amid the vineyards close by the Corbières region, between Narbonne and Toulouse. An excellent background, some might consider, for a tough Béziers forward of the era. He was born to a desperately poor family with seven children. They were so poor, as a child he slept in pits or ditches, not a bed. He saw his parents only for one month a year during his time in the correctional facility.

'It was hard physically and morally. The priests were violent towards us,' he said.

When he was thirteen, he was shut in a dungeon for a month, alone in the dark with only bread and water. But at eighteen, he was able to go back to his parents at weekends. Then, an outsider saved him. Rugby football. The Castelnaudary club found him a job so he was able to leave the institution. He helped his parents financially and enabled them to forge a new path to a better life.

Fortune smiled at last on him. One day, purely by chance, he boarded a train at the tiny Pexiora station. It was heading towards Narbonne, and on board was the French rugby star Walter Spanghero whose parents ran a farm at nearby Bram.

'What are you doing?' Spanghero enquired.

'Nothing,' was Estève's response.

The great man assured him, 'If you come to Narbonne someone will find you work.'

So he did. Every Tuesday and Thursday, the two would meet on the train and go to Narbonne for training. It was a bigger club with more money. Propitious circumstances for a young man who had known only hardship and deprivation all his life.

Estève was, remembered Spanghero, a very tough man.

But after five seasons with Narbonne, their near rivals Béziers beckoned. The philosophy at that club seemed to fit Alain Estève like the perfect-sized boot. He remembers one Béziers-Narbonne match: 'What a fight. Everyone was running everywhere. I was knocked out.'

Initially, Estève worked in the business of the club president. Then he became a chauffeur to the mayor of nearby Agde. Rugby gave him 450 francs a month plus expenses. (This, of course, in the so-called 'amateur' era.)

He talked openly of his trade. 'I always preferred to be the butcher rather than the calf. If there is no intimidation, there is no rugby match. I can swear I never kicked anyone on the ground. But treading on ankles, the joints? That is part of rugby. Knees in ribs? Yes.

'Eliminating guys at a time when there were no replacements was a habit. The more violent you were with the Australians and South Africans, the more they respected you. It was virility. When I played at Narbonne, on the train home we trained by hitting our heads against the side of the train. He who did it the longest, won.'

Then there was the intimidation at Sauclières. That was legendary. He admitted once putting his hand on the buttocks of an opponent and saying, 'It seems you are a homosexual.' The fists, the verbal and physical assaults were a staple diet throughout his career. He'd handled adversity as a child, so encountering it as an adult was no big deal. Thus, he could negotiate a prison sentence, received for pimping. 'It was OK, like being at home. If you have money there [in prison], it's fine.'

He ran nightclubs and restaurants for thirty-five years, a tough training ground in France. Once, he said, he refused entry to a guy who then pulled out a gun.

'He made me kneel down and said, "Now what shall we do?"'

'"Fire," said Estève.'

After that, they became best friends.

At Twickenham in 1975 the night before the match against England, the French players were ordered to bed at 8 p.m. Estève and some friends stayed out until 4 a.m. but assured the French coach when they got back, 'We'll beat them.' And they did. With Estève at lock, France won 27-20.

Estève and the Béziers gang were not exactly French rugby president Albert Ferrasse's cup of tea. 'I told Ferrasse what I thought of him,' he told the newspaper. 'That is why I was suspended for a year. In the French team, the Agen mafia had everything at that time. Albert Ferrasse and Guy Basquet made the rain and good weather. They didn't like me.'

Estève's defence of his role in the brutal assault of André Herrero did not convince *Midi Olympique*. 'Estève has not told everything,' they claimed. They were almost certainly right. But after the paper appeared, the author of the Estève article received a chilling phone call. 'I am going to get you,' said the voice.

Whether it was Estève allegedly kneeing Herrero and breaking four of his ribs, one of them in two places, or Michel Palmié punching someone so hard they lost the sight in one eye, these were some of the acts that defined the Béziers team of that era. There were others, lots of them, too.

Yet the grandly named French Fédération de Rugby (FFR) appeared largely powerless in the face of this overt aggression. There was a historical reason for that. Violence had been an endemic part of the game in France since its inception. Béziers were by no means the initiators of this trend.

But it would lead not just to permanent physical damage in the case of some, like Racing's Armand Clerc, but other consequences unimagined at the time.

For the roots of that, we must go far back into the mists of time in the French game.

CHAPTER 7

Split Personalities

A small town, a quiet South of France café.
For reflection on the violence...

For those under the misapprehension that violence is solely the preserve of the French game, I offer this small newspaper snippet.

'The game known as rugby football will soon destroy itself. It is played principally by violent souls who inflict upon each other the most callous deeds without even so much as a word of apology.

'It is said that this game is practised only by gentlemen, but its manifestations are those of the very lowest class. No gentleman to be sure will regret the passing into oblivion of such an evil recreation.'

Those words were written in a newspaper in Devon, England, in 1904. So, given that Béziers was not founded as a club until 1911, the French club is off the hook in this instance.

But by now in this book, you should have got the point. Violence and rugby in France seemed manacled to one another

167

since earliest times. The violence on the terraces at the 1924 Olympic final, as the USA beat France 17-3 in front of 30,000 spectators at Stade Colombes while French fans beat up American supporters, was an early example. They also hurled bottles and rocks at the American players on the pitch. One American player was knocked unconscious after being hit in the face by a walking stick.

Paradoxically, this from a nation that offered the world the beauties of the Belle Époque and its myriad refined cultural elements.

On the one hand, these are an elegant, suave people in love with culture, capable of great invention and exquisite contributions in all forms of the arts. On the other, many of those involved in their rugby have been violent, vengeful and downright brutal. Intimidation, as some call it, has ruled. The dichotomy can be exasperating.

But then, these wildly fluctuating emotions of the Gallic temperament, often exceedingly good through a natural flair for the game but sometimes appallingly bad, as witnessed by some grotesque acts of violence, are from the same source. Is it within their DNA to reveal both almost simultaneously?

Can you have one without the other? Yes, in a perfect world. But in this one, it is unlikely. After all, the two extremes of emotion arise from the same DNA. Alas, as with most human beings, that would appear to be flawed. If you want the median, you're better off following a nation less exciting and excitable without the Latin temperament. Like the English. Less prone to excessive emotions but far less likely to offer the intense moments of pleasure through entertainment by which the French can light up any stage.

Essentially, do you want a gentleman or a scoundrel?

As these pages have shown, violence has often stained the French game, like red wine a white tablecloth. But is it being selective to focus chiefly on that, to the exclusion of the positive elements? After all, if violence were omnipresent in French rugby history, so too were the many individual moments of great skill and elegance.

Do we not mentally play back in our minds images of some of the glorious tries they have fashioned upon the rugby fields of the world? Like Philippe Saint-André finishing off a move under the English posts at Twickenham in 1991, which began on France's dead-ball line. It was later voted Twickenham's 'Try of the Century'. Then there was Serge Blanco completing a brilliant try in a World Cup semi-final against Australia in Sydney to put France into the 1987 World Cup final. And what of that memorable try in Auckland, started from deep by Saint-André and ending with Jean-Luc Sadourny's touchdown, to help defeat New Zealand 23-20 on France's 1994 tour? They called it *l'essai du bout du monde* (the try from the end of the world).

The list goes on endlessly.

Let's be honest. When the mood takes them, no side in the world does high-class skill and entertainment on the rugby field like the French. But perhaps in pursuing that Valhalla, doubtless egged on by the urgings of an excitable but demanding and impatient audience, it is inevitable that many will fall short. After all, we can't all be Jo Maso or Antoine Dupont. Therein lies one source of frustration.

Sometimes, the two emotions collide head-on in the same game. Occasionally in the same movement. A moment of supreme skill can be followed instantly by the ugliness of punches or a brutal assault. Two explosions of great drama and excitement. But each of a very different nature.

The French Championship final of 1971 provided a classic instance. Béziers and Toulon were old adversaries, clubs with men who had long memories and frequently saw such matches as opportunities to settle old scores. The French Don Corleones taking care of family business.

Late in the game, Béziers full-back Jacques Cantoni ran back close to his own line to collect a downfield kick. Instead of returning the kick, he ran from near his line on a dazzling counterattack. The heartbeat of thousands all but stopped in anticipation.

Hair flying as he raced out of defence, Cantoni produced two mesmerising sidesteps, like rabbits from the conjuror's hat, which utterly defeated opponents. Suddenly, he had found the open field. Except that a third Toulon defender now approached. His intent was very different. Cantoni drew him before freeing wing René Séguier outside him. Long after the pass had been made but with Cantoni still running, he was smashed in the head by a stiff-arm assault by the Toulon player who was off his feet. You couldn't call it a tackle. It was a vicious, pre-meditated flying leap, an act of pure violence. No more, no less.

Cantoni was knocked off his feet by the blow and lay senseless as Séguier ran on to score. The try won Béziers the final but the assault by the Toulon player was dreadful, a slur on his club and the French game.

But then, French rugby men have been knocking six bells out of one another virtually since the day the game was introduced to the country. The fact that the game was played from its inception by all classes of society and was seen almost as tribal, especially when matches were played between local rivals, all but guaranteed a version of warfare.

As former New Zealand and Oxford University blue of the 1960s Chris Laidlaw, who played club rugby for Lyon OU in 1970 and 1971 while studying at the University of Lyon, wrote, 'What seems to be forgotten... is that rugby is by nature a game based upon violence. It is a series of constant physical confrontations which are extremely provocative, particularly when a high degree of tension is thrown in.'

What is more, Laidlaw made no attempt to absolve his fellow countrymen from responsibility in this field. 'Obstruction and intimidation have both played a vital part in rugby at international level for many years. Every All Blacks team I ever played in happily used brute force to dampen the ardour of its opponents if necessary.'

The same applied to every other serious rugby-playing nation. Colin Meads, that late, great New Zealand All Black once summed up with remarkable accuracy French capacities in this regard during a tour of France.

'Those frogs certainly know how to dish it out – they never stop. But then, they never stop taking it either. I love it here.'

It's an undeniable fact. If you wanted colour, drama, excitement, flair, panache, violence, war and wilful assaults all rolled up into one package in your rugby, then France for most of the past century should have been your No. 1 destination. French rugby has had the lot. Nowadays, they call it 'essential viewing'.

At times, watching a rugby match in this country has been matched only by the dramatic twists and sounds of an opera. One moment the flowing aria, the next, blood everywhere and corpses strewn across the stage. The audiences have loved it, revelling in the drama and gore.

It's next to impossible to nominate THE roughest, most violent game there has ever been involving French rugby men. There are many worthy candidates for the title. After all, remember that the French national team was thrown out of the Five Nations Championship in 1931 by the other nations.

In part that related to ongoing reports of amateurism being ignored. But violence on the field was already legendary in the French game. All at the same time, the French seemed mad about rugby and rugby mad. Try this little soupçon of information to confirm the latter.

In 1943, in the middle of the Second World War, 28,000 spectators turned up at the old Parc des Princes in Paris to attend the final of the French Championship. With most of France occupied and all the free world and humanity fighting for its very survival, those brave men of the French Fédération de Rugby met on 5 June 1942, just seventeen days before the Germans launched Operation Barbarossa, the assault on the Soviet Union, at which the whole world trembled. But, comfortably ensconced in a small café, doubtless fortified by a pastis or whatever, they made the momentous decision to resume the French Championship...

The Battle of Britain? 'Which match was zis, Monsieur?'

Stalingrad? 'Ees zis a new team, Monsieur?'

So they kicked off the 1942/43 French Championship with much enthusiasm. Forty teams from the German Army occupation zone competed together with another fifty-five from the (at that stage) unoccupied zone. There was the small matter of the Germans annoyingly occupying the so-called free zone in November of that year, halfway through the Championship. But those determined men of the FFR were not to be discouraged.

'Call eet off, Monsieur? Are you mad?'

They just changed the name of the two zones, to 'North' and 'South'. *Voila!* How simple was that? And the teams, like the German marching bands, played on. It must have been like living in a surreal outer world utopia.

Disregarding the pitiless slaughter at Stalingrad, the *really* important news from 1943 was that Bayonne beat Agen in the final to lift the coveted shield.

They were at it again the following year, Perpignan downing Bayonne by twenty points to five in the final, again at Parc des Princes, in March 1944. Just twelve weeks later, the Allies hit the Normandy beaches. But, I have to report, it wasn't all plain sailing for French rugby men attending that 1944 final. The start of the match was delayed due to an air raid alarm.

Finally, in 1945, Agen, with a team that included the future president of the FFR, Albert Ferrasse, beat Lourdes 7-3 in the final. In all, around 93,000 people had turned up for the three wartime finals in Paris. Watched over, in the first two cases, by the Nazi oppressors. All very curious.

But then, when you think about this whole issue, perhaps it is just another example of how the game had got into the very soul of France and Frenchmen even by 1942... and even with a world war going on.

The 1950s were a whirl of post-war *joie de vivre*, the extension of friendships and the increasing popularity of the game. With rugby league largely out of the way, a victim of Vichy, union prospered. From 1947, France was back in the Five Nations Championship. French muttering about the mischievous '*Rosbifs*' across the Channel stilled. For a while!

From around 1957, the famous Blackheath club in England would play an annual fixture, on Boxing Day no less, against the renowned Racing Club de France. This was the crème de la crème of European fixtures at the time. Blackheath, the most famous club in England, against the slick Racing Club from Paris.

Visitors from post-war Britain, where rationing remained up to 1954, who were invited over to France for a short tour came home astonished at the high standards of hospitality afforded them. Not to mention a few thumping heads from the vats of wine they had collectively worked their way through on the trip. There wasn't any shortage of foie gras, either.

In 1954, the London Scottish club, based in Richmond just outside London, made a visit to France, arranging matches in

Paris and then in the Dordogne. One of their party was the Scottish international Logie Bruce-Lockhart, who had served in France during the Second World War with the 9th Sherwood Foresters and 2nd Household Cavalry.

But one player boasted still greater qualifications in the eyes of the exiles' hosts. A member of the Scottish squad had descended into the Dordogne region by parachute before D-Day to help organise the local resistance. What is more, he had been awarded the Légion d'honneur and the Croix de Guerre by the grateful French. They threw out the red carpet for such a man.

So, after their game in Paris, the London Scottish party went to Montparnasse station and caught the night train down to the Dordogne. They were met early the next morning at the station by the town band, officials from the local *mairie* plus the men of the Saint Cyprien Athletic Club, their rugby hosts, who were celebrating their club's 50th anniversary. Just to add to the delight, two local beauty queens presented garlands and waved flags.

The players were taken off for breakfast which consisted of ham and eggs, truffle omelette, pâté de foie gras, two bottles of *vin bleu* each (blue wine is fermented from a combination of red and white grapes with pigments and sweeteners added). That lot was followed by rum and coffee. Welcome to the Dordogne.

While they were there, the locals organised two dances and a banquet for their visitors, besides the match. Bruce-Lockhart said later, 'The rugby, like the pitch, seemed to have something of the pageantry and dash of a bullfight without the bloodshed.'

The club president, Jean Ladignac, was a renowned character besides also being the local mayor when the Scottish exiles arrived. On the second day Scottish were there, he invited some of the players for a private lunch: 'rich pâtés, strange cheeses, rare local wines,' reported one player.

As for Bruce-Lockhart, we are indebted to him for the delightful picture he painted of Ladignac. Describing what he called 'a true rugby man of Saint Cyprien', he said, 'Well over six feet tall and broad-shouldered, he was readily identified by his loose-fitting light grey suits, rakish beret and sunglasses. Even when invisible you could pick him out at extreme range by his strangely penetrating, hoarse whisper. His voice had been worn to a rasp by the over-use, ceaseless smoking of Gauloises and by late nights. Nevertheless, Monsieur Ladignac was a dynamo.

'He seldom rose before lunch or got to bed much before dawn. Most of the intervening hours he spent planning, administering and watching rugby, entertaining and above all, talking. Passionately interested in fishing, food, wine and politics, he had a finger in every pie.'

In all his spare time, Monsieur Ladignac ran the local *pharmacie*.

But even after a banquet the night before a game, some of the Scottish players would be taken aback by the level of physicality from the home team. Friendships that blossomed off the pitch were never allowed to intrude into extreme levels of physicality on it. That was the French way.

Meanwhile, on the international stage, in 1954, France beat New Zealand for the first time, 3-0 in Paris. A young André Boniface from the Mont-de-Marsan club in the Landes region, was selected on the wing and had a special memory of the game.

The man destined to become a legend of French rugby remembered, 'Bob Scott was a very attacking full-back for the All Blacks which was most unusual for that time. We organised a very tight defence against their backs. I tackled Jardine fifteen times in the game.

175

'I don't think France deserved to win against them. I was a bit embarrassed to beat them that time. But at least I beat them once.

'The night after that 1954 Test match was fun. The New Zealanders wanted to enjoy Paris and we helped them. I went to a bar and talked all night. I love to talk with fans and supporters, people that love rugby. We would take some French artists like Anouk Aimée, quite a famous actress. She was crazy for "Les All Blacks"!!!'

In 1958, France toured South Africa for the first time and, remarkably, won the series 1-0, with one match drawn. Later in the year, they also beat Australia, 19-0 in Paris. These were famous, fabulous results, and key signposts along the road to French rugby's emergence as serious performers on the world stage.

Yet always there was this undercurrent of violence in the French game. You couldn't have the aesthetic beauty without the fisticuffs.

With players like the Boniface brothers, André and Guy, plus a host of others like the flying Christian Darrouy (all of them from the Mont-de-Marsan club), and the great Michel Crauste in their back row, there was a guaranteed element of genius in any French national team of the era. Yet lurking around the corner, like some mugger in a dark alley, lay the men of violence. Alas, in the 1960s, that exploded catastrophically across the world of French rugby.

If you trawl through most of YouTube's panoply of French rugby's Championship highlights back in the day, you're risking accusations of being ghoulish. XXX-rated videos have nothing on these scenes of violence. Players are kicked, punched, assaulted from behind. Fists land flush on faces, knocking down grown men with the ease of snipers. Senses are scrambled, jaws broken, teeth lost.

Foreigners, even those with considerable experience of the game even at the highest levels, were sometimes taken aback by the levels of violence. The New Zealander Chris Laidlaw wrote thus of such occasions.

'A nasty taste is sometimes left in the mouth... by the violence... and the first few matches I played in France almost completely alienated me until I realised that there is a certain ritualistic quality to the fighting and not a lot of it is premeditated violence. One is nevertheless treated to some memorable sights, and I have seen two players actually arrested during a match, one for clobbering the referee and another for sorting out an irksome spectator.

'This of course raised the question of whether an arrested player may be replaced and this led to lengthy arguments between players, officials and Gendarmerie in each case.

'The Gendarmerie are always on hand and quite often are to be seen on the field bringing a little heavier authority to the aid of a hapless referee.'

I'm not sure how that great former Welsh referee Nigel Owens would have handled having police on the ground to strengthen his authority.

One critic talked of the French 'split personality' and went on, 'Observers throughout history have noted the Gallic penchant for loudly proclaiming the need for law nationally and quietly slipping away and breaking it individually.'

Well yes, perhaps. But this is the way of a nation. It is the people. It is the characteristic. It is pointless to wish they were different. They are what they are and ever will be. Just like the British. And each country must live with its historic legacy.

By the 1960s, the violence was all but out of control in French rugby. The 1963 Championship final brutally emphasised the problem. Dax met Mont-de-Marsan at Bordeaux, the first time the two local rivals had met in the final. They called it 'the clash of the Landes'.

Local rivals, local friends? No, sworn enemies.

It was, initially, a sweltering hot June day at the Parc Lescure, on the Atlantic coast. Before the match, thousands of fans roamed the pitch, letting off fireworks which exploded in all directions. It was a carnival-type atmosphere. Before the rugby started...

Some Dax fans had made a papier mâché bull, stuffed full of fireworks. As they dragged this across the field, smoke belched and explosions were set off from its front and rear. Others burned effigies and a group of Dax fans, wearing their berets, walked around the ground on stilts. To complete the colourful scene, the famous Dax band belted out just about every number it knew.

These definitely weren't scenes you would find at Twickenham in those days. It was, quite frankly, one of the reasons why I fell in love with French rugby.

When the pitch was finally cleared and the game began, not everyone was filled with praise for the rugby. Winning was all that mattered. But with both sides scared of mistakes, there was a plague of kicking into touch. In those days, you could kick directly into touch from any position on the field.

The crowd began to keep the ball among themselves for long periods, forcing constant stoppages in the play. Sometimes, they lasted five or six minutes. It was mind-numbingly boring.

All of which raised frustrations even higher. The referee, a portly gentleman, would have been more at home adjudicating on a bowling green rather than a rugby field. He never suggested a figure of authority or control.

The violence exploded, typically, after a brilliant, weaving run by Dax fly half Pierre Albaladejo deep into the Mont-de-Marsan half. The elegant side-stepping footwork and dummying showed French rugby at its best. What followed was the game at its worst.

When the referee blew his whistle for a technical offence, a couple of players scrapped mildly for the ball. Unknown to the Dax prop André Berilhe, his opposing prop, Pierre Cazals approached him from behind and smashed an unseen fist into the Dax forward's face. Cazals, a forest firefighter later in life who died in 2015 at the age of eighty-four, was guilty of one of the most cowardly assaults anyone has ever seen on a rugby field.

Rest in peace with that legacy, Monsieur.

Berilhe was eventually dragged up by his teammates, at which his legs completely buckled. The punch had shattered his senses. Finally, after copious quantities of smelling salts had been forced into him, he managed to play on in a kind of half world. Later, as if to play its part in the dramatic day, even the weather turned violent, the summer heat exploding with thunderstorms and hail. Somehow, it just said everything about the drama, violence and spectacle of a French final.

If you ever saw one, you were forever ensnared, captivated by the whole event.

Mont-de-Marsan won the final 9-6. Extraordinarily, later in life, Cazals and Berilhe would sit together watching derby matches between their two clubs.

But if 1963 was a bad year for violence, it would get worse. In season 1965/66, disciplinary action was taken by the FFR against 390 players.

The French Fédération begged in a round-robin message to the clubs, 'It is to the club leaders that we appeal. You know the offenders better than we do. Act against them yourselves. Empower your captains to take action themselves.'

That season, in the first two rounds of competitions, fifty-two players were punished by the authorities for acts of wilful violence on the field. Most received two-week suspensions for dirty play or foul language to referees.

Midi Olympique newspaper seemed unconvinced this would work. 'We don't think the scourge of rough play will disappear next season. It was a problem forty years ago.'

There was only one word to describe the 1966 final. Disgraceful. Agen met Dax at Toulouse and won the match 9-8. But long before the end, the scoreline was the last thing on most people's minds.

Alex Potter, the legendary French rugby writer of the day, had penned these words about the game in general earlier in the season. 'In the south-west, rugby is among the reasons for living.'

But as the final exploded, Potter, who was watching the game on television in an apartment in Montmartre, was shaken by what he was witnessing. He wrote, 'Three French friends and myself were momentarily staggered, petrified, stupefied, bewildered, flabbergasted, confounded, wide-eyed and open-mouthed.

'We could see neither the ball nor the referee on the screen but we could see most of the forwards and they were punching and kicking each other.

'Stop it,' shouted Gaston.

'Thugs,' yelled Pierre.

'Dirty,' hollered André.

'Hooligans,' bawled I.

'Someone said they were settling accounts that way, thinking they would dodge punishment.'

In the 41st minute, a hooker was knocked out by a kick in the stomach. In the 78th minute, a player was laid out with what seemed to be a boot in the face.

The Agen player Michel Lasserre had his chin opened up by a rogue boot. Punches were ubiquitous.

One onlooker said, 'It was a dreadful display and blame should be shared equally by the teams.'

Another called it 'The final of shame'. *Midi Olympique* opined, 'It was a match that turned into a street brawl.'

One observer wrote later: 'This final left a very bitter taste due to a violence almost unbearable, pitched battles before and after half-time. The knockout of Cassiede and Berho, a kick on Michel Lasserre which split his chin, sneaky... assaults... and multiple screams.'

The FFR called it 'the cancer of brutal play'. They suspended two Dax players, hooker Léon Berho and prop Christian Lasserre, plus the Agen prop Marius Lagiewski for life. But tamely, the sentences were lifted a few months later...

Lagiewski had history, especially against Dax. In the 1962 semi-final, Agen beat Dax despite having Lagiewski sent off, thus forcing him out of the final and denying him a Champion of France medal when Agen beat Béziers. Someone wrote of him, 'He was formidable and feared.'

It wasn't as if the men of violence were unaware of the damage they were doing to the game all over France. They probably even realised the IRB were appalled by such scenes and wondered whether to ban France once again from the Five Nations Championship. The fact that they didn't probably owed more to their fear of rugby league once again gaining popularity in France at union's expense (a point the FFR would have made volubly to the IRB) rather than their own distaste for the brutality.

But this wild, lawless era represented the entire sport's nadir in France. What it revealed was twofold: firstly, that the game was out of control and secondly, the game's so-called authority, the FFR, feared it was largely powerless to do anything about it.

Why wouldn't the FFR be revealed as weak and largely leader-less? Their pusillanimous lifting of the lifetime suspensions within a few months represented a green light to the men of violence to continue as they pleased. Thus clearing the way for a decade of Béziers dominance and brutality in the 1970s and first half of the 1980s.

Why should Béziers have feared swingeing punishments given what had gone before, especially in the 1960s? By their weak approach and the vacuum in leadership at the top of the French game, the FFR invited another era of intimidation and brutality in their club rugby. And they certainly got it.

The election of Albert Ferrasse as the new president of the FFR in June 1968 (he would keep the post until December 1991 and win re-election seven times) seemed to promise something more substantial in the corridors of power. Ferrasse, while accepting the natural physicality of the French game, made clear his distaste for violent acts like kicking people on the ground.

Although he presided over Béziers' era of dominance, he made sure that some Béziers players, like Alain Estève and Michel Palmié, would pay a substantial price for their misdemeanours on the playing field.

Ex-Lourdes and Tarbes prop Michel Cremaschi said, 'Ferrasse was one of the old school, the patron. He was the boss. A real old-school president. When you played against his team, Agen, you knew you couldn't win because of the referee. Maybe Lourdes were winning 12-8 and then suddenly, a penalty. Agen would score from it. 13-12!!'

It was not just outsiders who were confounded and confused by the frequent explosions of violence, given the grace and beauty with which at other times the game could be presented. Even many of those playing rugby in France found this side of the game distasteful.

Alain Lorieux, for one.

Why does he think there has always been an element of violence in French rugby?

'It's because French rugby has always been an image of French society. That's to say, conviviality, joyfulness, loving people, revolutionary, and all that. At the same time, the Frenchman defends his jersey. I believe violence started quite early. In the Olympic Games, early on, France was excluded because of violence. There was this attitude in French rugby.

'I started playing rugby at twenty-two years old. Before that I had been a lifeguard. I really liked the world of rugby, but it was necessary to defend myself. For the spectators, there was a lot of passion towards the field. In fact, in an afternoon there would be grabbing, all the violence would come out and they would go home happy even if their team had lost. So they would feel much better and the players had defended their territory.'

Did Lorieux, still a physically imposing man, approve of the violence? 'No,' he insisted.

'After leaving Grenoble, I played in the third division and every Sunday, I got my head bashed in! It's not the same spirit as the British. In France, you have to prepare yourself for the war. It may take a couple of days; maybe two hours before the game you are smashing the walls. I didn't like that. I was a second rower and a runner. In the French team in the first part of my career, I was not integrated in the team because I was more a player who wanted to run, not to fight.'

Ask Pierre Villepreux, former full-back par excellence for CA Brive and then Stade Toulousain as well as the French national team, which club he hated facing the most. Lavelanet, was his response.

'Always it was a fight, it was impossible to play. The Englishman Roger Shackleton played there, also Patrick Estève, the French wing. But always this team was fighting. Not my rugby.'

There is no doubt that nowadays French rugby has cleaned up its act. To a degree. Incidents like the collective fights of

183

the 1960s and 1970s are now rare. A blatantly violent act will almost certainly earn a red card. In a professional sport that is usually suicidal.

Professionalism is a key factor, especially in matches with a glut of TV cameras operational on the ground. Even amidst the confusion of a ruck or maul, the sly punch can be detected with forensic accuracy by the television match official (TMO) and the referee's attention drawn to the incident.

Yet even so, French indiscipline can still be ruinously expensive. In March 2020 France went to Edinburgh hunting a rare and coveted Six Nations Grand Slam. Alas, the pressure-cooker atmosphere was again too much for some players of 'Les Bleus'.

First, France back-row player François Cros was sent to the sin bin for ten minutes for dumping a Scottish player on his head in a tackle. He was lucky, it could have been red. But worse followed just before half-time.

Prop forward Mohamed Haouas punched the Scottish back-row forward James Ritchie and was promptly sent off. He later received a three-week ban for the incident. Haouas's act was self-destructive. France could not cope with fourteen men and lost the match 28-17, another Grand Slam campaign in ruins.

Something similar had wrecked France's 2019 Rugby World Cup hopes just five months earlier. It was astonishing that French players had clearly not learnt the lesson from that disaster. With France in control of their quarter-final against Wales in Japan, lock forward Sébastien Vahaamahina elbowed Welsh flanker Aaron Wainwright in the face, having already grabbed him round the neck.

France were leading 19-10 at the time and seemingly poised for the semi-finals. But the sending off turned the game on its head. Wales revived, sensing a comeback, and they achieved it against France's fourteen men to win 20-19. All France seethed at Vahaamahina's act of lunacy.

Although it wasn't on the international field, a French club game in February 2020 confirmed that old habits die hard in the world of French rugby. There was uproar throughout the French game when seven players were sent off, as well as both coaches, in a Fédérale League 1 match between Tarbes and Lannemezan, two clubs separated by just 22 miles.

The derby match of the Bigorre region exploded into violence when players and management became involved in a brawl, firstly on the field and then spilling over off it. Numerous punches were thrown and the game was held up for seven minutes.

The referee banished both coaches and picked out five players for instant expulsion. That meant a game of thirteen against twelve, but the brutality and violence had not yet been fully sated. Two more red cards were subsequently waved, and the match finished with twelve against eleven.

Ulrich Pretorius, Tarbes' South African hooker, said after, 'It must be said, it is dangerous for everyone; things can turn very quickly.'

The president of the League Occitanie de Rugby said their competition was now 'the laughing stock of rugby'.

It was the old story of French rugby. Local rivals. Local bragging rights at stake. *Plus ça change, plus c'est la même chose*...

Perhaps this rogue gene that seems to exist in some French rugby men is forever lurking, just waiting to emerge. Take the club playing, years ago, against local rivals down in the south-west. Allegations of biting were made during the game which led, all too predictably, to fist fights. Alas, that gene was still vibrant even at the end.

It was the tradition of most clubs in those days to line up thirty glasses of a drink, normally a pastis or wine, which the players could consume in each other's company. But one of the victims of the biting was in no mood for socialising, even long after the final whistle.

Eyeing his assailant across the table, he picked up his own drink and hurled it over his foe. Inevitably, the mother of all fist fights broke out again.

The danger to France at a World Cup is obvious. There will be no shortage of opponents keen to wind up the French players as far as they can. Just one rogue boot or one punch, launched in anger at an opponent or in retribution for some unseen act, could cost France everything. The players of every major rugby-playing nation know this French weakness exists. Can they exploit it? You can bet your life they will try every trick in the book to do so.

That is professional sport. Every tactic and trick are used to gain an advantage. Fair and foul.

France's players had better understand that immediately. If they don't, and if even a single moment of indiscipline is spotted, the perpetrator might cost France a first Rugby World Cup title. Vahaamahina could have done that in 2019 in Japan. It is something with which he must live.

In some senses, this almost police state-like existence in modern times on the international rugby fields of the world is unfair. Rugby union remains a highly physical, challenging and mentally sapping game. Is it fair to excoriate and punish a player for one single moment of frustration that has led to madness? Perhaps not in every case.

But under the present rules, referees have little room for their own interpretation. They are as much a prisoner of the system as the players. If a single player commits a single transgression, the penalties can be catastrophic for his team, not to say his country.

French players at a World Cup are going to need to be squeaky-clean from the first kick-off to the last. If they're not, wily opponents may lure them into a scenario that becomes disastrous.

What is plainly apparent is that France has the players to win any World Cup. But then, they have had them before and never done it, for a variety of reasons. Self-discipline, perhaps more than any other factor, will be the key to their bid for future titles in the world of rugby.

CHAPTER 8

The Elixir of Life... and a Force of Nature

Béziers–Narbonne

One element of French life and culture seems almost as axiomatic to rugby as the ball itself.

Le vin.

Wine is the elixir of life in France. It flows as freely as a stream, crossing all geographical borders and social classes. It fuels passions. It is the stimulant to those who dabble in the creative trades, like the writer and artist.

Listen to tales from men and women of rugby the world over, of their visits to France and the sumptuous hospitality. Everywhere, wine – red, white, rosé or even champagne – is the delectable liquid that melts barriers, warms souls.

Perhaps the strangest thing of all is, the more the non-French-speaking visitors consume of the stuff in convivial French company, the greater their command becomes of the national language. Or should that be worse...?

189

It is all but inconceivable to sit down for a meal at a French table without a bottle of wine in sight. But how the British and French handle that bottle is very different. Most thirsty Brits gulp the stuff down, the French sip. That makes a considerable difference by the end of a long evening.

So join me at this table, set beautifully for the six guests and their host. I should sketch the scene, for it is one of the loveliest you will find in the South of France. Journeying south, you leave the A9 motorway at Junction 37, Narbonne East, and head away from the town, out towards the hills. Very quickly, you come to a small roundabout and see a sign 'La Clape'. Do your homework on wine and you know this is nothing to do with your health.

Immediately, vineyards surround the road on both sides. I am forever intrigued by how meticulously straight the rows of vines always are. And in the autumn sunshine, the leaves are a riot of colour. Deep yellows brush stunning reds: older, deeper brown leaves hang limply from their stalks.

Earlier in the year, in early summer, the winds of the Mistral make the miniature dandelions, the pretty yellow flowers that grow everywhere on the rough, stony, rocky ground in these vineyards, dance like Wordsworth's daffodils in springtime. The tall grasses bend in the wind towards the sea.

The road twists and turns until reaching a plateau. Here, you can see the short distance across the hills to the Mediterranean. Very soon, you see a sign 'Château Hospitalet'. It is the home, the base of Gérard Bertrand, the most famous winemaker and grower in this part of France.

It was always likely two activities would feature strongly in the life of Gérard Bertrand. Rugby and winemaking. His father grew vines on the land between the town and the sea. Also, young Gérard's birth seemed to coincide with the start of the greatest era in the history of Narbonne rugby club.

He was born in Narbonne in 1965, spent the years from 1984 to 1993 playing for RC Narbonne as a back-row forward, before enjoying a single, promotion-winning season in Paris with Stade Français.

But before his own senior level playing days began, an excited fourteen-year-old looked on as Narbonne won the French Championship title, the Bouclier de Brennus, in 1979. Before that, they had been runners-up to Béziers in 1974, narrowly losing 16-14. He well remembers the triumphant return of the 1979 team, Christian Trallero among them of course, to Narbonne the day after the final.

But Narbonne really took to the Challenge Yves du Manoir. The club won the trophy in 1968, 1973, 1974, 1978, 1979, 1984, 1989, 1990 and 1991. They were runners-up in 1967, 1982 and 1992. For an increasingly rugby-mad youngster living close by the town, Gérard's progression to the club to represent first the lower-grade teams but then the 1st XV was expected. Bertrand was to play in three of those Yves du Manoir trophy-winning sides.

It is an oddity that so few former rugby men seem to have made their mark in the French wine business. Former French wing and full-back Jean-Baptiste Lafond has built a career in the wine trade as a *negociant*. But the mythical image of countless numbers of gnarled former rugby men, ears rubbed smooth and noses rearranged by years of conflict in the nether regions of scrum, ruck and maul, spending the remainder of their lives in the vineyards, is precisely that. A myth.

But Bertrand is not surprised. 'It is not easy to get into. I was already a vine grower when I was twenty. I managed my rugby career at the same time. But now people have to make choices. Also, it is not an easy job. There are thousands of details that are important.

'People say, "Oh, Gérard Bertrand is very successful now." But they forget the twenty-five years when I did not make any money. It took time, it was a long journey. A long battle before starting to be happy and make money. Also, it is a constant battle. It is a passion, but it is for seven days a week. Over the last thirty-five years, I have worked seventy hours a week. Really, a full-time job.'

Anyone wish to apply?

Bertrand shares my view that back in the day, the wines of the Corbières were often like Béziers forwards. Full on, in your face, confrontational. Not very refined.

'In the 1970s, it is true that the quality of many of the Corbières wines was a little rough because people did not have any expertise in quality. My father Georges, who was also a rugby player and a referee, was one of the first to believe in the potential of the region. He made good wine [like their Domaine de Villemajou which has been popular ever since] and taught me about the excellence of the wines in this region.

'We developed a lot of skills and aged our wine in oak to order to produce great quality.

'I think things changed in the 1990s when we started to have some international success with our wines. More recently, in 2021, one of our wines was selected the best red wine in the world in the Japan Wine Challenge (for their 2019 L'Hospitalitas). We have had a lot of recognition from the most important markets.'

In 1987, suddenly and quite unexpectedly, Gérard's father, who had begun to pass on his knowledge of growing grapes and making wine to his young son, died in a road traffic accident. It was a shattering blow for a young man who, not that long before, had received his Baccalaureate and had started studies in business administration and sport. It literally changed his life. At twenty-two, he began to take on the task of running the vineyard, something he was hardly qualified to do at that age.

But from the tragedy emerged the flowering of the man.

Today, Bertrand owns sixteen estates where a variety of grapes are grown and a vast assortment of wines made. Among them is Le Forge, a Syrah/Carignan red blend where the Carignan grapes come from vines over a hundred years old. The wine is a tribute to Bertrand's father. They also make a successful Pinot Noir, Domaine de L'Aigle which was first made around 2006.

One of the rosé wines they make, Clos du Temple, Languedoc Cabrières 2019 vintage was described by *The Times*'s wine expert Jane MacQuitty as 'delicious... and the world's priciest pink'.

At £238 a bottle, it should be delicious!

Bertrand manages 400 people in the business and they have established the Bertrand brand in 160 countries. Not bad going. But tonight, his guests are concerned chiefly with something else. A challenge!

We gather in the warm autumn early evening, before the sun goes down. A large white tablecloth covers a table that contains place settings for six and three bottles, their labels completely hidden. All we know for sure at this stage is that they are reds. Our task, set by quiz master Monsieur Bertrand, might appear straightforward. Guess the vintage of each wine.

Straightforward? Finding your way safely through an old Vietnamese minefield whilst blindfolded would probably be easier.

With each label covered, we try to glean meagre clues. Such as studying intently the colour of the wine as a little is poured into each glass. 'Browning' in colour denotes considerable age; a vibrant colour perhaps suggests a more recent vintage. A crude, basic philosophy, I know. But we're under pressure here and struggling for ideas.

The first one? Fruity and rich with a vibrant colour. It clearly wouldn't be the oldest but it was by no means made last month. My guess? Probably around the turn of the century, say 2000.

LE COQ

It turned out to be from the 1980s. Oh dear. Missed by almost twenty years. Must try harder.

The next has a deep after-taste on the palate, a lovely mature velvety wine I estimate from the second half of the 1970s. Hell, that's about thirty-five years old. Venerable indeed!

Er, that one was from the 1960s. I have to say, for someone who drinks enough of this stuff, this is a pathetic attempt.

So, one final one to come. Gérard will offer few clues. But I note he does pour this one with even greater care and precision. Well, we know it isn't the latest vintage. By the law of inevitabilities, it's going to be the oldest. But how old?

I decide to go for broke. After all, it tastes fantastic, a beautifully matured wine with a long after-taste and hint of browning but nothing to suggest it is past its best. So I offer my estimate. The late 1940s/start of the 1950s. Perhaps it might even have been made in the year the Second World War had ended.

Most of my fellow guests sup and swill and think along similar lines, it transpires.

The answer? 1929. Ye gods. But here is the awful part. As we left the table later at the end of the evening, a couple of us looked back in longing. The 1929 vintage still had a quarter of the bottle left. Unused. A scandal!

But I have a question for him now. In a sense, it's as tough as trying to estimate the age of his red wines. 'Today, you have over 1000 hectares of grapes being grown on sixteen estates and you sell your wines in more than 160 countries around the world. Would you exchange all that for having won the French Championship title with Narbonne?'

He blows out his cheeks forcefully. 'It's a tough question but it's true. I have one regret from my days in rugby and that was being in two French Championship semi-finals but not winning the trophy. I also won the French Cup three times. But never the Championship.'

It irked and irritated him, that unfulfilled pursuit over so many years. But everyone has to move on.

'I realised one day I was chasing something impossible. Now, I don't have any more ghosts in my bedroom. I am at peace because I realise rugby was just an important part of my journey, my life. The result is not the most important thing but the human adventure, like making friends for life as well as sharing emotion.

'You can chase the dream of being an international but the most important thing for a rugby player in France is to share the Bouclier de Brennus with the city because it's a communal spirit. I saw that in 1979 when Narbonne were champions and I was just a teenager. People felt like they were kings of the world for a month.

'That feeling goes on. Rugby keeps you young, even now. As soon as you think about the rugby and capture some of its emotion, you are filled with emotions and good spirit.'

But Narbonne today? Well, it has one of the best indoor markets in all of France. The selection of fresh meat, fish and vegetables beside the huge array of cheeses and preserved meats, is simply astonishing. The fresh fish stall is mouth-watering.

The town itself, so close to the Mediterranean, is also renowned as a starting point for those sailing the Canal du Midi, perhaps all the way across southern France to Bordeaux on the Atlantic. Old Riquet's ditch...

Just inland in this historic region, you can unearth cultural gems, such as the Abbaye de Fontfroide, a former Cistercian monastery 15 kilometres south-west of Narbonne which was founded in 1093. In a setting of exquisite calm, peace and beauty, it is a unique place. Those who come here to see the great buildings and beautiful gardens, to take a little time out of their lives for reflection, seem to depart in peace.

Around 118 BC, Narbonne was the capital of Gaul. It was a major grain exporting centre with traders sailing from there right across the Mediterranean. The port was always critical to Narbonne's fortunes so when it silted up in the fourteenth century, its relevance began to decline.

But Narbonne today? The question has a very different connotation for Bertrand and he knows why. 'There is still the spirit of rugby to be found in the smaller centres like Béziers, Narbonne and Perpignan. So at Narbonne we have a present. But I don't know whether we have a future. [They were relegated from Pro D2 in May 2022.] We cannot reach any more the Top 14. The budget is five times or more higher with most of the Top 14 clubs compared to ours.

'Rugby is still professional in Pro D2 these days. But for me, I believe that after you have professional clubs in the Top 14, the rest should be only semi-professional. It's important for players below the Top 14 level to have a job. I don't want to see players losing their best years, breaking their bones and then at thirty-five having nothing to do. For 90 per cent of the professional players, they don't earn enough money to be able to do nothing after their playing careers. They are not prepared for the second part of their lives. Yet, the second part is longer.'

Bertrand sells his wines around the world. He has great swathes of land under his control and runs a multi-million-euro business. So why wouldn't he put millions into his beloved old club, buy good players and get them back to the summit of French rugby?

He offers a rather more pragmatic approach than that emotional idea. 'I put some money into the club to keep it at a decent level. But the problem is not only just money. It is to find a business model. You have to try to find some resources and in Narbonne you cannot find €25–30 million just like that. It's just not possible.'

Pierre Villepreux, former French international player and coach, sadly agrees. Does he think these one-time leading clubs will ever revive significantly? 'I don't think so, no. Today, they do not have the money. The economy now is in the big cities where you have a major sponsor. Also now, the presidents of the clubs are people coming from the financial world.

'Before, the presidents were coming from rugby. That was very important. Today, the president of Montpellier said, 'I am available to go to the World Cup to help them [the French] with things.' But his company also sponsors the All Blacks!

'When I coached Toulouse, the president was Jean Fabre. He was a captain of the French team. You can share many things with people who are coming from the financial sector but I am not sure you share the same values.'

As Gérard Bertrand concedes, the mentality has changed. 'When I was playing, perhaps twenty-three of the top twenty-five players at the club would be from Narbonne. They had been there since they were youngsters. We had the jersey in our blood and the colour of the jersey was in our skin. We were ready to fight for that. Always. It was a battle just to make sure you were in the bus with the first team when you went to a match.'

Ready to fight? Surely not. *Mais oui*, even here at Narbonne. Bertrand smiled at the memory. 'Violence was always a part of the game. Each town or city had their own style of playing and their own character. Bayonne played in a different way to Narbonne who were different to Clermont. But now we have seen a unification of styles of the game.

'But years ago, they played with their own traditions and intimidation was a part of it. In my time, intimidation was a key. We tried to intimidate people before going into the stadium. A lot of things happened in the tunnel before we even reached the field.'

No finer example of this exists than the 1991 French Championship semi-final between Bègles Bordeaux and Toulon at the Stade Mayol. The lunatics had taken over the asylum long before a ball (how silly of me, I meant a body) had been kicked. Eyes were rolling in heads, bruises from heads and limbs smashed against dressing-room walls already developing as the two sides lined up. As they walked out on to the pitch, some had to be separated by the referee. The fight was on. The combatants couldn't wait for a starting whistle.

The team given the kick-off deliberately kicked the ball straight out, miles over the touchline. Why? So there would be a scrum instead and the fight could begin, the originators of the detonation unseen deep in the bowels of the scrummage.

Ah ha! It wasn't just the players who were switched on. The referee knew full well what was coming and blew his whistle before the scrum went down. A penalty was awarded – who cared to whom it was given and for what alleged offence – to defuse the inevitable explosion which the referee knew he could do nothing to stop.

But that only delayed the violence. At one point in the game, backs were rushing into a general melee to boot the bodies of opponents lying on the ground. Fists were flying everywhere. It was shameful, appalling stuff.

The large influx of overseas players in the French game has inevitably diluted or even defused much of that local pride and spirit. After all, fighting for the honour of your local town or village was the start, one of the key structural elements of this game from its earliest origins in France. Mercenaries, from wherever they come, seldom possess such passion as the locals in the team.

Narbonne's 1979 try-scoring hero Christian Trallero concurs with Bertrand's view. 'Today, the problem with rugby in France is too many foreigners. It's life at a work level, it is globalisation. But the public cannot identify themselves with a team of overseas players. At Montpellier one year, there were so many foreign players. Plus a foreign coach.

'Players used to stay at clubs like Narbonne or Lourdes all their lives. But you cannot fight this globalisation. My shirt comes from one faraway country of the world, my watch from another. This is globalisation.'

Manifestly, rugby cannot exempt itself from this trend, even if it so wished. But, unlike most of western society these days, at least rugby and rugby men and women are not all made in China.

* * *

The hands are like buckets. Great big firemen's buckets. He proffers one and my own hand disappears as it shares his greeting. When you get it back, you count the fingers. Just to be sure.

The face, with that great bulbous nose, looks like its owner has lived three lifetimes. It is weather-beaten, craggy, characterful. Lines run up and down and across it like railway tracks. The eyes penetrate like lasers.

At seventy-eight, he has a head of hair as thick as a thatched cottage. Greying, yes, but that's all. Then there's the thigh. Well, therein lies a tale...

Nothing can prepare you for the sight of this great Frenchman's right thigh. Unless, that is, butchery is your trade.

It is not exactly normal to see a seventy-eight-year-old man drop his trousers two minutes after you meet him for an interview. The lady with us covers her eyes... or pretends to, anyway. There are gasps in the room at the sight.

The scars run from the top of his thigh bone down to the knee. In between, there are ravines where the flesh has been unevenly joined. It is like someone chopped up his whole thigh and then, much later, forgot where the various chunks belonged. So one piece of flesh runs one way, the next the other way with parts of it just folded over.

Those in Monsieur Walter Spanghero's office, just outside Toulouse, are then invited to inspect the inner parts of his thigh in technicolour. The photo is all but stomach-churning, a grotesque sight. Taken in an operating theatre, it shows the bloodied interior of the thigh when a major infection was threatening to destroy his whole leg. You wouldn't want to show this around after a good plate of cassoulet.

Walter Spanghero.

The story is, one of French rugby's greatest ever forwards went into hospital in Toulouse for what was expected to be a simple hip operation. Alas, an infection got into the thigh. That was the start of a three-year nightmare for the great old Narbonne and Toulouse lock and No. 8 forward.

By the time he was finally cleared to go home, he had been operated on twenty-two times, had received care in five hospitals in and around Toulouse, had spent ten months in isolation, suffered three heart attacks and two strokes and encountered two viruses that were unknown even to the medics.

'Every time I thought I might leave, I had another virus. The surgeon said, "What can I do with someone who has such mammoth bones?"

'I thought I would have a better life upstairs, but they didn't want me,' he joked. Christ, if you can joke after that run of misfortune, you must be a special person.

Walter Spanghero certainly is. Between 1964 and 1973, he won fifty-one caps for France and was voted, by legendary All Blacks forward Colin Meads, the toughest opponent he ever met. Coming from Meads, that was right up there in the Croix de Guerre class of honours. He was a fabulous, fantastic ball-handling forward of immense power who just wanted to get his great hands on the ball and run, support others and help keep the ball alive. At 1.87m tall and 100kgs, he had the muscular frame and speed to trouble all opponents. He was a freak, and freakishly good.

Once, on a tour of South Africa, he even played at prop.

The son of an Italian bricklayer, the Spanghero family left Friuli, near Trieste, to settle in France's Aude *département* in the 1930s. In time they began to farm, a perfect environment in which to rear and toughen up the six boys born to Madame Spanghero: Walter, Claude, Laurent, Guy, Jean-Marie and Gilbert. There were also two daughters, Maryse and Annie.

When he'd finally recovered from the twenty-second and last operation, someone asked him if he felt he owed rugby his life for making him tough enough to survive all that. 'Rugby training did not get me through it. I was working on our farm in Bram, driving a tractor and carrying heavy weights when I was fifteen. It was the fact that I worked in those conditions that got me through it.'

But at a cost. He confesses his memory is not the same and his hand was shaking. He had to force himself to learn to write again. But, he says, the discipline to survive it all came from his family and education. 'Members of my family were very disciplined. Nobody would ever complain. You just went forward, never complaining. If you don't have the will to do something, you can't achieve anything.'

That was how it was back in those times.

Spanghero was always a huge, powerful man with enormous bones. When he was fifteen and still playing soccer, they asked him to stop because he was breaking all the ankles of opponents. Not illegally, just through the force of his tackles.

But he might have been lost to rugby almost before he had started the game. 'I didn't want to play rugby. The first game I played my nose was broken all over my face. I said, "I don't want to play this game any more."'

He was persuaded to persevere, but then suffered a broken rib in his first senior match against Dax. But working on his parents' farm continued to toughen him. 'Sixty years ago, the farm was far more important than playing rugby. But farming was tough.'

He earned the respect of every opponent, cheerfully or grudgingly. Then, in 1972 came a watershed moment. France arrived at the great old Stade Colombes for their last international match on the ground. It was a spring day, warm and inviting. France had lost several recent games, partly because the petulant French selectors had omitted some key players like Spanghero.

Forced by media and public criticism, the selectors backed down. Spanghero returned as the senior forward and captain. But first, there was what we might call a conflict of philosophy.

Full-back Pierre Villepreux, on his final appearance for 'Les Bleus' insisted they attack with ball in hand from everywhere. Spanghero promised, 'If you do only this, you will never have any ball in the backs. I will keep the ball.'

But Spanghero knew rugby. He could see possibilities and eventually signed up to the approach. France attacked from almost everywhere that day, slicing open the English defence like master butchers at their trade. The attacking lines they ran, not least featuring Spanghero off the tail of the line-outs and back of scrums, overwhelmed the Englishmen. 'The first thing we wanted to do was attack, put speed in the game,' he remembered.

France scored six tries to two, won by thirty-seven points to twelve, and anyone who was there that day has never forgotten it. The rugby played by France was simply sumptuous. Even the English were opening champagne bottles that night in Paris. You just felt privileged to have been there.

French style and elegance at its zenith.

Those French players, Spanghero told me, were special performers. No surprise there with names such as Maso and Villepreux in the backs. Plus with mobile forwards such as Spanghero, Benoît Dauga, Élie Cester and others, France ran rampant. 'The best team of that era was in 1972/73,' he thought. 'We beat England in 1972 and New Zealand in 1973 in Paris and drew a Test in Australia, losing the other by a single point.'

But the open, attacking, running style demanded great fitness.

'It was no problem for me to run 20 kilometres in a game,' he smiled. 'Also, the scrums were much tougher than today. I had more than enough fitness from working on the farm. At twelve years old, I would be milking the cows at 5 o'clock in the morning before I went to school. Then the same in the evening when I came home.'

But the violence? Well, Spanghero knew all about that. If an opposing team could get to him and reduce him by injury or some violent act, the outcome could be affected. Take Narbonne's 1974 French Championship final against the feared Béziers at the Parc des Princes.

From Béziers' kick-off, Spanghero was engulfed by a pack of human animals, tearing at their greatest foe. When play eventually stopped, Spanghero was seen limping heavily from some blow to his thigh. His shorts had been ripped to pieces, as if by a pack of hunting dogs. 'They all smashed me,' he said. 'I had a testicular problem afterwards. But they had planned it from the kick-off. They wanted to take me, like the Springboks... had tried. Do that first before playing rugby.

'When you do not accept this intimidation and you answer, it becomes even more violent. But then, violence has always existed.'

'But why?' I asked.

'Because we are French. Stupid people are everywhere, particularly in rugby. I never punched people but for certain others, rugby without this... violence... could not exist. It comes from indiscipline. The French are not disciplined. But now you have television, and there are three referees. Everything has changed.'

Some victims of this violence back in the day continue to pay the price. Spanghero tells the story of his brother Claude, like him a French international from Narbonne. In the line-outs during one club match, he was being illegally prevented from jumping by an opponent. Claude told the referee, 'Do something about it or I will.'

Nothing changed, so when it happened again, Spanghero punched his foe. From the blow, the opponent was paralysed in the face.

Walter remembered being at the 1971 French Championship final when Béziers met Toulon and André Herrero had his ribs smashed in. The notorious assault, allegedly by Estève. Spanghero's 'take' on it was frank.

'Herrero would do exactly the same thing as they did to him. It was part of the game. You had to tell yourself that. It was part of the game. It's like foie gras: at first, you don't know what it is. But then you get used to it...'

But French rugby has other attributes, many others. What, I asked him, has France given the rugby-playing world? 'To begin, the playing revolution of the game. It has given open field rugby rather than just strength up front. In our time, the main thing was to avoid opponents, to find space. We wanted to play a complete rugby rather than just forward-based. Otherwise, we would never have beaten teams like New Zealand.'

That elegance, that flow has been the legacy of that generation and men like Spanghero, Dauga, Maso, Boniface, Villepreux and others.

There are occasional exceptions, as we have seen. But by and large, the legacy of excessive and omnipresent uncontrolled violence has not survived the passing of a generation.

For that, Spanghero, now seventy-eight, is happy. And his happiness extends to a life well lived. He and his family knew tough times in the early years. Not least when Walter was sent to a boarding school and struggled with an academic life. The story is amusing.

At thirteen, he found himself at the Saint Joseph de Limoux school. But these were different times to the modern day. One day, a teacher tried to kick young Walter. He avoided the boot and the teacher smashed his ankle against a bench.

Walter's father was summoned to the school. Hearing the story, he told his son, 'If studies don't suit you, you're going to come with me to the fields.'

His school education was over. At thirteen, Walter Spanghero became a farm boy. The rest, as they say, is history. But whatever happened to the French national team and their ability to produce that mesmerising rugby so beloved of Spanghero and those of his era?

Happily, France's ability to play sumptuous attacking rugby, with a philosophy and will based on seeking space, fluidity, movement, sparkle and creativity has again emerged in the last few years. It may have gone into hibernation for some years, but it is far from moribund. Undeniably, it is not seen on every stage, at each performance. Some displays fall below expectation. Inevitably.

But modern-day audiences have glimpsed again the mesmeric qualities this innate Gallic skill can bring. It can illuminate a field as vividly as any floodlight pylon.

CHAPTER 9

La Ville Rose

Narbonne–Castelnaudary–Toulouse–Auch

The A61 autoroute connecting Narbonne on the Mediterranean Sea to Toulouse, the so-called 'Pink City' in the Haute Garonne, runs for 91.7 miles.

Heading west, initially, it snakes its way past the vineyards of the great Corbières region, like an endlessly slithering tarmac-coated reptile.

In early 2022, it was a pain in the neck, given the omnipresent roadworks and speed restrictions. Trying to stay in a reduced width lane with huge trucks cruising alongside you, often in heavy rain, was no pleasure. Fun on some electronic game screen, no doubt. But not for real.

But when the motorway work gangs have packed up and gone off to some other road to put more unknown thousands of motorists in peril just to repair a hard shoulder or paint some fresh white lines, you can enjoy the majesty of this ride. Old, abandoned castles built by the Cathars line the route, invariably constructed, of course, at the top of hills to deter invaders.

Then at times, you glimpse the beauty of the Canal du Midi, ambling gently along beside the autoroute-rushing vehicles. A world within a world.

In modern times, Toulouse, with its famous terracotta-coloured bricks, has been the rugby capital of France. In twenty-five years since the dawn of professionalism, Stade Toulousain have been French champions nine times. The next most successful club is Stade Français with six titles.

But before we get to Toulouse, we will see motorway exits to some great rugby towns, past and present: Castres, Mazamet, Carcassonne. You also spy an exit to a town renowned as the home of one of France's greatest dishes. Castelnaudary and cassoulet.

The French will cheerfully spend hours debating the merits and contents of this one dish. It seems to go so well with rugby; both are as much traditions of the winters in these parts, as frosty mornings and muddy fields.

We once dared to cook cassoulet for a French artist friend and his wife at our home in the south. This was a bit like preparing rotting herrings for the Swedes, or telling an Aussie to clear off and leave us Brits in charge of the barbecue.

A brave but risky enterprise.

Mind you, we were spurred on to great culinary heights by the sight of a magnum of St Emilion Grand Cru, his generous offering to the feast. He deserved a meal commensurate with such elan.

Anyway, after consuming two giant portions from the huge earthenware pot full of the stuff, our guest wiped a napkin across his mouth and declared confidently, 'This was the best cassoulet I have ever had.'

Cassoulet is almost as historic in France as the castles of the Cathars. Indeed, it is said to have originated from the siege of Castelnaudary by Edward, the Black Prince, in 1355, during the

Hundred Years' War. The people of the town are said to have collectively pooled the little food they had left and cooked it all up in a giant cauldron. Perhaps they then cracked open some of the wines stored in the town's cellars.

Or maybe it was a cunning plot to lure the invaders in for supper and end the siege.

I once stopped an elderly lady in the centre of Castelnaudary and asked her a simple question. 'Where is the best cassoulet served in this region?'

She directed me two or three miles out of town, off the road and down a muddy side-track. I thought it was a joke until I arrived in the car park. Every single car, and there were about twenty-five of them, had local number plates. The restaurant itself served nothing apart from this single dish.

When I'd eaten my plate, served from a giant communal pan kept warm on the stove in the middle of the restaurant, I understood why. It was sensational.

The only sad part of the story is, this was about thirty years ago and I could never remember its name to go back. So you can't, either.

Cassoulet has certain essential ingredients and others by choice. Indisputably, you need chopped up onions, some garlic, sliced pork belly, sausages, confit canard, two tins of white beans and stock. You can, if you wish, put in a chunk of lamb, preferably neck, plus a few strips of streaky bacon and two tins of tomatoes. You can also put breadcrumbs on the top. If you don't want to put in tomatoes (and they say you never see tomatoes in a traditional cassoulet), you can use tomato puree.

Raymond Blanc's own recipe suggests SIX garlic cloves, left whole. Which may send your friends running for cover, considering what your breath is likely to be like after that lot. But prepare for a siege if you follow this recipe. It takes five and a half hours to cook.

With ours, it takes about three hours. Which equates to about two bottles of wine consumed by the chef. BEFORE the dish is served...

Gérard Bertrand licks his lips at the prospect. He admits he is a huge fan. He loves the recipe at Restaurant Comte Roger in Carcassonne and says, 'I like this dish because all the chefs have their own recipe.' At Comte Roger, they make their cassoulet with confit canard, Toulouse sausages, pork belly and white beans from Castelnaudary.

Bertrand's preferred red wine to suit best the richness of the cassoulet is his own Château La Soujeole Grand Vin 2018. It is from an estate just outside Carcassonne.

A journey through France without regular stops to enjoy the food would be like a trip to Cairo without seeing the Pyramids. In the case of Toulouse, no visit to this great rugby ground and institution is complete without experiencing the food.

There are, as I said earlier, reasons why Stade Toulousain are one of just two clubs never to have been relegated from the top league of French rugby. One is money but another is more difficult to define. But it revolves around two words. Class and expectation. They are the Real Madrid of French rugby.

Everything this club does speaks of class. Developing the entire matchday experience is one way. You can book a seat in the smartly designed and furnished large brasserie in the main stand at the Stade Ernest Wallon, and choose your meal. When I was last there, they were offering the choice of four starters, five main courses and six desserts.

This is a proper restaurant, not just some matchday catering outlet.

Perhaps you would choose, as a main course, steak tartare, Basque pork with a sauce, or maybe entrecote steak with wine sauce or a cod steak with clams and samphire. Or maybe the chef's speciality, a mixture of shellfish and white fish. The *entrée* and *plat* costs €24. Add $5 if you include a dessert.

Afterwards, you can order a coffee or fortifying Armagnac (it originates from the nearby Gers region) prior to the game. When you have finished, you stroll out into the stands and take your seat.

Eating out at a sporting event is certainly not the sole preserve of Stade Toulousain rugby club. But the last time I checked, English Premiership clubs like Gloucester and Newcastle weren't quite offering this quality of food. As for the range of wines, not even the finest football clubs in England can match them. This is exceptional for a sporting organisation.

Nor is this quality confined solely to those booking a table in their restaurant. I arrived at the ground one evening for a Championship match, against Brive. But before the game, I toured the mobile food stands inside the ground. There were the usual baguettes of *jambon* and *fromage*. Toulouse and *merguez* sausages, too. But there was something else.

One stall was doing a roaring trade in confit duck. A girl wearing hygienic plastic gloves was busy slicing each pre-cooked leg and arranging the cut pieces on to a baguette. It was bursting with meat by the time she had finished. The taste was exquisite. At €6.50, it was superb value.

The smell of those ghastly, stinking onions that emit from almost every cooking outlet at English sports grounds, like odours from drains, is nowhere to be found here.

Toulouse ensure this type of quality goes down to the tiniest detail. I requested exclusive interviews with their star players and internationals, captain Antoine Dupont and Romain Ntamack, plus the recently retired New Zealand All Black Jerome Kaino. I stipulated I wanted to talk with each player individually, not in a group.

Ask most clubs or provinces in Britain and Ireland to make its best players available for exclusive interview and, in most cases, the absolute best you will get is a collective interview with the player put up for the entire media corps. Stade Toulousain did want to know to whom Dupont and Ntamack were talking and for what publication. But, the details settled, at an agreed hour each presented himself. About half an hour with each, on his own, followed by the next one. Then Jerome Kaino arrived.

That level of assistance was matched by the help forthcoming from the office staff. 'If you are attending the match, would you like a car park pass?' It was duly provided.

I'm not saying none of this ever exists at other clubs in France, or in the UK or Ireland. But in everything they do at this formidable club, they demonstrate, subtly and without fanfare, their sheer professionalism. They set standards on and off the pitch here that others struggle to match.

Nor were those examples one-offs. With a film crew alongside for a night match against La Rochelle at the 36,000-capacity Toulouse Stadium, we shot pictures around the ground before the start. But afterwards, we needed one interview. Antoine Dupont. This wasn't easy.

The guy was weary after a tough match. He had to do TV immediately after. Then shower and change, and head upstairs to the special supporters' lounge to do a 'question and answer' session and sign autographs. Finally, at 0025 hours, he comes across to us for an exclusive interview.

Why? Purely because of the efforts of Lorène Guillot from the club's media department. She simply epitomises the meaning of the phrase 'media assistance'. 'It may be difficult,' she warns us. But because of her efforts and professionalism, it happens. Outside of North America, where do you find a club's media people prepared to go to these lengths to give you what you want? Stade Toulousain seek to help, not hinder.

Of course, Toulouse rugby club is in prime position to maximise its proud position as one of the top clubs (or provinces) in the northern hemisphere. The city is home to the multi-billion-euro Airbus Industrie, with its base just down the road from the ground in Blagnac.

Final production and testing is carried out at Toulouse, although parts for the planes are made all over the world. But Toulouse is increasingly Airbus, and Airbus, together with all the offshoot companies that have followed in its wake, is Toulouse. Inevitably, some of the vast sums generated by this business have found their way into the coffers of Stade Toulousain rugby club through sponsorship and other means.

Few clubs enjoy so global a multi-billion industry on their own doorstep. It gives them a rock-solid base, a reliable launching pad to help fund their own organisation. Other clubs, perhaps subject to the whims and fluctuating interests of individual multi-millionaires, cannot be as sure that their chief financial backer will always be there for them. Wealthy men can get tired of expensive toys. They'll throw them out of their pram when they get bored.

Thus, most years the club enjoys the biggest budget of any French club. Or it is within touching distance of the biggest spenders. In season 2021/22, Toulouse had €37.3 million at their disposal, just shy of Stade Français's €39.1 million. These sums matter. Usually, they decree success or failure. Although, not always...

On a hot June night in Nice in 2022, the club tenth on the list (out of fourteen) regarding budgets for the year, Castres Olympique, confronted Stade Toulousain, with the second biggest budget, in the Top 14 semi-final. Much against expectation, Stade Toulousain were beaten, 24-18. It reminded us that financial supremacy does not ALWAYS transcend to achievement on the field. It also underlined that the zealous

The stadium at Brive, in the beautiful Correze.

fires of competition continue to burn fiercely throughout the world of French rugby.

That same season, Brive could boast a budget of just €17.6 million. Below them were Perpignan, with €17.4 million. Finally Biarritz, scraping together a paltry €12.8 million. And as February's aesthetically stunning hoar frosts arrived across France in 2022, Biarritz faced a harsh, cold reality. They were stuck at the bottom of the Top 14 table, already with little hope of survival among the elite.

The Top 14 season was to end in precisely that same order of finances. Biarritz ended up last, then Perpignan, then Brive.

This is how it is in French rugby. Indeed, most professional sport.

But then, Brive is a well-run club, professional in its ambitions and behaviour. Part of the reason for that is the way

France's top clubs are monitored by the FFR financial experts. Brive's English President Simon Gillham told an interviewer in October 2022, 'The financial discipline [within French rugby] is incredible compared to the things I read about England. If you say, "We are signing Beauden Barrett next week," you have to prove you have the finances.'

There is, too, far more money available to French clubs. Their deal for TV rights with Canal+ is worth £100 million annually, shared by the top thirty clubs. In England, BT Sport pays just £35 million per year for rights to the Gallagher Premiership.

The growing reputation and allure of French club rugby was confirmed in October 2022 when Gillham announced that UK millionaire Ian Osborne had agreed to buy a share in Brive, rather than investing in an English club. Gillham said, 'Ian's thinking was that he wanted to invest in French rugby not English rugby because he found it is a much healthier place to be.'

It was a remarkable testimony to the growing appeal of the French club game and the ultra-professional way it is run compared to some other countries.

* * *

It was good to be back in Toulouse again, queuing for lunch or dinner at the famous L'Entrecote or sitting down watching your meat being cooked over an open fire at the atmospheric L'Aubrac in Rue de la Colombette. Both are right in the centre of the city.

There was, too, a great man of Stade Toulousain whom I had long wanted to meet again. Alas, he lives now in Limoges, in the Haute-Vienne *département*. It is a six-hour round trip drive from Toulouse. But I'd travel a lot further than that to spend an afternoon talking rugby with Pierre Villepreux.

We had known each other a long time. Back in the day, when he was Toulouse coach and I lived in Bath, I met him at a Toulouse Championship match one spring. He asked me where I was now living. The name 'Bath' made his ears prick up. 'We are looking for two pre-season friendly matches. Would Bath play us?' he asked.

I told him I'd check, find a second club interested in a game and get back to him. Bath were keen and my contacts at the Welsh club Neath similarly excited interest. So, in time, Stade Toulousain ran out on the famous Recreation Ground at Bath with a team littered with star names.

Three days later, they lined up at Neath, the venue once dubbed the 'bag-snatching capital of the world' by Australian coach Bob Dwyer after his Wallabies had had their, how shall we say, private parts closely examined by their foes. Dwyer recalled years later, 'One of their quaint activities, I assume to "distract" our players, was to apply the "monkey grip" [a hand full of nuts] in the ruck/maul.

'It worked in fact, but, in the end, we won the fight and the game!'

But this was years later. Surely that sort of thing wouldn't happen again here? It couldn't, could it?

I understood that Toulouse were subject to similar treatment in the nether regions of the scrum, ruck or maul because the match turned into a humdinger of a fight. As far as I can remember, a couple of players were sent off and the bad blood lingered to the end. Some 'friendly' match. I felt pretty ordinary about having fixed up a sporting World War III.

So the instigator of these games watched two huge crowds turn up and walked away without a penny for his match-making skills. Furthermore, he was happy to do so. But someone cared. Pierre Villepreux brought me a smart Stade Toulousain jersey as *un petit cadeau*.

Back in the day, Villepreux was so respected as a coach that England, through their then director of rugby Don Rutherford, sought his services in an advisory capacity. Rutherford had seen Villepreux and his colleague Jean-Claude Skrela steer Toulouse to three French Championship titles in 1985, 1986 and 1989. What is more, they had achieved it with a glorious incarnation of the style Villepreux always espoused with the French international teams for whom he played thirty-four times between 1967 and 1972.

Villepreux coached Stade Toulousain from 1982 to 1989 and for most of that time his teams purred like the club's resident cat. With a forward base that was strong but always highly mobile and a shrewd, powerful ball player in Albert Cigagna in the influential No. 8 position, they unleashed backs with

At Limoges, the author (left) with former French player and coach Pierre Villepreux (centre) and ex-French journalist Serge Manificat.

217

the pace and talent of men like Denis Charvet, Eric Bonneval, Guy Noves and Serge Gabernet. It was a sight of great beauty to watch. They flowed like the mighty Garonne, in full winter flood.

Villepreux was asked by the RFU to fly to London to take a couple of England rugby training sessions. They fixed his flight to Heathrow, drove him to Bisham Abbey and off he went, cajoling and urging his philosophies into the minds of the England players. No money was ever mentioned – well, after all, this was a game that was still 'strictly amateur' at the start of the 1990s. At Twickenham, anyway. Although someone did make some money out of it.

A couple of years later, with France playing at Twickenham in the Five Nations Championship, a spectator who had flown in from Toulouse to watch the game, a Monsieur Pierre Villepreux, walked into the England Rugby shop inside the ground. He was mystified: he thought he'd heard a familiar voice.

Turning to a TV screen, he saw a familiar face. His own. There, captured on video tape, was Villepreux's training session with the England team. Being flogged at £15 a pop. Cheapskates!!!

Not that Pierre Villepreux would ever bear a grudge. The man wouldn't understand the emotion.

Through his playing skills as an attacking, running full-back, and later as an innovative coach, Villepreux's name eventually became synonymous with Toulouse. But he wasn't from there. He was born in Pompadour in the Corrèze region, during the Second World War, and originally joined CA Brive.

He tells a lovely story of the rugby philosophy ingrained in youngsters in those days. They lived in Pompadour and his father played the game. It was a small club in the bottom division. They had a schoolmaster who also played, so at break times there was always a game. The Sunday social life of the town in those days was at the local rugby club. This was 1950–

53 and Pierre was about eight or ten. They played what he called a free game, in the space behind the goalposts. No set positions, no referee either. 'We just played for the pleasure of running, passing. Sometimes there was a fight.

'We learned this rugby because life allowed us to do that, to be free. If you are free, you take the initiative, the decisions.'

Why does he think this country so loves rugby?

'Firstly, there are two cultures of rugby. There is the culture that arrived with the universities in Bordeaux and Toulouse. But there is also the culture which I call the fighting spirit, the will to play rugby because it is a moment of fighting and very often not always a correct fight.

'So there is this sort of ambivalence. People who like rugby to be more in movement, and others who prefer rugby where you play against the other team with the will to destroy them.'

No prizes for guessing the mantra, the creed Villepreux has followed all his life. They put him in the first team at Brive when he was eighteen but the youngster had a character strong enough to write his own terms of engagement. 'They told me, "You will play full-back, not fly half."

'I said, "OK, but if I play full-back I want to run with the ball. I won't waste the ball and kick it away like full-backs everywhere."'

Wow, the cojones of the young man. At eighteen. Which is exactly the way another young man plays in contemporary times. Stade Toulousain's Romain Ntamack.

The rugby culture of Brive changed with that decision. 'Before, it was only the forwards who played at Brive. Afterwards, it was the backs. We gave another spirit, and we ran with the ball more than we fought. It was another way of thinking rugby, another sense not only to the players but to the public who accepted the challenge to change their way of thinking about rugby and the way to appreciate it.'

For Villepreux, it is a clash of cultures. The most glorious illustration of this 'free game', of a philosophy forged on attack, pace and movement, came at London's Wembley Stadium in 1998 when his French team destroyed Wales 51-0 in the Five Nations Championship. France's fleet-footed runners under Villepreux's tutelage amassed seven tries in the game.

Could it be replicated today, this fast-flowing rugby? It is already. Observe the way in which Antoine Dupont, Romain Ntamack, Damian Penaud and others are dragging France to levels of attacking excellence we feared might have been lost forever from the French game. Thankfully, France found a coach in Fabien Galthié willing to embrace this mentality.

Could others do it? Yes, if they had a coach of sufficient courage, willing to offer just a basic structure, the lightest of hands on the tiller, but then give the best players their heads to make their own decisions. To play with spontaneity. But too many coaches lack that courage. They are control freaks, seeking to infiltrate every element of their players' minds. Alas, innate caution defeats courage in such men. Under them, too much modern-day rugby has become like chess...

You stand here, you wait there for the second or third phase and then you bring him into this position, etc., etc.

Villepreux, who played for Stade Toulousain from 1965 to 1975, concedes, 'My philosophy is the philosophy of liberty for the players. When I played with Jo Maso and also the forwards, we had two principles. One was, it is necessary to go forward and two, it is necessary to support the ball carrier. That is all. Going forward and support is the basis of this game.

'We could adapt our game but the players decided. It was up to them to understand the game, why they should pass or kick or just keep the ball.

'The principle of going forward and supporting are the only constraints. But today, they have a game plan and they must follow it. It's completely different. But I was pleased to see Ntamack play the ball from behind his own line against New Zealand in November 2021 in Paris. It is the capacity to seize quickly that opportunity which the game gives you. For me, this was a crucial moment. But if it had been another player, not Ntamack, I am sure he would have touched the ball down.'

Does this new French team have the capacity to play like Villepreux's teams?

'Yes, completely. But for that, you must train like you want to play and play like you have trained. Not spend five days in the gym. For me, there is still too much structure in rugby. At one time when I played in the Brive team (from 1963 to 1965), we had no coach. We had one man who chose the team, that's all. The training sessions were taken by the players. We talked together and we had this liberty to play like we wanted. Yes, the liberty to make mistakes.'

Intriguingly, Villepreux cites current French coach Galthié as one of the few people in French rugby's recent past brave enough to confront the coach. 'For me, the players have not been brave enough to say to the coach, "No, no. We will not play this way, but in another way." But Galthié was this player. He had the capacity to understand quickly and to play this sort of rugby. For me, if you have an opportunity even on your goal line, you try.'

It is, he insists, in the French DNA to play in this manner. 'In France, we have always had this capacity to understand the game better and quicker than many other nations. In England they call it the "French flair". But we are not the only nation to have flair.

'When I coached the England team, I said, "OK, go, play."

'The players did not understand. But after two or three sessions with them, they began to have this flair because I gave them this possibility to understand the situation, to change, to take their own decisions and not the decisions of the coach.

'The No. 10 now of England [Marcus Smith], I would take him immediately. Please let him play like he wants. Not say that he has to do this, that and that.'

Who would be the best player he ever played with? 'Each time he gave me the ball it was the right moment. But if the ball was not good, he would keep it or kick it. But it was always the rugby adapted to the situation. His understanding of the game, his technique and skill were remarkable.'

Jo Maso.

*   *   *

So, from one great Stade Toulousain man to another...

France used to call its leaders by specific names. Back in the day, there was Louis the Pious, Charles the Bald, Louis the Stammerer. And Louis the Lazy.

It might be a fun exercise, I thought, to apply something similar to a few French rugby men down the years.

Jacques Fouroux? Jacques the Wily.

Michel Palmié? Michel the Violent.

Jean-Pierre Rives? Perhaps, Jean-Pierre the Philosopher.

You had to be careful when you stayed with Rives in his younger days. There was always the propensity for, what shall we say, a little misunderstanding. Like the time I arrived before 8 o'clock one morning at his Paris apartment, ready for a day's work with him on his biography.

'*Bonjour* Jennif—' the name froze on my lips. For this beauteous creature in black lingerie answering the door certainly wasn't the one I was expecting.

Inside the apartment, we had the chance to talk between ourselves. Jean-Pierre explained. 'Ah, Jennifer is *en vacances*. This is the new Jennifer.'

Well, I'm glad we cleared that up. Back to the coffee.

It's a few years now since that little moment of surprise on the doorstep of his apartment. More like decades. All of which reflects his words when he answers the telephone.

'Jean-Pierre, it's Peter. How are you?'

'STILL ALIVE,' he cries, with rousing enthusiasm.

I know the feeling.

So we talk and make a plan to meet. The location is perfect. Along the Mediterranean coast heading west from Nice, you take the A8 motorway and come off at Le Muy. Just a little distance from the coast is Grimaud, near which is a stunning private golf course.

When you stand at the top of a hill and look down at a generous wide fairway dropping away below you, with the sun-kissed Mediterranean as a backdrop and St Tropez just across the bay, then you know someone's doing it tough. But then, as they say, someone has to...

For a long time, Rives was a regular player on this beautiful course. But these days, you are more likely to see his seventeen-year-old son Jasper out on the fairways. We meet at the clubhouse for lunch and Jean-Pierre shakes his head when I ask if he still plays.

'No, no more. But Jasper plays well. He can hit a drive up to 320 metres.'

At seventeen? Ye gods!

He's arrived on this warm, sunny day in a large, outsized, tropical-style floral shirt, with baggy white linen shorts. Hair tousled, as it always was. The famous blond locks are now white.

But the colour of his hair really does not concern Rives these days. The brush with death two years ago which so nearly engulfed him and his family straightened out any misplaced priorities in his life.

The author (right) with Jean Pierre Rives.

Rives and his second wife, Sonia, and their two sons, Jasper and Kino-Jean, were in bed when the fire took hold. By the time they realised its severity, Jean-Pierre and his wife were scrambling to safety just in the clothes they wore, while Jasper jumped out of a window into the garden to escape. They believe the fire had started in a battery attached to one of the boys' electric surfboards.

By the time the flames had finally been extinguished, nothing remained of Jean-Pierre Rives's home. His mementos, the art he had recently completed, all his books and photos plus his clothes were gone. Everything was lost. Literally, he stood in the street in a shirt and shorts. All he had left was what he stood up in. But he had his family. They all survived. 'We were just happy to be alive,' he said.

It's just like the old Jean-Pierre as he shows me the vast building site where the new house will be erected. He shrugs at the memories, the lost items. Even the Légion d'honneur and National Order of Merit medals awarded to him by the French government. But then, he was never one for baubles, possessions, stuff. It didn't float his boat.

He did lament the loss of all his photos from his youth and playing days. The many pictures taken at the Parc des Princes on French international days, with his great friends. Brothers in arms.

But I have come with a surprise for him.

When we worked on his book, all those years ago, he gave me a vast file – of pictures of friends, on the rugby fields, on the golf courses they shared. These were happy times. Alas, some, like Robert Paparemborde and Jacques Fouroux, have now passed away.

But there were others: Blanco, Sella, Skrela, Dintrans, Ondarts, Bertranne and many others. It wasn't until quite recently I came upon this file, as you do, in clearing out more of that *stuff*.

Some memories from those times, I told him, handing over the large envelope. He opened it and his face was instantly wreathed in smiles. 'Oh, this is fantastic. Thank you so much. I thought I had lost all of these. What a wonderful surprise.'

It is not the only surprise of the day. As we work our way through a light lunch and sip the sparkling water in the outdoor clubhouse restaurant, the conversation starts not with rugby, but golf. He has some special memories from back in the day.

'I played with Seve Ballesteros three or four times. Charity events, pro-am special golf days, you know the kind of thing. Seve was so nice, a wonderful guy.'

But someone else he played with in that era was at the other end of the spectrum. 'I played with Nick Faldo, too. But he was

Stade Toulousian players celebrate another French championship title win with the Bouclier de Brennus in the bath.

not very nice. *Sir* Nick Faldo!! He never said hello, goodbye or anything. What an a***hole.'

Perhaps the loss of much of his art in the fire has propelled him to work longer hours subsequently. He takes me down some steps in the temporary house they are renting, just a stone's throw from where the new, bigger home will be built. Stacked up against the walls of this vast underground room – it extends to the entire size of the huge, sprawling house – are scores of paintings.

'I moved to abstract geometric paintings some time ago,' he says. 'It is simpler than to work on sculptures. I must go somewhere else, to a workshop about ten minutes' drive away, to work on those. With my paintings I can work at home.

'These... [he points to a stack of half a dozen large canvases] are waiting to be sent to people in America.'

His sculptures have been found in various towns and cities

226

of France, such as Lyon, Paris, Toulouse, etc. And to live on the Mediterranean, a haven through the years for so many of France's great artists in part because of the beautiful light, is something he regards as a blessing.

He resists the temptation, perhaps we should say inevitability, of so many of his generation to criticise modern-day rugby. Rives seizes the artist's brush; hence, he sees a broad canvas which contemporary players can fill as they wish. Besides, he grins, many of the myths, the legends of past times were just that. Myths.

'We thought we were world champions at rugby just by passing the ball. But I remember some games when we never passed the ball at all. No one passed in those days.

'The important thing is to fight and win. It is the same today; rugby is rugby. You know the French – they are always fighting. Welcome to France. But for me, what matters is the spirit is still there. Whatever style your team plays, only with the forwards or to find space for the backs, keep the spirit.

'I hope we will stay like this because when you see someone today from rugby, it is clear the spirit remains. Perhaps the styles change a little sometimes. But the spirit, the comradeship among the players, is the same.

'When I met you today, after so long, that is rugby, that is the spirit of rugby. I don't care if we pass the ball like this or like that. Or if we use the foot. The friendship and spirit are the most important things in this game. These are the values of the family of rugby. That is the same today as when I played. [He represented Stade Toulousain from 1974 to 1981.]

'So I wish them the best, these new players. I hope they will enjoy the game as we did. It is not the same game today but that is OK.

'When I see players like Antoine Dupont, Romain Ntamack and Matthieu Jalibert of course they are different. But it is still the same spirit that we knew. The spirit, the desire to fight for your team, your friends around you. The same rugby family that we knew all those years before. For me, the family of rugby is the most special thing of all. For this does not end when you stop playing. It continues forever, throughout your life.

'I have so many friends from rugby.'

He has, and always had. He played just a single match for the esteemed Racing Club de France, right at the very end of his playing days. A Toulousain all his career, he only went to Paris in response to a call from his great friend, Robert Paparemborde (nicknamed Patou) who was already at Racing.

'Jean-Pierre, will you come and help us?' asked Patou.

'OK, I come,' said Rives. But his idea of helping did not extend to actually playing for Racing. He intended it to be an advisory role, perhaps with tactics and a little coaching. After years of physical exertions, Rives knew his body wouldn't take any more.

He was settled at his Paris digs when, early one Sunday morning, the bell rang. Rives, half asleep, was bewildered as to who would be on the doorstep at such an early hour. When he finally opened it, he was confronted by three of the Racing Club players: Jean-Baptiste Lafond, Yvon Rousset and Franck Mesnel.

They arrived carrying bags of croissants, pains au chocolat and coffees and juices. As they sat at Rives's table, the purpose of this curious visit became clear. They had come to persuade Rives to play in Racing's match that very afternoon.

He'd sworn blind he wouldn't, that was it and a large curtain had fallen on his career. But here was the dilemma – Rives hated ever saying no to his friends. So, shortly before 3 o'clock that afternoon early in the season of 1984/85, a very familiar figure took the field in the famous light blue and white stripes of Racing Club de France. He played. But only once.

By then, his body must have been in physical torment. Perhaps he never did as much damage to it as on a July afternoon in faraway Sydney back in 1981. Rives, first capped by France in 1975 as loose forward, had just played a fulsome part in France winning the 1981 Grand Slam in the Five Nations Championship. Alas, he suffered a bad shoulder injury in a match building up to the first Test against the Wallabies at Ballymore, Brisbane.

The diagnosis, a dislocation, ought to have ended Rives's participation in the tour there and then. Instead, those of us on the tour had a scenario almost akin to a royal birth, with regular updates and announcements on the situation and his progress. Except that, in his case, he wasn't trying to push something out but force something back in.

In the event, Rives just couldn't play in Brisbane. He shouldn't have played any more on the trip, but Rives being Rives – captain, inspiration, idol and figurehead of the French team – decided he would.

I've seen a few grotesque sights on the rugby fields of the world in my time. But Rives's appearance that day would have to be right up there with the worst.

He ran out for that second Test with one arm hanging useless by his side. His whole shoulder was swathed in bandages and padding, a futile attempt to alleviate the pain of more multiple impacts. Half-stooped, a grim expression on his face, he looked like the Hunchback of Notre Dame on a bad day.

He could barely do anything constructive – well, have you ever tried playing in a top-line rugby match where you catch the ball under pressure with one arm or hand? Or tackle with just one arm?

Apart from that, it wasn't too bad until half-time. But that was when the effect of the powerful painkillers at last wore off. The second half represented forty minutes of undiluted agony for the French captain.

Legendary Frenchmen and women have demonstrated bravery in a multitude of situations down the centuries. But if you wanted a stirring example of sheer guts and bloody-mindedness in ignoring physical pain for the French cause, this would be among the best. Months later, Rives was still in pain from the after-effects.

Today? Some of the aches and pains may remain. But Rives prefers to remember the good times, the friends he made the world over. 'A wonderful game that gave us all so much,' he says.

No better way of putting it than that.

* * *

But from the past generation to the present.

Who better to outline their philosophies on the game, past and present, and on life per se, than the two brightest stars in the new French rugby firmament.

Antoine Dupont and Romain Ntamack.

The first thing that strikes you up close about Dupont is his powerful, squat frame. He may be just 1.74m tall, but the 84kgs weight is evenly spread. Much of it is muscle-bound, too. He might lack a few inches but few seem keen to pick a fight with him.

It is true, he is no modern-day incarnation of the 1.62m lightweights Jean Gachassin or Lilian Camberabero, champion French players in their day. Dupont is no frail, fleet-footed scrum half liable to get smashed off the field at the first collision with some opponent. The width of his neck alone is testimony to the frequent gym workouts demanded of every player in the contemporary game.

His torso is intrinsically a compact power unit, more than able to withstand the heavy physical batterings specially

Antoine Dupont.

designated for him by fearful rivals. He is chunky all over. Indeed, it is frequently the opponent who comes off worse. Times have changed.

Cool, calm and confident. Very polite. He ticks all these individual boxes, too. And I like his respect for his elders, those who went before him in the Toulouse and French international teams. Then there is his wish to interest himself in other, non-rugby activities. So for Antoine Dupont the rugby player, substitute Antoine Dupont, the builder.

'Rugby does take up a lot of my time but it is a passion. But I also like to spend time with my family and friends. I come

231

originally from a place about an hour outside Toulouse. Now, with my brother, I am helping to renovate a family property [a hotel once owned by his grandparents] where we will host marriages, birthday parties, etc.

'Rugby takes up much of my time but I think it is important to do other things, to talk about other things. It is good for the brain.'

Born in Lannemezan, he grew up in a small nearby village named Castelnau-Magnoac. There, his rugby story began at four years of age with Magnoac FC.

'That was the youngest you could be signed up to a team. I wanted to start even earlier but it wasn't possible. My grandfather played rugby and my mother and father used to watch the games. I immediately got caught up in this sport. I never wanted to stop.

'The south-west is the heart of rugby in France. There are the most clubs here. When I was young, I was a fan of Stade Toulousain and I liked very much Frédéric Michalak. I also watched the All Blacks and I admired Dan Carter. Luke McAlister, too.'

For Antoine Dupont, add Romain Ntamack, his fly half partner for club and country.

Dupont's nascent career began with Auch, the club of the Gers where Jacques Fouroux played. Like most young men of that region, he soon came to acknowledge that duck, and cassoulet, were his favourite meals.

He was there three years, learning the game and developing physically, before switching to Castres as an eighteen-year-old. His senior career began there before Stade Toulousain came calling in 2017.

But he isn't like some brash, young contemporary sportsmen, focused solely on themselves and their burgeoning bank balances from a life in professional sport. He respects the past and pays homage to those who left their significant legacy on the game.

'I know pretty much about the old players, the generations who made French rugby famous. Players like Jean-Pierre Rives, Jean Gachassin, the time of the Grand Slam of 1968 and then, with that pack of forwards, in 1977 and 1981. There have been several generations of players who had great results for France and we know all about them.

'We often watch old clips of tries and actions which marked French rugby. We don't often watch whole games which is a shame. But we saw once a game, I think in 1994, when France won in New Zealand. It's good to see these old games; I enjoy watching them.'

Romain, too, is a striking young man. He stands 1.85m, weighs 86kgs and has a thick shock of dark hair. On his left forearm, he has the date 1 February 2019 tattooed in Roman numerals, the date of his senior Test debut for France.

He is, too, familiar with many of the great men of French rugby. Well, with a father as famous as Émile Ntamack, the ex-French wing, he should. 'When you play in the Toulouse jersey and also the French jersey, you are inspired by the history of the rugby before us and the inspiration of old players.'

The roots of rugby, according to Dupont, run deep in French culture because it's a sport which has been played for a long time, more than 100 years now. 'I think that is particularly true in the south-west and because the French team has had such good results internationally. When growing up in this country you realise two things: how long this sport has been growing and how much people love rugby in France.'

These humble words reflect a respect for the past, an acknowledgement of those who laid the path for others to follow. There is, too, an awareness that leading professional rugby men today are public property. They have a duty to embrace that. Does Dupont mind all the fuss that can accompany those in the modern game? Or does he crave solitude?

'Sometimes you just want to have some rest and not speak to anyone. But it is part of your job to open your life to the public. It's not the thing that I prefer. But it is necessary.'

It will be increasingly so, he can be sure, in a Rugby World Cup year. Especially on French soil. But just winning it might not be enough to satisfy the purists, those still in love with the flair and style of great French rugby teams past. Dupont nods his head. He understands that sentiment.

'We still want to keep those qualities on the field but we must adapt to the adversary and to the conditions on the field. We cannot always play a game which is pretty to see. It is important to be able to win in several ways. But of course, if it is with panache, it's much better.'

How important is it to play with that *joie de vivre*, for club and country? Is it practical nowadays? It is, he avows, his favoured way of seeing things. 'My job is my passion and I have always taken great pleasure on the field. As much, in fact, when I was fifteen playing with my friends, as nowadays playing at the Stade de France. I will always try and keep that passion.'

As a guardian of that culture, Dupont shares the view of Pierre Villepreux that Stade Toulousain benefits hugely from one factor. No one, apart from a former Toulousain, has ever coached Stade. Ugo Mola is the latest to follow that trend. 'I think it is important to continue that tradition,' says Dupont.

'Given that there are so many great former players and coaches in Toulouse, it is probably easier for Stade Toulousain than other clubs.'

One of those ex-Stade Toulousain greats is Philippe Rouge-Thomas, now Director of Training for youngsters with the FFR. They have eight coaches in a programme that works throughout France and involves 600 youngsters: 450 boys and 150 girls.

His name might not be a Blanco, Rives or Villepreux. But Rouge-Thomas has enjoyed a fabulous rugby career, as both player and coach.

As outside half, he was Champion of France with Stade Toulousain in 1984, 1986, 1989 and 1994. He won the Yves du Manoir with the club in 1988 and 1993 and earned two caps for France in 1989. As coach at Stade, he was Champion of France in 2001 and 2008 and won the Heineken European Cup three times, in 2003, 2005 and 2010. In all, he was coach at Toulouse for ten years, from 2000 to 2010.

We stand and chat, over a pre-lunchtime glass of rosé, at Rene's convivial wine bar in the Marche Victor Hugo in the centre of Toulouse. Does he accept Dupont's view about home-grown coaches at Stade Toulousain?

'Yes, it is important in our culture. What is important for us is to have players who are capable of respecting the instructions but also to be capable of changing on the field. Because what one previews in the game is not necessarily what will happen on the pitch. The players must be able to react intelligently to the situation that faces them on the field.'

Which probably explains why there are no English players in the Stade Toulousain team.

Rouge-Thomas went on, 'It is a question of liberty. They have to coach the same way they have been coached themselves. If you have lived something, you must reproduce what you have lived already. You have to have continuity between the generations. Generally speaking, it's a question of brotherhood, whatever your age.

'Another demand is about going up to the highest level and staying at this level. If you are able to reproduce this level for years and years, it is fantastic.

'The Top 14 requires so much of players it is necessary for us to prepare at least three players per position who can maintain the level. They can replace young players with other ones so the guys are not exhausted. It's a question of finding the right balance.'

Romain Ntamack concurs with such a philosophy. 'It is part of the history and culture of our club always to have a manager or coach who has passed through the club. That is as important today as ever.

'It is also very important to me that we continue to play with that *joie de vivre* for Stade Toulousain and France. It is the pleasure of playing and training together. All the group is very close. We meet up outside rugby to do other things and to talk about non-rugby things.

'In the French team, there are players very close to each other. I think today rugby is so much more professional and there are more restraints. But we try to keep this pleasure of playing.'

Ntamack attributes much of his talent to the tuition of his father. 'I began to play rugby at five years old and my father taught me a lot of things, like the technique of rugby as I was growing up. He showed me the importance of doing things quite early, which I still do today. We watch the old videos of rugby and the legendary tries of the French team. These things inspire us and we try to emulate them.'

Quite often they succeed. No more so than in November 2021 when France put New Zealand to the sword with a much-prized 40-25 victory in Paris. The critical moment, not just in that match but as a reaffirmation of glorious French dash and adventure which has flavoured the French rugby dish down the ages, came when Ntamack ran back into his own goal area to collect an All Blacks kick ahead.

To the conservative Anglo-Saxon eye, the young man seemed to have only one option. Touch the ball down and concede

Romain Ntamack.

the 5-metre scrum. But to the opportunistic Gallic eye, the situation was rich with potential.

The young Frenchman stooped to collect the ball with the ease of a child, picking daisies in a summer meadow. He glided back towards his own goal line... and then stunned every observer by brushing aside a tackle and setting off on an attacking run that took him out of his in-goal area, through the French 22 and towards the halfway line.

Jet-heeled, he surged clear before finding support and offloading. The movement continued to flow until the All Blacks killed the ball at a ruck. From there, France kicked a penalty goal. Ntamack's brilliant inspiration had captured the moment. It wasn't so much a single illustration of French verve but a fulsome statement, a pledge, as to France's enduring rugby pedigree. It told the audience, 'The legend of this game, carved out by so many talented rugby men for a century or more, is safe in our hands.'

As for Ntamack senior, talk about banishing the old man's reputation in a single movement!

The young man offers a charming, modest recollection of the moment. Did he think to pass or kick?

'No, I thought of nothing! It was so quick, I didn't have time to think at all. It was two seconds... in which time... I took the decision to try to get myself out [of his in-goal area] and from the moment when I broke the first tackle, I just accelerated downfield. But I had no time to reflect on what to do.'

Which was even better. It proved that spirit of adventurism, the innate pleasure of feeling ball in hand, remains a critical element of the French rugby player's DNA. Welshmen, Irishmen, Englishmen, Australians and New Zealanders – we should all celebrate that. For the game is immeasurably richer for such talent.

Is it Ntamack's first instinct in any game to run? 'In that action, I turned on my left foot and I am right-footed so I didn't think of kicking. But for Stade Toulousain, I always think of getting myself out [i.e. of running out of defence] rather than kicking.'

How Pierre Villepreux will smile at that remark.

Romain Ntamack enjoys other pleasures in life. He doesn't like rugby to occupy 100 per cent of his time, he concedes. So he makes visits to the cinema, restaurants. Even shopping. As he says, it is relaxing to do other things sometimes.

But he does enjoy watching rugby from around the world. Meanwhile, he keeps close to himself an ambition that may one day make headlines. 'I would like to play in another country in the world. Maybe New Zealand or Australia for the culture which is so different in the southern hemisphere.'

Ntamack is a serious thinker on his rugby life. 'The joy this club brings to the whole city is something crazy. I've always had only one dream: to be part of a team that could generate that level of enthusiasm. And my dream now is to win again. When you win, you have only one desire and that is to relive those moments. It's like a drug actually.'

He believes fervently that his club's identity is its secret. 'The Stade has always had a solid course of action and that has been perpetuated at every level of the club. The players respect this identity more than anything and everyone who wears this jersey wants to be worthy of its history. That is why this club has been a step above the rest for so many years.'

* * *

Playing in another country had always been something that great former New Zealand All Black Jerome Kaino wanted to do when he signed for Toulouse. But right now, Kaino has a different problem on his hands...

It takes rather a lot to beat Jerome Kaino at anything.

At 1.96m tall and 110kgs in weight, the eighty-three-times capped former New Zealand All Black World Cup winner and twice Top 14 champion, as well as a European Champions Cup winner with Stade Toulousain, offers an intimidating presence. Not without reason was he known as 'The Enforcer' in his playing days. Some opponents had rather more earthy descriptions for him.

But one person has the big man's measure. His twelve-year-old daughter, Milan. Truth to tell, Kaino looks a touch uneasy when it comes to discussing the exact field in which she masters her famous dad.

'She is probably the best French speaker in the family,' admits Kaino with a slight expression of pain. 'The majority of her friends' parents work at Airbus and they're mostly Spanish. So she's learning a bit of Spanish as well. So that gives my confidence (in learning French) a bit of a knock. I am still battling on with French.

'Rugby French, I understand pretty much everything. But when they're just having a conversation among themselves, it's French slang and I'm gone.'

But ask Kaino what the whole Toulouse experience has given him and his family and he is effusive in his praise for the opportunity.

'It's huge. The experience that my kids have had here in Europe is immense. We've been to London, driven down to Spain... many things. We're learning a different language and a new culture. You can't get these experiences anywhere else and they're so valuable for the kids.

'When I was younger, I would have loved to have experienced this. So what we're giving our kids is incredible. I just wish I'd come earlier. It's not only about the success I've had with Toulouse. It's how the city and the country have embraced us. I would like to have played here longer.'

But since his retirement from playing, he has been working with the academy youngsters, the 'Espoirs' and Under-23s. You see him too in the 1st XV's dressing room for major matches. 'I'm glad I am not playing any more watching the games of these guys. Seeing some of the confontations I'm very glad I retired.'

How do some of the less-muscled guys, the backs, survive this immense physical examination each week? Take a player like Stade Toulousain outside half Romain Ntamack.

'A lot of them are quite small of frame but they're actually quite physically robust. Ntamack is 1.86m tall and weighs 86kgs. Antoine Dupont is only 1.74 metres tall and 84kgs. He's a little ball of muscle really. The kids these days are conditioned for these tougher games we have. They are robust and strong.

'A couple of years ago I saw these guys play and I said then, French rugby is entering into a golden era. My only doubt was whether the French coaches could bring the best out of them. Individually, just seeing the way they express themselves within their clubs, they've got a lot of X factor there. But then, we saw in Paris against the All Blacks in November 2021 the French management and coaching staff are able to get the best from them.

'They are young leaders, decision makers. But they've got a good structure. I think they're quite spontaneous in the way they play. They play whatever is in front of them. Antoine Dupont is definitely that type of player. He's a natural leader, doesn't need a structure. He will see some space and play accordingly. They are definitely decision makers.'

What is more, Kaino signs up to the theory that Shaun Edwards is playing a fulsome part in this French renaissance. He does not accept indiscipline is still a potential Achilles heel of French rugby men, not at this level, anyway.

'That has changed a lot. Look at their defence. I think Shaun has made a huge difference with the discipline in their defence. William Servat, the ex-French international, has also done a lot of good work looking after the scrum but also their attack breakdown.

'You can see how ferocious they were on defence and attack but disciplined at the same time. I think they're only going to get better.'

Another factor has impressed Kaino about the game in this country. 'It is incredible the support for rugby, especially here in the south. The supporters are so passionate for each little

241

region. Each club has its unique style of support, like the songs they sing during the games.

'I found it incredible and being here in Toulouse you see how many registrations they have in terms of the girls' game and the younger teams. I was blown away by how much support there is behind the game here.'

Truly, the roots of this sport run deep and far into the soil of the land.

* * *

There are some areas of France positively injurious even to the health of strong rugby men. You can negotiate the rich food or omnipresent wines of regions like the Auvergne, with its cheese, Bordeaux with its wines, and Normandy, with all that butter, cream and cider.

But then comes the Gers and you think anew.

In Gascony, only about 50 miles south-west of Toulouse, you'll find a gastronomic feast laid before you at every turn. The region is renowned for it. In no particular order, you can eat cassoulet, foie gras, duck, wild mushrooms. These are local specialities. For drink, you're unlikely to go thirsty with the light, fruity and aromatic Côtes de Gascogne white wines, Floc de Gascogne, a fortified sweet wine and, most famously, Armagnac brandy.

Which is partly why I chose it for a long weekend trip. We'd been there before, as guests of the French coach Jacques Fouroux for an international between France and Romania in 1990. After the match in Auch, capital of the Gers, Jacques had invited us for drinks at his home. We sipped a pleasant wine on a terrace at the back of the property which looked out to the Pyrenean mountains.

It was an idyllic spot.

We adjourned from there to the restaurant of the elegant Hôtel de France, owned by the renowned André Daguin, one of France's leading chefs from 1960 to 1997. If you'd never had lightly cooked foie gras inside a pumpkin, this was the place to try it.

Two of the many virtues of Jacques Fouroux, captain and coach of the French national team during his playing career from 1972 to 1977 and coach from 1981 to 1990, were his endearing optimism and sense of fun. So, on this particular Saturday night, he leads us into Daguin's restaurant. Alas, it looks like half the Pyrenees has come to dinner. There is not a spare table in sight.

But Jacques is not concerned. A booking? For Monsieur Fouroux? Please, be sensible. Jacques is Mr Spontaneous in disguise. He doesn't book. But they'll find him a table.

Led by our host, we go straight through the restaurant and through the door into the kitchen. There, after a brief conversation, a small garden table is put up for us, together with four chairs. We sit down and instantly four glasses of champagne arrive.

As flambés flare, steaks sizzle and foie gras gently fries at the hands of this award-winning chef and his team, we tuck in. A Grand Cru is served, almost with the fanfare of the King's arrival. Jacques pours, and liberally. The food we are served is sensational: foie gras, *magret de canard*.

By 11 p.m., tables have become free in the dining room. So we pick up our wine glasses and relocate for the cheese and dessert. We're there until 1 a.m., the last to leave.

This was hospitality, Jacques Fouroux style. It was completed the next day when he emerged from his wine cellar with a bottle of cognac from the 1930s. A gift for me. As if dinner last night was just a snack.

A little less than a year later, we're wrangling with where

to go for the lady's birthday. She'd like somewhere quiet, nice country around, good food, relatively easy to reach. With no rugby matches in sight.

'Why not Auch?' I suggest.

'Because there will be a rugby match on.'

'No there won't. We won't mention it to Jacques so it'll be a rugby-free weekend.'

She looks dubious. But we book.

Gascony is in all its glory. Late summer sunshine and warmth, the apple orchards laden with fruit above a vivid green carpet. Cows chew contentedly in the fields, some surveying a field of 'Tournesol', the famous sunflowers that somehow define France.

At 6 p.m. on a warm, sunny evening, we're sitting outside a café in the centre of the town, sipping a couple of kirs. What could possibly go wrong?

Alas, my attention is caught by the sight of a figure heading into a shop close by. No, it couldn't be. But then he emerges and looks down the street to the café.

'Peter, what are you doing here?'

'Hi, Jacques. Well, it's the lady's birthday so we thought...'

'Ah, you must come for drinks; 7.30 at Claude Laffitte's restaurant.'

The dark looks I get from my companion are life-threatening. But what can we do?

At the appointed hour, we arrive at the restaurant to be confronted by an enormous punchbowl. It is three-quarters full. What is in it is a source of wonder. But after two or three glasses, either a strong wind has suddenly got up from the mountains or the walls are moving of their own volition.

What follows is another sumptuous feast. Plates of foie gras, *mi-cuit*, and then *jambon*, followed by a rich duck dish as the main *plat*. Cheese to follow, naturally, and a dessert afterwards.

At one point, I spy Jacques leaving the room, clutching his mobile. But I dismiss it... until, sometime later, there is a knocking on the back door. These diners are optimistic. It is nearly midnight.

After a short interlude, an extraordinary sight greets us. One of French rugby's great men and Auch's renowned restaurateur file into the room, trousers rolled up to their knees. Each has a chair slung over his shoulder, a wicked, impish expression on his face as they sing the 'Gay Gordons', walking around the restaurant.

Behind them is a somewhat bemused-looking local patissier carrying a freshly baked cake. In the middle of the birthday cake, in marzipan, is an enormous phallus...

My only consolation when I heard that Jacques Fouroux had died in Auch exactly eight days before Christmas, 2005, at the absurdly young age of fifty-eight, was that he'd crammed about four lives into his one.

CHAPTER 10

Peter Pan and
The Legend of Lourdes

Auch–Lourdes–Bagnères-de-Bigorre

I bring the car to a halt after the ninety minutes, or 60 miles, journey south-west from Auch down towards the Pyrenees. I am non-plussed, bemused at the sight before me.

It's barely 4.30 in the afternoon but darkness is everywhere. Not to mention silence. No people on the streets, hardly another car in motion.

Huge towering blocks of hotels stand forlorn and empty, not a light to be seen in one. Similarly, most of the houses are dark and shuttered. What happened here?

A fast-flowing, malevolent river rushes through the centre of the deserted town. Steadily, a bitter sleet slants in on a burgeoning wind.

Welcome to Lourdes in midwinter. If you didn't know, you'd assume the scene had been created for a sci-fi film. But whatever, it is deeply depressing. Even the pilgrims stay away at this time of year. The grotto that lures untold numbers is dark, empty. Silent.

Everything has shut down. Winter is nigh yet the snow that will bring skiers and life back to the town has yet to fall.

Next morning, I join a little road, giving a sweeping vista of the mountains that provide a dramatic backdrop to this Pyrenean town. But it is a fleeting moment of inspiration. For a visit to the Antoine Béguère stadium can do little to raise spirits among rugby men with imagination.

It is hard to believe now. But from 1948 to 1960, FC Lourdes were champions of France seven times. Then, they won another title in 1968. This little ground, nestling in the valley beneath the mountains, was the epicentre of French rugby. At one stage, they went undefeated at home from 1948 to 1960, an astonishing period of ascendancy. In 1948, they had eight French internationals, and seven in 1958.

FC Lourdes (officially Lourdais) rugby ground today.

Paintings of former Lourdes greats at the stadium.

Such rugby excellence created a vibrancy, a passion that infused everyone in the town. You didn't have to be an FC Lourdes fanatic, a rugby nut, to feel the wave of success wash over you and all you surveyed. In 1955, with Lourdes in the years of their pomp, 20,000 people once filled this ground for an ordinary Championship match, against Mont-de-Marsan. Listen carefully to the cold wind blowing off the mountain peaks and perhaps you can hear the last cheers and cries of those who attended that day. But in truth, there is nothing but silence.

Today, there is seating in the ground for just 2800. Alas, they seldom come anywhere near selling all those.

This is a club that produced or developed internationals and legends of the French game at will. It was the Rolls-Royce production line for French rugby.

Jean Prat and his brother Maurice, Michel Crauste, Jean Barthe, Robert Soro, Arnaud Marquesuzaa, Roger Martine, Claude and Pierre Lacaze, Henri Rancoule, André Campaes, Jean Gachassin, Pierre Berbizier, Jean-Pierre Garuet, Louis

Armary, Michel Cremaschi, Alain Caussade and many others all played for France. At times, it seemed like the Lourdes rugby factory would never fail to produce players.

But after 1968 when they won another title, it stopped. Just as Béziers' formidable ascendancy from 1971 ended abruptly in 1984. Never to be repeated in either case, although in 1981 Lourdes did reach the final of the (now discontinued) Yves du Manoir competition, beating their old rivals Béziers 25-13. Lourdes had also won the Yves du Manoir in 1953, 1954, 1956, 1966 and 1967. It meant something in those days.

Between them, from 1948 to 1984, these two great clubs won nineteen Bouclier de Brennus French rugby titles in thirty-seven years. But today? Lourdes have disappeared, even off the slippery slope from the top. In 2022, they were playing in Fédérale 2 Pool 6. Where once they faced the likes of Toulouse, Racing Club, Agen and Toulon, today they encounter, with all due respect, teams such as Balma Olympique, US Morlanaise, A.S. Pont Long and St Girons SC. How the mighty have fallen. Anonymity has covered the old stadium like a blanket to hide its shame.

Béziers entered the 2021/22 winter in Pro D2, the second tier of French rugby and still professionals. Yet their glory days are long gone, too.

Another sad tale is of SU Agen, eight-time champions of France. They upgraded the old Stade Armandie, doubtless hoping the team would revive. Alas, Agen spent that long, hard winter battling to avoid falling out of D2. But then, they were used to adversity.

In the 2020/21 season, they played twenty-six matches in the Top 14 and lost every single one. Their points tally was 315 for, 1101 against. The club of the great Philippe Sella, once one of the best clubs in France, ended the disastrous season forty-four points behind Bayonne, who were next to bottom of the table. For a club with Agen's history and one-time prestige, it was humiliating. Sella, and others of his time like Daniel Dubroca, Pierre Berbizier, Philippe Benetton and Abdel Benazzi, looked on in despair. As for Albert Ferrasse, once dubbed 'Monsieur Agen', he must have been turning in his grave.

But then, so dramatic a decline had also been the fate of clubs like Dax, Tarbes, Mazamet, La Voulte, Cahors, Tulle and a host of others. Even in Pro D2, a host of once-renowned clubs peer anxiously over their shoulders at the impending doom of relegation. There is little they can do about it.

But does any of this matter? Some would point to history and other sports, recounting instances of a once-esteemed club falling away. So what...?

What was sad about the decline of many of the once-illustrious French rugby clubs was that it represented much more than just the changing fortunes of individual clubs. That happens. Remember that immortal phrase. 'King Rooster one day, feather duster the next.' They know a thing or two about roosters in rural France.

This trend signalled the end of an era, the passing of a time when even clubs from small French towns could win the mighty Bouclier de Brennus. Their demise affected everyone – supporters, young and old, the local *mairie*, the townsfolk and local traders. Part of the life, the vibrancy and spirit of the town, disappeared with the rugby club's demise.

Back in the day, clubs from towns like little Bagnères-de-Bigorre, deep in the Pyrenees, could put together a rugby team capable of going all the way to the final. They did that twice, in 1979 and 1981, and an entire Pyrenean town descended on Paris.

Dax reached five finals, although disastrously losing each one. Tarbes reached few finals but in 1973 achieved lasting glory by beating Dax in the final.

But today, the list of small-town clubs capable of winning the title has shrunk almost to nothing. When a smaller club has attracted the financial largesse of a wealthy businessman, in the way Biarritz lured multi-millionaire Serge Kampf into their fold, they have prospered. For a while. Indeed, with shrewd recruitment, they have been able to buy some outstanding players and beat even the powerful city clubs.

Biarritz, fuelled by Kampf's finances, won the French Championship (their first since 1939) in 2002, 2005 and 2006. They even reached the final of the Heineken European Cup in 2006 and 2010, albeit losing each time. They were the grand days. They hired Spanish La Liga soccer club Real Sociedad's Anoeta stadium, just across the border in San Sebastián, for their Heineken knockout quarter- and semi-finals. These were seismic days in the heart of the Basque lands.

Players like Serge Betsen, Joe Roff, Imanol Harinordoquy, Dimitri Yachvili, Jean-Michel Gonzalez, Thomas Lièvremont, Damien Traille and Philippe Bernat-Salles made Biarritz a powerful team, whatever the opposition.

But since then, reality has bitten. Kampf passed away in 2016 and the club's fortunes withered. No new sugar daddy could be found. The dream died.

Despite promotion to the Top 14 in June 2021, they struggled all the following season to justify their place among the elite. In the end, they couldn't. Biarritz were relegated. There is a reason why only two clubs, Stade Toulousain and Clermont Auvergne, have never operated below the top flight. In a word, it is... money.

Money has oiled the wheels of rugby union in France virtually from its inception. The reality of French clubs paying their best players down the decades has been the sporting world's worst-kept secret.

Listen to the words of one of French rugby's greats, François Moncla, who passed away in 2021, aged eighty-six. Three years before his passing, I sat down with Moncla at his home in the suburbs of Pau and reminisced about his rugby times.

What he said revealed fully and frankly, without emotion or drama, the reality of rugby in France all those years ago. To put it baldly, France was living a lie. Its rugby men were being paid, in strict contravention of the rules of the so-called amateur game. They always had been.

France had been ejected from the Five Nations Championship as far back as 1931 for, in part, paying its top players. Yet once they returned to the fold, in 1947, the old system was quietly reintroduced. Thus, for almost fifty years, until professionalism was announced in 1995, France operated under false pretences. Mind you, other countries began to catch up with French traditions long before the IRB finally declared the game 'an open sport'.

In the twilight years of his life, Moncla made little attempt at obfuscation. 'I was with Racing Club de France for nine years and we were champions of France in 1959. Then I returned to Pau [helping them win the French title in 1964].

'Yes, there was a little money changing hands in those days. Not like now but...

'I should have gone to Lourdes but the president of Racing Club, Roger Lerou, told Arnaud Marquesuzaa, Michel Crauste and myself that if we all signed for Lourdes, it would be a sign of professionalism.

'The president of Agen [Albert Ferrasse's club] wanted to sign me and told me what I would get. It was a good offer, enough money, but I wanted to move to Pau for business reasons. Then, Pau gave me the same as Agen proposed.'

This, Moncla hastened to remind me, was in 1959. The small matter of thirty-six years before professionalism was officially sanctioned in France and everywhere else. Yet club presidents all over France knew precisely what was going on. So, of course, did everyone else in French rugby, and plenty of those beyond the country.

But in his last years, François Moncla, an outstanding, powerful and fast back-row forward in his day who was made captain of France in 1960, was concerned about money in the modern-day game. 'I am very worried,' he told me. 'Youngsters get large amounts when they are very young but if they don't save or they get injured, they may end up with very little. We had a job in our day, it was a big difference.'

In case anyone thinks it was only the star names, the big fish who were receiving money for playing rugby union in that era, listen to the words of our old friend Marius Lagiewski, Agen prop of notorious fame in French Championship matches of the early 1960s.

'I had a fixed [wage],' he told an interviewer years later. 'Then there were the match bonuses.'

Of course there were...

But you know what? To me, the French were right all along about amateurism. It was the rest of rugby that was deluding itself.

Amateurism at the lower levels of the game, was fine. It was, after all, chiefly a recreational sport in those days. But among the top players, it was a sham, a joke, a complete farce. It deserved the derision it received down the years in France. As the IRB continued to pontificate about their 'strictly amateur game', banning people like Gareth Edwards for writing books after they had retired that 'professionalised' them, the French quietly got on with their own way of doing things.

World rugby's mantra was fundamentally flawed for several reasons. If you want to see the best in any walk of life you tend to have to pay for it. To try and get by for sixty or seventy years as cheapskates, unwilling to equate merit, commitment and supreme skill with financial remuneration, was absurd.

Whoever turned up at La Scala and found that Pavarotti wasn't charging that night?

In rugby, the nettle should have been grasped long, long before 1995 by which time the whole game was just being deceitful and making itself look absurd.

Asking the best players in the world to give up their spare time so that they could train harder and fill international grounds to make millions for the individual Unions while they received not a dollar or pound, was disingenuous. In the UK, that disingenuousness lasted over 100 years. Only in France did they see sense virtually from the start.

Pure 'amateurism' at the top level was flawed for another reason. It was intrinsically unworkable.

Whatever the year or the location, if you were a wealthy businessman in, say, Lourdes or London, who wanted to help your favourite club, what was to stop you buying a top player who represented your company at, say, five or ten official functions in a year? You could pay him whatever you wished for as much or as little work as you required. After all, his employment was solely with your company. You owned him.

But naturally, if he was working in the town and was a top player, nothing would stop him joining the local rugby club.

Of course, even if the club knew full well about such an arrangement, what was it to them? They weren't paying the player. Officially, they were amateurs. Yet he was working in that town or city, earning money from a local company, chiefly because he wanted to play for that club. So no one could prove he was doing anything wrong. Sure, he was being paid to, in effect, play rugby. But the club wasn't paying him so that was OK.

The whole system was about as clean as a Paris sewer. Which is probably being unkind to sewers.

Why, are we not entitled to ask, did England lock forward Nigel Horton suddenly up sticks and take off for Toulouse in 1977 for a couple of seasons? Once there, he found himself working in a bar, Le Donjon, in the centre of the city. For recreation? For fun? But he also played for Stade Toulousain and continued to represent England for another three years. One wonders how all that worked out. I'm sure it was all perfectly innocent...

Then there was the case of England lock Maurice Colclough taking himself off to Angoulême to play for a few seasons. As we have read earlier, Scot Damian Cronin was invited to join Bourges at a time when the game was still officially amateur. Perhaps for the weather. Or the coq au vin. That was clearly superior.

This farce of turning a blind eye to a fundamental strut of the old, so-called amateur game undermined most of the values that the game's rulers espoused. You wondered at times how they managed to keep a straight face while proclaiming strict amateur principles. Meanwhile, rugby people throughout France were making their own plans, by dint of their own assessment of the regulations. Clearly, they didn't think much of those rules.

What the IRB did, of course, was go after the easy targets, the small fry. I remember working for a London radio station in the 1970s and we sought to introduce a 'Man of the Match' award for the club 'Game of the Day' which we had covered. The winner was hardly going to buy Buckingham Palace on the proceeds. We got a sponsorship deal and handed over a bottle of whisky.

Or at least we did for a week. Suddenly, the IRB came hammering at our door. 'Make the player give it back or we'll professionalise him,' was their message.

Meanwhile in France, players were laughing all the way to *la banque*.

The French made no fuss about it. The media didn't particularly write about it but they knew what was going on. No one wanted the calamity of a 'world exclusive' splashed all over their newspapers. They just looked the other way. For about seventy-five years...

Back in the day, when he was a young man, money was the last thought on Jean-Pierre Garuet's mind.

He walked into the Lourdes ground for training one day and saw what he called 'the spiritual sons of rugby', Jean Prat and Michel Crauste, who was the captain. They prepared, he said, like professionals. Funny thing, that...

Garuet began in 1969 as a cadet. Lourdes' last French title was the previous year, 1968. 'I played No. 8 like Crauste and wanted to be like him. But from the back row, I passed to prop because of my size. I was 77 kgs.'

He found a novel way to turn much of that weight into muscle. 'As an amateur, I also worked. I handled lots of 50 and 80 kilo sacks of potatoes. I was working in the open air, hauling these potatoes nearly every day. That gave me natural muscles. Also, going into the Army reinforced my neck and my body, naturally.'

Michael Crauste and Jean-Pierre Garuet at Lourdes.

There was another mentor in his own village. He lived 15 kilometres from Lourdes in a small place called Pontacq where 'Papillon' Lacaze (French full-back) was. 'I would see him train practically every day.'

But by the time he finished, in 1991, FC Lourdes was in decline. What did he think French rugby lost with the demise of such great clubs as his?

'It has lost the identity of French rugby. It is now globalised with players from Fiji, Tonga, New Zealand and South Africa. Ever since the game turned professional, a world of people arrived. It was sad that we, the old players, weren't asked to give our teachings. There were good props in all the clubs. But it became the world of money.'

He worries about the possibilities of severe injury to front-row forwards these days. 'The scrum is like a war. It is another world, yet it is refereed by the young. But I am sorry to see the world of refereeing asks nothing... of former players.'

To emphasise his point, his facial expression darkened. 'Four days ago, I was at a game in Fédérale 2 and I saw a young player who was disabled. He's a coach now but in a wheelchair. So there needs to be like a passport for the young, an X-ray to know if their necks are strong enough. If a scrum is badly formed, you are in danger. I have seen that many times.'

Michel Cremaschi was another from the south-west France production line. He won eleven caps for France at prop forward between 1980 and 1984. The mercurial Jacques Fouroux was his national coach, Jean-Pierre Rives his international captain. Not the worst mentoring duo in the rugby world.

Cremaschi, like Garuet, gave Lourdes a strong forward pillar from which to construct their teams of the 1980s. But when he surveys Lourdes, the ground and the club's status nowadays, he is dismayed.

A painting on the wall at Lourdes of ex-French prop Michel Cremaschi.

'I am disappointed with how things are now. But one is confronted with reality. Lourdes is a town of only 14,000 people because the young people leave for the cities. There is no work; it is difficult now for the juniors. There are still some talented young players who come through from this region. But they go to join Toulouse, Pau or Castres because they have training facilities.

'At Lourdes, there is no longer the means to finance the club.'

Why did he go there in the first place?

'Lourdes had a history. When I arrived, they had been champions of France eight times. At that time, Lourdes was number one. Also, Lourdes had its game of movement, of running and attack. We tried to lead and we had this generation of players of value.'

But the writing was on the wall. In 1985, Pierre Berbizier left for Agen, Cremaschi joined Tarbes where he contested a French Championship final in 1988. It got worse; five or six players left for Grenoble. 'I went to Tarbes because I felt there was more chance and means of keeping a good team.'

Already it was clear that Lourdes had no money and the consequences were inevitable. But Cremaschi laments the decline of clubs like Lourdes. 'These old clubs have lost their identity. It is associated with the value of the regions. Agen had a style of play, Lourdes had their own style. Bagnères had a style of play. Toulon were different again – more aggressive up front.

'So each region had its own style, but we lost that because now everyone plays the same. There is less freedom for the players too.'

Can there be any future for these grand, once mighty old clubs? Or is their fate to become widely shared anonymity?

Cremaschi has at least one idea. 'You could do like in Ireland and make regions. You could put together Lourdes, Tarbes and Bagnères and take the best players. Jacques Fouroux suggested that many years ago and he was right. Fouroux was the most advanced thinker in French rugby. He had a very good vision.

'The problem today is, the director of Lourdes says, "Oh, but I want this", the leader of Tarbes wants something else and the top officials at Bagnères want something else again. You could make a training facility and keep the best players, like in Ireland. But I think in France we have not understood this.'

Around the turn of the century, with this trend increasingly apparent, there was talk of amalgamating Dax with Mont-de-Marsan. A XV of the Landes region, they speculated. But even then, a projected budget of around €20 million was, as someone pointed out, totally insufficient. A club needed €50 million a year just to be in mid-table. So the idea collapsed.

Ex-Dax and France outside half Jean-Patrick Lescarboura said, 'I am more Dacquois than Landais. But this is no longer our generation. Now it is time for businessmen.'

Cremaschi had a valuable point to make. 'To me, the roots of rugby are established in French culture by the value of the regions and their solidarity. I think even companies... they take their values from that. Now in businesses, they take the spirit from rugby. It is the solidarity of people, friends.'

Are these roots damaged today by young players, some of whom are more interested in money? 'Yes, but that is normal,' he says. 'There was a bit of passing of brown envelopes in our day. At Lourdes, we had the advantage of being able to train in the afternoons. We didn't work in a factory, we had a quality of life. At the time we were happy. We didn't earn millions but we had a quality of life.'

* * *

A quality of life. Well, they certainly know about that in these parts.

So now, dear reader, a light interlude. I am off on the trail of a pig. Not that guy who smashed someone in the face recently on a rugby field and got sent off. I mean a real pig.

I take the road from Lourdes to Bagnères-de-Bigorre, the D937. It twists and winds, up hill and down dale, as you skirt the Pyrenean mountain chain. Even on this cloudy, bitingly cold day late in the year, the scenery is dramatic. The mountain peaks are all covered in snow.

The road passes through Loucrup and then a series of hamlets. Farming is the main occupation here but already many of the animals are inside for the winter. In summer, when the wild flowers are profuse, this is a beautiful part of the world. But under this grey blanket of cloud and in these temperatures, it is uninviting.

In time, I come to a town, Pouzac. It has only 1100 residents, but a vast, sprawling supermarket. Bagnères is barely 3 kilometres down the main road. But in Pouzac's supermarket, at the butcher's counter, there is a product for sale that is revered throughout the Bigorre *département*.

For the fact is, the pigs in this region are worth their weight in gold. Almost literally. The story of the Noir de Bigorre is fascinating. It has been rooting around these parts of south-west France since the time of the Greeks and Romans. These black pigs are indigenous to the foothills of the central Pyrenees; quintessentially, the Bigorre region.

You can trace their history right back to the times of the monks who raised these animals in the many Benedictine abbeys that proliferated in this area. The soil and humid climate ensures that grass grows for most of the year here, so the animals feed on grass, fallen apples, chestnuts, acorns, worms and such like. Put together, they offer a succulent meal for the pigs which in turn produce highly flavoured meat.

Yet astonishingly, given their history, at one stage the black pigs of the Bigorre nearly became extinct. The introduction of so many white pigs into the region from across northern Europe threatened the entire future of 'les Noirs'. By 1981, only two boars remained (together with thirty-four sows). That was how close they were to dying out.

Happily, a handful of local enthusiasts were alerted to the danger and ensured the animal's future. Fortunate, not least for the farmers and tradesmen of the area who now have on their hands a creature of incredible worth.

After slaughter, the meat is dried and preserved for almost two years or more. It begins to be sold at twenty or thirty-six months... depending upon your budget.

And what a budget you will need to buy! Naively, I once wandered into the Victor Hugo market in Toulouse and stopped at a butcher's. 'What is Noir de Bigorre?' I asked. They lure you into business and draw you on here like a fly fisherman with some tasty bait, seeking the trout.

I tasted a morsel, ordered a few slices – and afterwards, felt I should have made a call to the bank manager to OK the deal.

One thing is for sure. Once you have tasted this meat you don't forget it. But you also remember the price. Ouch! Yet as Alan Jones, erudite Australian rugby coach of the 1980s, once observed, 'It's the Gucci factor. Long after you've paid the price, you remember the quality.'

You certainly do with Noir de Bigorre. In both senses.

Today, if you fancy black ham de Bigorre, twenty months prepared, you will pay around €90 a kilo. A boneless but not large offcut of the ham, thirty-six months matured, will cost about €150 a kilo.

Pork sausages? €69.50 a kilo. A whole leg of the black ham, with the bone, twenty months prepared, is €368 a kilo. A whole black ham (boneless) will cost €400. If the latter is thirty-six months prepared rather than just twenty, expect to pay €565.

This is a seriously expensive animal. Not even rugby players back in the day were considered as valuable a lump of meat.

* * *

Talking of expensive, just imagine how much money one of the greatest former French internationals there has ever been would make from the modern-day game. Unknown riches would be strewn before him, in the style of the Roman conquerors.

The town of Bagnères-de-Bigorre is both the birthplace and home of Jean Gachassin. A legend of French rugby. To find him, you don't have to go far from the town centre. Head out of town, take a small side street and it opens up. On the left stands a good-sized, wooden constructed house. At the back is a small swimming pool.

He comes to meet me at the door. At once, there is the nimble step, even of a man who is now eighty. He bears a neat frame, is dressed tidily and smartly. His rugby memorabilia remind us of another time, another era. A Grand Slam-winning trophy, small yet much prized with the golden cockerel standing on a black plinth, is just one of his favourite items. There are plenty of others.

An old man with his memories?

There was never very much of Gachassin. Born a small baby just two days before Christmas, 1941, he only ever stood 1.62m when fully grown. He weighed, by modern-day standards, a paltry 62.1kgs. What is more, he played the game in an era largely devoid of TV cameras, which meant there was little protection for smaller players against the foul deeds and sly physical beatings that proliferated on a French rugby ground. Sometimes, too, it was more dangerous without the ball than with it.

Yet Gachassin had one critical attribute. He was fast. Lightning fast. So much so that he made thirty-two appearances for the French national team between 1961 and 1969. He was a member of the 1968 Five Nations teams that helped France win her first Grand Slam title. It was an era in French rugby when skill trumped physicality as an attribute. Hence, the selection of the Camberabero brothers, 1.7m and 1.62m respectively, in that 1968 Grand Slam season, as well as Gachassin.

There was an ingenuity, a crackle about their collective efforts.

We settle comfortably into the leather sofa in his home. Here, deep in the Pyrenees, it is already grey on an early November afternoon. Before too long, the light will begin to fade.

Painting of Jean Gachassin at Lourdes ground.

The author (right) with the great Jean Gachassin.

But there is light to be seen. It illuminates his expression. A broad grin spreads across his face when I ask how he handled the tough, grizzled forwards of those times. 'It wasn't at all a problem for me because I was so fast. I was Champion of the Pyrenees at 200 metres. My biggest advantage was that I was so small. And it has not died out. Now you have little Antoine Dupont from Toulouse.'

Dupont is modern-day rugby's version of the small warrior of the French game. As said, he is 1.74m tall and weighs 84kgs. But that makes him massive by Gachassin's stats.

He played for Lourdes from 1967 to 1972, before returning home to join Bagnères from 1972 to 1978. Nicknamed 'Peter Pan' in French rugby, the diminutive Gachassin didn't mind where he played. So in any team at any given time, you might see him at full-back, wing, centre or fly half. Or you might not, given how fast he moved.

He rather played that way, too, popping up like a 'jack-in-the-box' anywhere at any time. If a movement seemed about to die, his vision would take him to the critical place to ensure continuity. It didn't always mean France would triumph. But he was forever exciting, always unpredictable. Somehow, he encapsulated the French game of that time. Rich in *joie de vivre*, a splash of unpredictability and always laced with entertainment.

French rugby, he insists, is a mirror of French society. 'For sure. Rugby in this area is like a religion, particularly in the south-west. Rugby existed by region. In my time, we had the best years of freedom and the joy of playing. In those times, there weren't fifty sports to engage you in your local town. Rugby was the game, the religion.

'When I was young, you dreamed about playing for the first team of Bagnères or Lourdes. If you didn't play rugby, you were not normal. At Bagnères when I made my debut, there were

100 players who wanted to play in the first team. For nothing!! They came for the pleasure.

'Now, young sportsmen go skiing, paragliding, playing tennis, volleyball, handball. That multitude of leisure pursuits did not exist fifty or sixty years ago.'

At eighty, it is too easy, too clichéd to paint an image of an old man in his dotage, both the chair and individual gently reclining. Gachassin, who is also a former president of the Fédération Française de Tennis, is sprightly, upright, alert. I've known men of fifty in worse shape.

But in this part of the rugby-playing world, nostalgia is seldom far away. He concedes his sadness at what has happened to the Lourdes club, a scenario that hangs like a pall over this region. 'I do not understand, with the past this club has had, that there are no longer people who could continue to restore this club, which has been one of the biggest clubs in France and has had extraordinary results.

'It was Jean Prat who signed me for Lourdes. I remember thinking, "It is Jean Prat who came to talk to me. I'll sign! I'll sign!"

'My parents warned me and said, "Well, what are the conditions?"

'"I don't care, I'll sign," I said. To sign for Lourdes was extraordinary. Just think of all the internationals they had had, of whom Jean Prat was the number one.'

Prat was the colossus of the French game. He was born in Lourdes and played for the club his entire career, from 1944/45 until 1959. In that time, as a formidable back-row forward, he won six French titles with the club and three Yves du Manoir titles. He played fifty-one times for France and was awarded the Légion d'honneur. He was also the first head coach of France in the 1960s. He died in 2005 aged eighty-one.

No wonder Jean Gachassin was impressed! In those times, they played just for the pleasure of it. Few were concerned at much else. 'If we had any gift, it was an evening aperitif,' he smiled.

'But now, there are only the big city clubs which can live and have good teams. The middle-sized towns like Lourdes and Tarbes; we can tinker, we can amuse ourselves but no more.'

He knew life was changing, would probably never be the same, when one day he went to see a promising young player in his role as president of Stade Bagnérais. 'I went to a local village called Tournay to sign a promising young prop. I asked him if he would sign for us and he said, "Oh yes, sir."

'But then his parents said, "Wait. It is not free. You must pay a surety or our son can't come."

'It was then that I knew there was a change in the system of recruitment. I felt this deeply and the next year I resigned as the president because that was it. If you gave something to one player, then there were fourteen others to pay.

'I signed Roland Bertranne and Jean-Michel Aguirre at Bagnères for nothing. They were young and happy to come and play at Bagnères with the system of play that I had put in place when I came back from Lourdes. [Both would play leading roles in France's Grand Slam team of 1977.]

'They had a little something, but it was nothing really...

'It was the pleasure, the honour of playing for Bagnères, for the club was ascending in power in the *département*. We didn't replace Lourdes and Tarbes but we became equal with them. There were some players who had first-team places with other clubs but they preferred to come to Bagnères for the playing system, even to play in the second team. The spirit was amazing.

'But one thing we did give the players, something fantastic which lasted all their lives, was the offer of employment, a career. I had a friend with an equipment company so when Bertranne signed for us, he gave him a job. I remember saying to Bertranne, "Be careful. It's not just all about rugby, life is about having a job and working hard." They [his family] had a breadwinner for life. But with rugby, even for ten years, you don't earn enough to pay for your whole life.'

Jean Gachassin was the epitome of two words out on the rugby fields of his day. Attack and spirit. The first was inculcated by the immortal Jean Prat in their days together at Lourdes. 'Everyone dreamed of playing like Lourdes,' he remembered proudly.

'We, the French, always had a certain spirit which was always rugby the French way. It is true, when we play countries like Wales or South Africa they are worried because we attack all the balls. The game of attack is organised by us.

'But when I arrived at Lourdes, Jean Prat said, "Look out, first attack, ball to the wing. The second ball, the same."

'"Why?" I asked. "To create something?"

'"No," said Prat, "it is to study how the adversary defends his opposite number."

'He was right. It is an important technique to study and analyse what the opponents will do.

'But for me, the best qualities that France has given world rugby are the game of the backs, the game of passing, of moving the ball. That is the work of the team, to free the wing. To set players free.'

CHAPTER 11

The Man Who
Put Men to Sleep

Biarritz–Bayonne–Perpignan

They're a hard, tough people these Basques. Immensely proud, too. They carry their injuries like war wounds.

Take the well-known Basque rugby man who broke his nose thirty-seven times in his career. All in the line of duty.

In 1987, Pascal Ondarts played at prop for France against Scotland in Paris with a triple fracture of the nose. He wasn't keen to stand aside because he'd only made his international debut a year before. When he was thirty. He never knew if he'd get back at that age. Grinning and bearing it was a much safer policy than admitting to the injury.

So Ondarts decided to put up with the pain. It didn't much matter. France won 28-22 at the Parc des Princes and Ondarts played his full part.

Alas, wily characters inhabited the dark world of French rugby in those times. Ondarts' broken nose became a matter of public knowledge. Then, eight days after the Test match, Ondarts lined up for Biarritz Olympique against Lourdes. Standing opposite him was a fellow prop and international Louis Armary, a man keen to exploit an opportunity.

'They knew I had a nose problem so when we went down for the first scrum, the first thing they did was punch my nose. It didn't occur to me until after the game that if I couldn't play in the next international, Armary would replace me.'

What scoundrels, what lousy sports. Yes? Well, no actually.

Ondarts had a confession to make. 'He was my friend, but I would have done the same thing to him.'

It was the law of the front-row jungle. Welsh international hooker Bobby Windsor remembers packing down against France at the Parc des Princes in the mid-1970s. There would be a strange sound as the two packs came together and settled, a French voice calling out 'Bobbeeeee, Bobbeeeee.'

Pascal Ondarts (left) with Serge Blanco at Biarritz.

Windsor, with his arms pinned around his supporting props, was helpless. He knew what was coming and who it was for. Seconds later, a giant fist from a French forward smashed into his face. Surely it could not have been our old friend, Béziers' feared Alain Estève. Could it?

Windsor said later, 'With the French at that time, it was like they wanted to kill you.'

If ever a single human being came closest to the epitome of life in all its senses, it would have to be Pascal Ondarts. He made his debut for Biarritz Olympique in 1976, did not win his first French cap until ten years later and kept playing for the famous 'B-O' until 1993. That was supposed to be the end of his career, a time when he could have his smashed-up nose finally repaired without fear of further rogue punches disfiguring it.

In fact, he played on whenever Biarritz needed him until he was thirty-nine. Even then, Jacques Fouroux tried to sign him for Grenoble where he was coaching. But he remained a one-club man to the end of his playing days. That was mostly how it was then.

His international record, thirty-four wins from forty-two Tests, was remarkable. Almost in tribute, once his playing days were over, *The Times* newspaper of London voted him one of the ten most frightening French players ever to represent the national team. It's true his fists are still like ham hocks. But Ondarts doesn't wield them very often these days.

He may be mine host at Biarritz's elegant café/restaurant in the town centre, Le Royalty in Place Clemenceau, plus owner of a hotel a few miles away, not to mention another couple of bars. But truth to tell, Ondarts, born on April Fool's Day in 1956 at Méharin in the heart of the Basque country, doesn't have a lot of trouble. Few are fool enough to take him on, even at sixty-six years of age.

One of the signature dishes at the restaurant in Le Royalty is a starter called 'Mimosa egg Pascal Ondarts'. Argue with this guy and the egg will end up all over your face.

Today, the frame is almost as familiar as in his playing days. Opposing props complained it was a nightmare scrummaging against him because those infamous sloping shoulders gave them no real target to latch on to.

England prop Jason Leonard, winner of a then England record 114 caps, called Ondarts 'the best, the toughest and the hardest prop I ever played against'.

Old rugby men wear tributes like that from fellow pros like medals on their chest. Yet there is something of even greater pride in Pascal Ondarts' life. His roots. They go back far into history for it is said generations of the Basques have inhabited this area for thirty millennia.

Strong, powerful Basques like Ondarts are as solid as the half-timbered, stone-built farmhouses of the region. They are called 'baserri'. The Basque country has its own language, customs, festivals and music. For the Basques love two things perhaps more than any other: singing and hill walking, or trekking. There are more than 40,000 members of the local mountain clubs, one of the highest concentrations in the world.

As for singing, the mellifluous tones of Ondarts' baritone voice in a French dressing room or at some stage during the night of a match, in Paris or Biarritz, were a familiar sound.

We're sitting outside the restaurant on a sunny June morning, amid the smell and sound of the ocean just down the road. I'm waiting to see whether he's a man of his word. But I needn't have worried.

We'd talked on the phone about a chat. 'Nine-thirty on Sunday morning is good,' he suggested.

But the morning after Biarritz had won promotion to the Top 14, I thought, 'That's never going to happen. He must have been up half the night, singing, eating and celebrating.'

I'd said I wanted to see Serge Blanco, too. 'He will also be here tomorrow morning,' Ondarts assured me.

So I sip a first espresso of the day in the warm sunshine and wait. Lo and behold, just before the appointed hour, Pascal comes out of the café. That familiar compact frame, the memorable rolling gait. Vast hands to shake yours. What is more, half an hour or so later, a sleek, grey Mercedes pulls up and parks directly outside. The King has arrived.

But there is no doubting which of these great men of rugby has aged best. Serge Blanco's frame all but obliterates those memories of that dashing, slim, fit full-back racing across the rugby grounds of the world, ball tucked under an arm as the other fended off would-be tacklers. When Blanco caught the ball, it was like the start of a movement from *Les Sylphides*.

Jean-Baptiste Lafond (left) and Serge Blanco.

But today, with a knee problem from inflammation, he needs a pair of crutches to get out of the car and leans perilously upon them as he negotiates a few steps down to the *place*.

Yet it is fascinating to see the reaction of passers-by to a glimpse of this great player. People nearly walk into tables and chairs as they peer at him. 'Yes, it's him,' is on someone's lips. No end of people are mesmerised by the sight of the two men. These are rugby's roots in the Basque country.

Does Ondarts regard himself as Basque or French, I ask?

'A good question,' he replies. 'Number one, I am a Basque, of course.'

There was a time, he insists, when all the best props were Basque. For in any village of this region you could find a rugby team. But these days, it's less and less. There is not much motivation now. Sometimes, he sighs, you find only one or two true Basques in either the Biarritz or Bayonne team. Almost as bad as one Pro D2 club once fielding eight or nine South Africans in their team. Honestly, how daft was that?

Ondarts says, 'There is no identity any more. I don't feel very good about that. Professional rugby kills everything.

'If we are not careful, rugby will die in the Pays Basque.

'There is a guy who wants to buy clubs. But you buy nothing. There is no value at all in Bayonne. Three years ago, Biarritz was bankrupt. So a guy got it for nothing. The debt was €3 million when he bought it. This is the problem in France. All the clubs are ruled by millionaires. Boudjellal [former owner of RC Toulon] spoiled everything.

'I would not put money into a club. It is not a serious investment. People today [running the clubs] are too far away from what it used to be. There are too many foreign players, so no identity. It is too easy for overseas guys to come, take the money and leave. In Biarritz, for example, there is no Academy for youngsters.

'Even a club as big as Clermont created an Academy... in Fiji. That isn't a fantastic idea at all for local youngsters.'

It is the future that concerns him most. 'When I stopped playing rugby, I created ten different businesses. Many people from that generation succeeded. But now I am afraid what the professional players will become in a few years' time. Because you don't buy a rugby player. It's a question of buying people.

'I am crazy when Biarritz lose but the youngsters, the players today don't care. It's a game and a job for these people who have been bought. For me, it is a passion.'

I idly stir my espresso and ponder my next question.

What has rugby taught him above all else? 'Respect. Respect for friends, opponents, visitors, people generally. Everyone has something to offer. Respect was the first quality I learned from this game.'

Yet he sees one club in France that bucks the modern trend. 'La Rochelle is the exception. The guy in charge has been involved for twenty-five or thirty years. He is the identity of the club. The people involved have the passion of the club. The audience in La Rochelle is the best in France. The other guys [those involved at most clubs] are not really interested in rugby.'

That may be true of some owners. But is there really a lack of passion for the game in the Basque country these days? Not if you consider the story from 2018 of Penarth rugby club's youth team in South Wales inviting a Basque Regional Youth XV for a match in the valleys.

The visitors brought players from clubs big and small throughout the region, including Bayonne and Biarritz. Passion? Well, an astonishing 160 players, officials and supporters made the journey to Wales. For a one-off, youth friendly match.

Ondarts followed in a supreme line of Basques who have scrummaged for the great clubs of this region and for France.

These were mighty men. They seemed almost crafted by nature rather than made by human hand. Hardship and tough physical challenges defined their lives. On and off the rugby field.

Iracabal, Azarete, Ugartemendia, Ondarts, Esponda, Etcheverry, Dospital, Gonzalez, Cremaschi, Lascubé – they were front-row men who came from the great Basque clubs of the region, like Biarritz, Bayonne, St Jean-de-Luz. They brought power and technique to their roles.

But of course, great men of the front row have been an omnipresent factor throughout French rugby. They have emerged from every corner of this rugby land. From Grenoble in the east to La Rochelle in the west, from the Paris clubs in the north to the likes of Pau and Castres down in the south. At every club, in every decade, strong, wily, committed front-row men have been a hallmark of the French game.

With faces often as disfigured as a scrunched lump of plasticine, their contribution has been fundamental. Even the fastest, most creative backs in the world are rendered largely impotent without the ball. Like a gun without the bullet.

The biggest joke of all associated with the Basque country, traditionally a hotbed of the game, where only pelota matches rugby for interest, is that sides from the UK, Ireland and the southern hemisphere used to travel here for games they called 'friendlies'. Indeed, overseas touring teams like New Zealand and Australia would play a team such as 'Côte Basque XV', or a 'French Selection XV' comprising a cluster of Basque rugby men. It was like signing up for an eighty-minute war.

Willie Anderson, a big-boned Ulsterman with large features and hands that turned into fists in a trice, was no shrinking violet as a player. From 1984 to 1990, he played twenty-seven times for Ireland as an abrasive, committed, ball-handling forward. You got up his nose as an opponent at your peril.

His first-ever recollection of French club rugby was when he was invited, as a promising youngster, to join Ulster for a match at Bègles-Bordeaux. He sat on the bench and never got on. But the experience was special.

'It was a different atmosphere altogether. We were treated like royalty. The food was magnificent and the band played during the match. I always felt after my career ended, I would have loved to have played or coached in France.'

Years later, an Ireland touring party was assembled in the second half of the 1980s to tour France and play matches at places like Auch, Biarritz, Lorient and La Rochelle. Tony Ward was on that tour and Willie Anderson was asked to lead them.

'It was one of the most enjoyable trips I had,' said Anderson. But any notion of 'friendly matches' was soon dismissed. There was an unofficial 'Test' match and Ireland won it, 21-18.

'After the match, there was not a single player in our dressing room who wasn't cut, bruised and bloodied on some part of his body. At one stage, Laurent Rodriguez and I stood toe to toe punching each other. You had to be on the border of violence... when you played them. In those days so many things happened. But you had to stand up to them. The respect we got from that was immense. I think we lived out the idea of the fighting Irish.'

But when the fighting subsided, Willie Anderson could appreciate as much as anyone the type of rugby French teams could play. 'They just kept the ball alive and their support play was superb. It was a pleasure to play that stuff.

'I played against France in 1986 at the Parc des Princes and they came at us in waves that day. It was shocking to be on the receiving end but something to watch. They played with inspiration and for the French, it is about always seeing where the space is.

'I am so glad that, in 2022, the French have come back with that emphasis on unpredictability. They are once again employing the Pierre Villepreux philosophies and it is a joy to see. By contrast, so much of recent rugby has been robotic. There are a lot of organisers in Britain and Ireland. But very few decision makers.

'I still coach and base a lot of my principles on Villepreux and his ideas of movement. I don't know why everyone doesn't look at Toulouse and see what they are doing.

'The French always employ that completely different way of thinking, rather than the Anglo-Saxon game. It's about keeping the ball alive, seeing what's in front of you, playing where the space is. But they have something else, too. Power. The toughest guy I ever played against was a French back. Philippe Sella. I remember him stripping the ball off Philip Matthews, our back-row forward, one day. I couldn't believe my eyes. Sella could have played back row, front row, anywhere. He was such a talent.'

Anderson noticed something else about French rugby men. 'When we played France in Paris, their players would take us down the Champs-Élysées for after-match drinks. They were dressed like movie stars. We looked like bin men.'

In their glory times down the years, Biarritz had players eminently capable of producing this flair. Until his retirement in 1992, the immortal Serge Blanco, born in Caracas to a Venezuelan father and Basque mother, was Biarritz's full-back. A king of a player with 93 caps for France but never crowned a French club champion. Like Villepreux, Blanco's first instinct was to run, to attack.

Would Blanco have swapped some of those French caps for a Champion of France title with Biarritz? 'No, I wouldn't, that is life. Let me explain,' he said.

'There are certain destinies in rugby. In playing rugby, there are joys and sorrows. If you sit at the table of those joys and sorrows, you appreciate your career. For me, all my career I had this luxury.'

Ask Blanco to define the Basque culture and his reply is pinpoint. 'The Basques are brave and strong, strong in the head also. What is great about the Basque region is the conviviality, the culture, the songs. It is a land of traditions. Always, we have a great welcome for everyone.'

One of those rugby men who was so 'welcomed' to the region was the Australian outside half Michael Lynagh. He first toured France with the Wallabies in 1983 and it left an indelible impression. On and off the field.

'When you played those French Selection teams before the internationals, you were basically being softened up. They chose all the hard guys and there were plenty of those in France.

'One match at Strasbourg was just a brawl from first to last. Our No. 8 Steve Tuynman had half his ear ripped off. I was on the bench that day with Andrew Slack and we both said, "Please don't send us out there today."'

But, under Sod's law, Lynagh did play the next match, at Agen, and badly broke his shoulder in a hard tackle. It was the end of his tour although he stayed on with the team. That gave him the chance to have a look at France and some destinations where the Wallabies played.

'It was a very passionate place for rugby to the point where it is frenzied passion. If you were a Frenchman within the sounds of the bells in your own town square, you never lost. Sometimes the passion went too far particularly with the forwards. It was brutal.'

Back in Lynagh's day, the tours were just chaotic. 'For my first tour (of three), the Australian Rugby Union agreed a ridiculous itinerary. After a game we would have an eight-hour bus trip somewhere else where, a couple of days later, we would get battered by another 'French Selection'. You were basically playing France every weekend. Everywhere you go, they are ready for you.

'They understand what playing for France means. It's not just another pay cheque. That is so important in this day and age. You have got to somehow link the present to the fabric and traditions of the past. Keeping that tie is so important. It's what makes rugby a little bit different.'

One trip to Biarritz was clearly something special for the Australian. Years later, around 1997, he was playing professional rugby in London for the Saracens club. They had a long weekend off and Lynagh suggested he and his wife go surfing. Biarritz was chosen.

'We spent four days there, met a few people and it was such a lovely, relaxed, calm place. It reminded me a little of the Gold Coast in Australia when I was growing up. Before all the high-rise buildings changed that.

'We loved everything about it: the people, the food, the atmosphere. Rugby was clearly such an important part of it. Down there, we were made very welcome, very quickly.'

So they bought a house, at a little place called Bidart outside Biarritz, and enjoyed it for eleven years. Their children experienced a different culture and loved the outdoor life with rugby and surfing. 'When you go there, with the Basque language, you feel it is a completely different environment to Toulouse or Bordeaux. We felt so at home and had a wonderful time.

'The Basque people are the nicest, most hospitable and generous hosts you would ever meet.'

Off the rugby field.

By the 2000s, Biarritz had a unique collection of players; some discarded by other clubs, a few acquired from elsewhere but some with real Basque pedigree.

There were fast, attack-minded players like Philippe Bernat-Salles, Nicolas Brusque, Dimitri Yachvili and the Australian duo, Jack Isaac and Joe Roff. Plus a big, strong, powerful pack with rock-solid operators like Jean-Michel Gonzalez, Denis Avril, Thomas Lièvremont, Imanol Harinordoquy, Olivier Roumat and Serge Betsen. They also had a prop forward named Sotele Puleoto. But more of him in a moment. His story is worth waiting for!

It was a multinational team with multi-talented players. And it gelled.

Roff spent almost as much time on his surfboard in the Atlantic breakers as on the training ground at Stade Aguilera. He was a fair-dinkum Aussie. But when Biarritz returned home in 2002 to an open-top bus tour of the town with the famous Bouclier de Brennus log, the French champions title after beating Agen 25-22 after extra time in a nerve-jangling Paris final, even a cool Aussie like Roff was stunned by the reception.

'Mate,' he told fellow Australian Isaac, 'I've won a World Cup, a Lions series and a Super Rugby title. But I've never seen anything like this in my life.'

People were hanging out of apartment windows as they drove in convoy from the airport into town. Many elderly people were in tears. Strong men, young and old, sang Basque songs.

Isaac explained, 'The whole town comes together. I saw one very old lady proudly waving a Basque flag out of her window. Until then, I hadn't realised how much impact what we were doing could have on the local people.

'But rugby is in the roots of this society. When you win the title, there is nothing like it.'

The roots, the traditions, the memories. Call them what you will. The plain fact is, they proudly remember their own in the Basque country. Walk into Biarritz's Stade Aguilera and you see a simple commemorative stone just beside the main stand, with an inscription. My translation:

Emile Lamothe
May 1944, Buchenwald.
Champion de France 1931 (with Toulon)
Biarritz Olympique
Voluntary fighter of the FFI.

Fernand Muniain
Disparu at Dunkerque, May 1940.
Champion of France 1935, 1939.
Winner Yves du Manoir 1937.

The words on these plaques which are to be found all over France and within its rugby clubs need no explanation.

Jack Isaac witnessed Biarritz's triumphs and tribulations, much of the time from a front-row seat. He was a player and then coach for the club. He even overcame the insult of his birthplace, Wagga Wagga, a regional city in New South Wales, being called 'Wanga Wanga' in the Biarritz club programme for the Heineken Cup match against Leinster in January 2004.

It's a long way from the Sydney Futures Markets trading floor to a rugby ground in the far south-west corner of France at Biarritz. But in mid-2000, Jack Isaac was working as a trader when he heard about a rugby contract being offered by the Basque club. He sent off his CV, got a reply within two days and a week later was on the plane to Biarritz via Paris.

He arrived in September 2000, little knowing it would be the start of an on-off eighteen-year association with the club. Literally, Biarritz and the Basque country became his home from home. Furthermore, it came to define his life. Just two years later, in 2002, he was in the Biarritz side that became champions of France. The stuff of dreams.

Mind you, Isaac had been taken aback when he had first arrived. Someone who knew the club had warned him, 'At your first training session, stand up for yourself.'

Before his first game, in the changing room, the new boy sat there astonished as most of the forwards fitted a box around their groin. Why, they weren't playing Neath, surely? Or even cricket.

Isaac said, 'I am sitting there thinking, "The eyes and balls are sacred in my culture. What's going on here?"

'But looking at this, I said, "I want one."

'I wore it for the rest of my career.'

It wasn't just at the top level that things tended to boil over. 'I remember going to watch the junior grades play at the weekends. The amount of all-in brawls was dumbfounding. These were young kids, fifteen or sixteen years old. But the fighting was part of the weekend, part of the game. That was what happened. Because it had existed for so long, it was part of the culture. They were expected to do that. Once you kicked off, everyone was in. Maybe even the coaches were inculcating that.'

But that wasn't all. Isaac watched most of his forwards snorting bottles of antiseptic mouthwash. Their eyes were watering from the fumes but it seemed to give them a high. Just in time, it would seem, for the pre-match coming together. That involved a lot of head clashing. It was, said the Australian, just the way they were. 'You thought, OK, that's what they need to do. I just went with it. I became such a better rugby player for it.'

The overall experience, I assume he meant, not the mouthwash fumes!

There was another notable player in Biarritz's golden era. His name was Sotele Puleoto and his name was known and respected through all French rugby circles. Nor was it just the size of the man that intimidated. True, he stood 1.93m tall and weighed a massive 135kgs. But there was a lot more to Puleoto than just size.

Born in 1967, he came to France from two of the most remote islands anywhere in the world, the Wallis and Futuna Islands of French Overseas Territory, deep in the South Pacific Ocean. It is said he was born in Nouméa, New Caledonia, but that seems unlikely. New Caledonia is 1900 kilometres from the two islands, which would have meant some hospital dash for his poor mother when she felt the baby arriving.

Mind you, the woman must have got used to childbirth. She had fourteen goes at it; Sotele had six brothers and seven sisters.

He first played the game for AS Mont Dore, a club in the suburbs of Nouméa. But when he left New Caledonia for France, he joined CA Brive before switching to Biarritz in 1996. It was there most of the fun began.

Puleoto, or 'Soso' as he was known, was a man of such natural strength he played both sides of the scrum, loose-head and tight-head prop. But he wouldn't throw his weight and strength around at will. After all, he was a law-abiding citizen, God-fearing too. But when it *was* needed...

Biarritz met Perpignan at Stade Aguilera one season and as the two teams lined up in the tunnel, Puleoto could be heard in conversation with an opposing prop. 'Make sure we push straight today, boys. Keep square and push straight,' were his words of advice.

Predictably, at the first scrum, a Perpignan prop tried to work Puleoto into a poor position by getting underneath him and pushing across. The scrum collapsed. They tried again, it happened again.

Puleoto stepped out of the scrum and wagged a finger in the direction of the USAP front-row men. 'Attention, attention,' he said. 'Be careful. I told you to push straight.'

At the next attempt the same thing happened. Except that when the two packs broke up, a Perpignan prop was seen to be lying motionless on the ground. He wasn't very well at all.

The USAP forwards turned on the referee, demanding Puleoto be sent off.

To which the official retorted, 'Well, I heard him in the tunnel warning you twice to push straight. So it's your fault. Penalty to Biarritz.'

Soso had another little phrase with which to warn any opposing props who might fancy dropping the odd scrum. 'Be careful, you're going to eat mashed potatoes if this goes on any more,' he warned one opponent. In other words, the victim would need a straw to eat pureed food for the next two weeks if Soso broke his jaw.

Jack Isaac wasn't a big centre so he'd had some comforting words from Soso before their first match together. 'Jacky,' he told me, 'don't worry, you'll be OK. I have your back.'

It was like a life insurance policy.

Isaac said, 'He had a hugely powerful punch but the trouble was for those about to meet it, you never saw it coming. It was a very short back lift. He threw it from just a few centimetres but the damage it could do was incredible. He had the ability to go "bang, bang, bang" and people would be falling over like dominoes. Yet he never worked out for any time in the gym or weights room.

'You couldn't say he was a great prop in terms of his scrum-maging but he was just so intimidating and powerful. He was feared throughout France, legendary in the competition.'

By general decree, another of the toughest men around in French rugby in those days was the Bourgoin and French international back-row forward Marc Cécillon. What is more, Cécillon had a temper that could flare uncontrollably. Like the time he went to a party in summer 2004 with his wife Chantal, didn't like something she said or did so (under the influence of drink), he drove home, collected his Magnum revolver and returned to the party.

In front of sixty witnesses, she was tragically shot dead and Cécillon was imprisoned for twenty years for murder. (It was later reduced to fourteen years on appeal.)

Yet strangely, in his playing days, Cécillon, who won forty-six caps for France between 1988 and 1995, was known as the quiet man of French rugby. But as hard as nails. That was a basic requirement for French forwards in those times.

Alas, he must have done something wrong in a match between Biarritz and Bourgoin. Because at one stage, Cécillon was to be seen out cold on the ground. Soso had left his visiting card once more. But the strange thing was, Marc Cécillon was a hero to Soso Puleoto. He was a player that Soso idolised, a hard, tough man. So much so that when Soso's second child was born in 1992, he named him Cécilion and the boy played two seasons for Biarritz from 2014 to 2016.

Nevertheless, Cécillon had to be put to sleep when he mixed it with Soso on this particular day. He was carried off on a stretcher and never returned. When Puleoto put your lights out, they were out for the night.

But that was then, this is now. Sadly, recent times have not been kind to the clubs of the Basque region. St Jean-de-Luz have declined (Puleoto finished his career there), Bayonne and Biarritz have swopped Pro D2 with the Top 14 but then tumbled back down again. Neither, it appears, is strong enough to survive over a sustained period in the top flight.

A realisation that was shared by Serge Blanco and Manu Merin, the respective presidents of Biarritz and Bayonne, back in 2015. Their solution? A merger between the two to create a so-called 'Basque Super Club'. Rather like Jacques Fouroux had suggested for Mont-de-Marsan and Dax. A 'super club' of the Landes and nearby areas.

Oh dear, the angst and rivalries that stirred up. There was more anger buzzing around than in the local hornets' hives.

In Bayonne, fans carrying huge banners, singing and chanting, marched around the town in protest. Biarritz seemed keener but when the Bayonne fans made it a case of 'over our dead bodies', both presidents stepped down and the idea died. Yet subsequent seasons have confirmed their views. At present, neither club appears strong enough alone to survive in the Top 14.

Alas, the issue has led to internal bickering. In April 2022, Blanco called for the resignation of several former players from the club's amateur board, including Dimitri Yachvili, Jérôme Thion, Imanol Harinordoquy and David Couzinet. Relations appeared far from harmonious.

Yet Blanco remains remarkably upbeat. Is it not difficult to see them struggling so much, I ask him? 'No. We are still living! When you love your club and you love rugby, you take pleasure at every level. Of course, I would like them to be at a higher level but in 2021 we went up from the second division to the first.'

Does Blanco believe there is a solution to this problem for Biarritz? For Bayonne, too?

'There are solutions but they have never wanted to find them. It concerns the spectators, the commercial partners, the players. It is necessary to find a plan together with the town council and the club.'

Was he correct to attempt a Basque country merger with Bayonne?

'The problem is that rugby is in the process of taking on dimensions that we could not have suspected. Today, they need a lot of money. If we have the possibility to have a proprietor who has a lot of money and is very interested in our rugby team and wants to become a majority shareholder, that would be cool. But if you don't have a large stakeholder, you just have to continue to play the rugby you love and stay alive.

'Biarritz can become a force on its own again but we must have good players and a top coach. We need to be in the Top 14 again but that is hard. When we are there, the town is brought to life.'

He agrees wholeheartedly with Irishman Ronan O'Gara, now coach of European Champions, La Rochelle. There are enough young men in the Basque country wanting to play rugby. The problem, as Blanco reminds me, is to keep those former Bayonne and Biarritz home-grown players who have left for other clubs.

His pursuit of a solution is maybe less intense now, since he no longer holds the president role with B-O. Perhaps the half-step back he has taken, plus maybe the heart attack he suffered in 2009, has invoked a more melancholic philosophy. 'I have been fortunate in rugby,' he says softly. 'The best thing rugby has given me is the friendship of other players and the sharing. You share the joy, the sorrow and the successes. It is about sharing all the moments of life.'

In the meantime, crackpot ideas laced the general conversation. Someone suggested Biarritz relocate to the north of France to play some of their matches in Lille. A daft idea. Like, in England, suggesting Manchester City play some home games in Penzance or Plymouth.

Yet consider this. How reduced would French rugby be, without the colour, tradition and pride of clubs like these? Lose Biarritz and Perpignan (both champions of France in the twenty-first century) as well as Narbonne (1979 champions) and Bayonne (1982 runners-up) and the French game would be so much poorer.

Who can forget the great days of those clubs? The pride, passion and panache. Plus the support of the local people.

Every town *en fête* on the night of their triumph. As Serge Blanco says, these towns are brought to life when the local rugby club succeeds.

As strong, sports-loving people, the Basques adore their rugby. Yet will they continue forever to follow teams unable to mix it with the best?

Basque rugby's collective glory era was in the 1930s and 1940s. Bayonne, created in 1904, were champions of France for the first time in 1913. They won it again by beating Biarritz 13-8 in the 1934 final. The following year Biarritz, or BOPB (Biarritz Olympique Pays Basque as they are now known), who had been founded in 1913, won it themselves. They were champions again in 1939.

Bayonne regained it in 1943, 3-0 winners over Agen. They finished runners-up the next year, too. But it was their last hurrah. Never again have they lifted the trophy.

By contrast, Biarritz were champions three times between 2002 and 2006. They carried the flag for the whole Basque region with pride. It was their greatest era individually as a club. But sad, envious eyes followed them from nearby. The men and women who have the blue and white of Aviron Bayonnais coursing through their veins...

There are many dilemmas here. It is necessary only to look as far as Wales to see the diminution of rugby by the decline of the great clubs. Under professionalism, the Welsh Rugby Union replaced clubs with franchises. But for most Welshmen today, more passion still exists for names like Llanelli, Cardiff, Swansea, Newport, Bridgend, Pontypool and Pontypridd than any of the franchises, the likes of Ospreys, Blues or Dragons.

Dwindling support has confirmed that suspicion. If the colourful old rugby centres of France, the likes of Biarritz, Perpignan, Dax, Lourdes, Tarbes, Bagnères and others are to be allowed to wither and die, French rugby may find itself greatly denuded.

There should be no reason why the major cities cannot support strong rugby clubs. But is French rugby of the future to be confined solely to those cities, the likes of Paris, Lyon, Toulouse, Montpellier and Bordeaux? It would be like removing certain clubs from the English football Premier League, such as Southampton, Leicester and Brighton, and just having the same handful of powerful major city clubs fighting it out for every trophy each season. How boring would that be?

A club like Leicester, which recently won both the Premier League title and FA Cup in five seasons after being in the third tier of English football as recently as 2008, proves the merit of clubs such as these. What rugby needs to help its growth is the support of wealthy businessmen, willing to invest long term in some famous old clubs. Béziers, with Christophe Dominici's plan, were on the right track. They just lacked a reliable partner/investor.

What is plain is that French rugby and the FFR will be helping to dig its own grave if it permits the likes of Biarritz, Bayonne and Perpignan to die away as serious clubs.

For it is a similar tale at the other end of the Pyrenean mountains at Perpignan. In recent times, USAP, the club of the proud Catalans, has mirrored Biarritz and Bayonne by bungee-jumping between the Top 14 and Pro D2. Although they did retain their place in the Top 14 for another season by beating Mont-de-Marsan in the play-off game in June 2022.

But they struggle for the same reason as their Basque rivals. A lack of serious money. As Gérard Bertrand says, towns in the South of France like Narbonne, Perpignan, Biarritz and Bayonne cannot find sufficient large businesses or moguls to underwrite vast investments in the town's rugby club.

None are big enough in terms of commerce to do so. What is more, even if they raised €20 million, it wouldn't be enough for sustained success. Yet some insist that the decline and virtual disappearance of clubs such as these should not be necessary. Ireland and Lions fly half Ronan O'Gara confesses he is somewhat mystified by the situation. After all, as he says, it isn't as if rugby is a dying sport in France. Very much the opposite.

'To me, clubs like Bayonne, Agen, Biarritz and Perpignan, are established clubs and I think the supporters are only dying to get behind their team. What they need to do is create a clear identity of what the project wants to stand for. Then they can take off again.

'But they have to be patient and build steadily. Sometimes, the projects have gone much too quickly (for these types of clubs). So they haven't had everything in place and ready for the challenge of the Top 14. Or they stay up for one season but then crash out because I guess they didn't have the Academy players coming through. Or they didn't do enough recruitment. It is possible to build more progressively.

'One thing I am certain about is, France should not go to franchises (like the Welsh). God, no. There is enough volume of players in France. There are plenty of players to go round. But it's hard enough to get French players to buy into their clubs. Having franchises would make it even worse.'

What O'Gara alludes to is the constant movement of players around the Top 14 clubs. In spring 2022, as the competition headed for the business end of its season, Perpignan were in the second potential relegation place, flirting with danger. At this time, their French international full-back Melvyn Jaminet announced he would leave at season's end – to join Stade Toulousain.

Although born in Hyeres, around the coast close to Toulon and not Perpignan, Jaminet had been with USAP since 2019.

They were his only senior club. Perpignan simply could not afford to lose their ace goal-kicker and star player. But it was a reminder that the best players will always be sought by the Top 14's wealthiest clubs. For when the likes of Toulouse come calling, few say 'No'.

O'Gara sympathised with Perpignan. 'As a coach, you are trying to get your players to love their club, love their teammates, to give everything together. But they would probably say, "Every July I have a different face next to me in the team. How am I going to get close to this guy?" The turnover of players at most clubs has probably been too big to create really strong bonds in the dressing room.

'That is the big challenge facing a coach like me. You are trying to get a little stability and a settled squad for a period of time where you can grow the project.'

For those involved with clubs such as these, the memories last a lifetime. Jack Isaac always considered his early years at Biarritz the best. He began to discover the language and culture of French rugby. 'I fell in love with Biarritz, the club and the life. We won the Championship in 2002 and I was playing alongside Joe Roff. Those first two years were the best for me.

'Later, in 2010, I helped coach them to the Heineken Cup final and it was a privilege to represent the club at that time. Bayonne is probably more a traditional Basque club. But I still had a real attachment to the Basque culture. It was a great honour to represent the Basque flag. I respected the culture and I love the way they live, the music, dancing and other traditions.

'When I started coaching, I tried to develop the fact that we were playing on Basque land, playing for the Basque people. I know some players really appreciated that. When you first meet Basque people, they are a little cautious. But then they open the door and are very warm.

'A handshake in the Pays Basque is a real handshake. They are an honest people and when I left, I felt a void in my life. It was hard to leave.'

One thing is crystal clear in Isaac's mind. 'Coming here was the best thing I ever did.'

But the Basque region kept drawing him back. He returned to Biarritz in 2016 as team manager and then in January 2019 joined Dax as coach. But their presence in Nationale, the third level of the French league system, is a silent rebuke for their decline from the top group.

Some great rugby men set out on their path in the game from this renowned club: Raphael Ibanez, Thierry Lacroix, Olivier Roumat, Olivier Magne, Jean-Pierre Bastiat, Jean-Pierre Lux, Jean-Patrick Lescarboura, Fabien Pelous, Laurent Rodriguez, Claude and Richard Dourthe, Pierre Albaladejo. French internationals all in their day.

But those days have long gone. Isaac sees the reality of the situation. 'It was just a natural progression, purely financial [that so many of Dax's best players left for other clubs],' he said. 'Young players move at an earlier age now.

'It is difficult to say French rugby has lost a lot... by the decline of once great rugby towns like Dax, Tarbes, Bourgoin, Bayonne, etc. The towns themselves have lost a lot. But it was inevitable under professionalism. I have to say, France is definitely stronger for that. Potentially, French rugby has never been as strong as today. They have a young group and amazing depth. There is a next generation of youngsters coming through.'

But for Isaac, who ended his association with the club in March 2022, it isn't all a picture of gloom even for Dax. 'The Nationale league is now a lot more competitive. Also, in Pro D2, there is some really good rugby played in that division. This division (Nationale) will go that way as well. But it's going to cost a lot of money and take a lot of investment.'

Which is, surely, where the FFR steps in and plays an increasing role.

Talk to any foreign rugby men who have played club rugby in France, and at some stage the conversation inevitably leads to one thing. The travel. In 2022, Dax, a town deep in the Landes region of the south-west, was sending its rugby men off in a coach for matches in places as far-flung as Massy (Paris), Chambéry (near the Swiss border), Nice (near the Italian border) and Bourgoin (East of Lyon). These represented gargantuan journeys.

Sometimes, grinned Isaac, you played a night match at such a location and then had to spend ten hours getting home. The coach would return to Dax but Isaac continued to live in Biarritz, nearly another hour away. 'After those night matches, it was crazy. Sometimes, I didn't get home until eight the next morning.'

What is more, when they got to faraway places for matches, that old French *bête noire* emerged once again, even at this level. 'The feeling of invincibility if you are playing at home and sense of disadvantage if you're the away team is a psychological mindset in French rugby,' said Isaac.

'At home it is our fortress. It shall not be breached. But somehow, it is not expected that you will win away. There is a sense that it will be OK if you get a bonus point (for a narrow defeat) when you go away. One or two of those seems to be acceptable in a season.

'It is an odd mentality. But hard as you try to change mindsets over this, it is difficult.'

He wasn't the first to try, but fail. He won't be the last.

But what of life in sunny Perpignan on the Mediterranean? Listen to a former New Zealand All Black talking about his time in Catalonia, where he spent a season, albeit most of it injured.

Dan Carter ruptured an Achilles in a match in Paris after just five appearances for the French club and could not play for the remainder of the season. But commendably, he stayed on in France, giving advice and assistance to his fellow USAP players wherever he could. Remarkably, in 2009, Perpignan went on to win the French Top 14 title that season, even without their star signing. But Carter was there with them that famous night at the Stade de France after their win in the final. The jig he danced on the team's lap of honour was of pure delight.

But why did Carter choose Perpignan when he could have gone to wealthy Toulon and joined several fellow New Zealanders. 'I turned down the chance to go to Toulon because I didn't want to be surrounded by other New Zealanders. I wanted to test myself, to go somewhere out of my comfort zone, somewhere I wouldn't be able to talk English all the time and relax with Kiwis.

'I wanted to make new friends and really challenge myself. I felt the only way to do that properly would be to go somewhere there weren't All Blacks.'

Once he could move again after his operation, he began to go to USAP training sessions. 'I couldn't participate but I could give some advice to individuals. We'd talk about the opposition, and I would try and contribute. I still felt part of the team in that way and it was important.'

They loved him for staying and doing that. 'The team were great; they made me feel at home immediately. I made some great friendships which is the number one thing I love about rugby. The friendships you make in this game last a lifetime and I made those friendships at Perpignan by staying.'

The Catalan supporters? 'They certainly love their rugby. Yet part of the reason I enjoyed being at Perpignan was I didn't find pressure from people generally. The Perpignan supporters are very passionate and there is still pressure on you to perform, with a lot of expectations.

'But I found that, after the match or away from the stadium, I could completely switch off. I was able to get away from all the hype. So despite the injury I got, it worked out well for me to go to Perpignan. I have never regretted that experience.'

The roots of the Catalan people are embedded deep in the town's rugby club. With their vivid colours of red, yellow and sky blue, on flags, rugby jerseys and even socks and berets, USAP supporters light up any stadium.

In Perpignan itself plus the villages of the Catalan region, you are never far away from witnessing spontaneous dancing, especially around lunchtime or early on one of those soft, warm South of France spring or summer evenings.

Perhaps there is something in the Catalan air that resonates with these New Zealanders. Across the world, just off the beach on the eastern side of Christchurch in New Zealand's South Island, a strong, tall-looking figure can be seen manoeuvring his surfboard onto the best breakers heading shoreward. Scott Robertson just loves to take on any personal test. He'd probably challenge a hungry shark to an arm wrestle just for a bit of fun.

You couldn't call Robertson a beach bum. He's got a lot more to do in his life than just lazing around on the beach or in the water all day long, much as he loves being out there on a board. As coach of the Canterbury Crusaders from 2017, he won five Super Rugby titles from 2017 to 2021. He won another in June 2022 and also coached Canterbury for three years, from 2013 to 2016.

Robertson joins our story because from November 2003, he spent two and a half seasons as a player at Perpignan. That followed an illustrious career, firstly with the Crusaders, for whom he made eighty-six appearances from 1996 to 2003, and then the New Zealand All Blacks, whom he represented twenty-three times between 1998 and 2002.

Typically for this super-fit, all-action Kiwi, he's stopped his cycle at the back of the beach to take my call. There's the familiar robust figure, headphones attached and ready to talk of his times beside another sea. The Mediterranean.

But it was hardly a life of luxury and ease for the arriving New Zealander. 'When I look back on it, I feel great pride that I went through it. It was tough for myself and my family. We'd been extremely successful in Canterbury but when we got to Perpignan, everything seemed to be flipped on its head.

'But once I stopped asking, "Why do we do these things?" and "Why are we training like this?" and I based it on their culture and what they do, I started to enjoy it. I began to learn the language and my wife settled into it more, too, so it was better at home.'

He began to grasp some of the cultural elements of French club rugby and saw things from a different perspective. 'Perpignan is special in its own way, being in Catalonia and near the Spanish border. But every club in France has got its own history, passion. There is a certain chaos attached to French rugby. Plus the lifestyle there is unique.

'I remember even now the photos we took of the kids cooking snails at home, and then having their photo taken under the Eiffel Tower before our 2004 final against Stade Français. Then there was the drummer singing a special club song – you don't get that in New Zealand!

'Stade beat us, 38-20, but we'd had a great year. The final was played in Paris before 79,000 at Stade de France. Unfortunately, our coach Olivier Saisset, the old Béziers player, was fired on the pitch immediately after we'd lost. It was Perpignan's first final for twenty-seven years but the president still fired Olivier because we'd lost. It was chaos.'

The pride is what Robertson remembers the most. They hadn't lost a game for ages at their tight little Aimé Giral stadium when Wasps visited for a European match – and beat them. 'It felt like the walls had closed in. You didn't lose at home.

'The contrast with Japan, where I went after Perpignan, was extraordinary. In France, players would come in for training at the last minute, grabbing a coffee. The Japanese boys are there training an hour before the start, just stretching. There were great contrasts.

'One of the reasons I went to France was to learn their language and understand about their culture. I did that, but now it is one of my personal goals to go back some day to win the Bouclier. Or even coach the French team. I would love to do that; it would be a great challenge for me. Something entirely different.'

At 1.9m and 109kgs Robertson is hardly diminutive in stature. But even he was stunned at times by the overt violence of the French game in those times. 'I remember there was a game we played against Béziers. It was an all-out fight; there were people coming in from all over the show. It was horrible. I went the other way; I wasn't used to it...

'I just didn't understand how quickly it could turn on its head. But I did understand that there was a sort of village mentality. You protected your own, you looked after your own. Of course, the laws allowed it then which was a shame. It was just part of the game, their culture.

'But I think it has changed a lot now. Things we used to accept, now we don't. A lot of behaviour has altered. The French are still aggressive but it's nowhere near as violent. It has changed with the world.'

All of which has certainly worked in France's favour. In the times when they would become so distracted by the desire to seek vengeance, concentration levels in their quest for victory, waned. They lost focus and consequently lost matches. Wily opponents (as we have seen with the English in Paris in the 1990s), knew they just needed to wind up the French and watch them lose the plot.

Today, with a rugby field as littered with cameras as an old country field with daisies, that is no longer possible. So French teams have given their complete attention to the game. The change in fortunes has started to become profound.

But Robertson fears one legacy of those brutal years may have not yet fully emerged. 'What caused it was a mentality to protect, to survive, to defend what is ours. We fight for that, we fight for our people. It's all in the DNA. OK, there was violence at times in almost all countries. But the French always had a bit more violence in their game. But it was sad sometimes, too.

'Playing at the top level was tough, honest. But that generation is coming through now with a lot of head knocks, many concussion issues. There is a lot of stuff that comes through from guys with concussion. That is a sad part of it.

'We didn't need to go there. Our game is too beautiful for us to get that hangover of that generation being in ill health. That's how I feel.'

But the New Zealander regards the many characters who fill these clubs as the essence of French rugby. Even in his time, Perpignan had Australians and New Zealanders, plus others from Morocco, Argentina and England. Also, great local talent such as Guilhem Guirado, then a rookie hooker. 'He was incredibly physical even as a youngster. We kept saying to the president, "Sign him." [Guirado would eventually become captain of France and, in his final game before retirement, a Top 14 champion with Montpellier.] There was a huge swathe of talent and rugby knowledge. There were so many characters and personalities, too.'

Like many French clubs of contemporary times, Perpignan based their game on the set pieces, especially the scrum. But on the good days, when the sky above matched the blue of their jerseys and the sunshine warmed their backs, Perpignan could be in the mood.

'It was about freedom,' Robertson maintained. 'They had a pretty special philosophy and unique way of their skill-set system. When they would find their offloading game and pass off the inside hip, it would fire. And they loved it when people talked about it, the French flair. But it seemed like they lost it for a while.

'Yet some of the teams you played, like Toulouse – wow, bang... some of the tries they scored and the way they played! They would light things up beautifully.'

When the time came and he sadly took his leave of his Catalan brothers, the New Zealander took home valuable lessons. 'Very much so. Definitely about them challenging around the maul and how much of a weapon it is. They can grind you down with the tries and penalties that they created to put pressure on teams.

'That is one of the Crusaders' foundation trademarks now. We have tried and tested it for five years. The French approach to this game really is unique.'

He loved life away from the field, too. It took them a while to respect and understand the French cuisine. But those patisseries and *boulangeries*? Memorable. Also, when he had time off, they travelled... surfing off the Atlantic coast at Biarritz, sightseeing in Barcelona, trips to Toulouse and other places. One indelible impression never left him.

'You have got to admire the French culture. It is strong and they preserve it well. It is about protecting their identity.'

Inevitably for this tough rugby man of New Zealand, the challenge of attempting to coach a French club to the Top 14 title stirs his soul. As he reminds me, only two foreign coaches have ever done that, in more than 100 years. 'So the chances of winning it as a foreign coach are stacked against you. Which is probably why I'd love to go back and try one day. To coach in the competition that I played in would be something special.'

So, on reflection, did the ways and habits of the French amuse, bewilder or frustrate him? 'A bit of everything,' he laughed. 'I was frustrated at the start because I kept wondering why they did specific things.

'Overall, it was beautiful, tough and physical. Sometimes all at once. They wanted blood for your money. I played a lot of the time when I was injured which I probably would never have done at home. I learned a lot of different skill sets and mindsets, plus made a lot of good friends. At times I was disappointed and frustrated but still loved it. There are a lot of different superlatives to explain your time and experience over there.

'But I wouldn't change them because I reckon I'm a better coach now... because of it. I understand the game differently. The French have got a special spirit that captures all of their people.'

CHAPTER 12

Way Out West

Mont-de-Marsan–La Rochelle

You go to rugby with your mates. Or you might go along with members of your family. Wife, son, daughter, brother.

But going to a game with arguably France's greatest living rugby legend is a rare privilege.

An entire region wants to be at this ground tonight. Mont-de-Marsan of the Landes, Stade Montois, to give the club its official title, were one of the signature clubs of French rugby. Founded in 1908, they were champions of France in 1963.

Sixty years has passed since then. But this accolade is not to be taken lightly in this country. The words 'champions of France' are spoken just as reverently today by any champion club's followers as back in the day. It is the way in French rugby.

But for my host *ce soir*, there is always a special meaning behind his journey to the ground. He leaves his home close by the sea and heads inland, to the 16,800 capacity stadium he knew so well as a young man. Here, they played for pleasure, for fun, but for local pride too. The genius of this man, together with his brother, captivated not just a town, a club or a region, but all of France.

Even today, all those years later, his name remains revered.

With their unique understanding as brothers, almost telepathic, they became a combination of vivid expressionism on the field, delightful in their vision and touch, lethal in their execution. Each developed a natural dexterity that was to become a fundamental part of their game. In addition, outside them was a man ideally suited to maximising their creativity.

Tonight, the field where they played is crammed. Stade Montois are playing their final game of the league campaign in Pro D2. Alas, although they will finish top of the league table, their dream of promotion will fail. Bayonne will topple them in the play-off game, to seize the ticket to promotion.

But for André Boniface, there are always memories when he comes here. The clue is in the stadium's name: Stade André-et-Guy-Boniface. Guy is the younger brother whom André – no, make that all France – lost, on the first day of January 1968. It was a day that changed André's life.

Townsfolk, outsiders, passers-by in Mont-de-Marsan: they knew something was wrong when they heard the bells. The mighty bells of the church of St Mary Magdalene tolling in the night. The team had won a friendly match at Orthez and the players had made their own way home, most by car. Guy was the passenger in a friend's car, his final journey. The vehicle crashed, hitting a tree at Hagetmau, and France's mercurial centre was killed. He was just thirty and had played thirty-five times for France, eighteen alongside his brother.

Even today, at eighty-seven years of age, André vividly remembers his emotions.

Stade André-et-Guy-Boniface at Mont-de-Marsan.

'Guy died on the night of 31 December. When I heard the news, it was like a bomb had exploded, an atomic bomb. I was stunned. When we heard he had died, all the inns in the villages immediately closed. It almost killed me. I stopped playing rugby for two years. I wouldn't watch any game. Guy and I always played twelve and thirteen, side by side. For thirty years we were so close to each other. It was more than anyone else.'

The renowned French rugby writer of that time, Henri Garcia, penned these simple words to express his sadness, a grief shared by a nation. 'When Guy died, something died in rugby – friendship, gaiety and generosity flavoured with insouciance.'

So when André comes back here now, like tonight? 'Yes,' he answers softly, with an expression of melancholy writ large upon his craggy face. 'Always there are the memories...'

There was no history of sporting excellence in their family. Yet their father bought a house at Montfort-en-Chalosse in the Landes region. It was propitiously sited. André lived there

307

until he was eighteen and even thereafter, he went back each weekend.

'Here, in this part of France, the countryside is very nice and the place where I was born, Montfort, looks like New Zealand. In most villages, the first thing you see, even from 2 kilometres away, is the church. But at Montfort, the rugby ground is right in the middle of the village. It is one of the first things the visitor sees.

'My father (Jean-Louis) bought the closest house to the rugby ground. From my parents' house, we could see the goalposts. Yet my mother never went inside the ground.

'We (Guy and I) always thought we were small All Blacks. We practised and practised. Every day started at school with ten minutes of rugby discussion by the teacher. Then, after school, the ground was the first place we went to each day. We would play barefoot until darkness came.'

But they played only for fun. Dreams of the French team and facing the great rugby nations of the world were just that. Dreams. Furthermore, before 1960, André says they didn't know what sort of game to play.

'We played at random. It was the British who invented the saying "French flair". We suddenly realised we could play a certain rugby. We realised how different we were, but before that we didn't know. Before that, we kicked as much as anyone else.'

André, the elder brother by almost three years, was to win forty-eight caps for France between 1954 and 1966. He was the key player as Mont-de-Marsan won the 1963 French Championship. But who was the best player. Guy or André?

The great Jean Gachassin played with and against them. 'It was the two, they were complementary. There was complete osmosis between them. I was a person who played alone but they played as a twosome. You couldn't change it.

'The night Guy died was terrible. A great friend had disappeared. It was so hard for we saw each other often. We were very, very good friends. He came here, I went there, our wives knew each other.'

Tragically, just three days after Boniface's death, another young French international rugby star was killed in a car crash in the Landes. Jean-Michel Capendeguy had won two caps for France and just been chosen to face Scotland in the 1968 Five Nations Championship. The wing from Saint Jean de Luz was aged just twenty-six when he lost his life in the accident.

South of Bordeaux, deep in the heart of the Landes *département*, is a chapel dedicated to three young rugby men who died in a horrific car accident. The trio, Raymond Albaladejo, Jean Othats and Émile Carrère, all played for Dax and in September 1964 were returning from a friendly match against CA Bègles in Bordeaux.

Their car hit a truck at Lesperon, between Mont-de-Marsan and Aire-sur-l'Adour, and spun off at speed, crashing into a tree in which it became embedded. All three were killed.

Albaladejo, a wing, was thirty-one and the brother of Dax and France outside half Pierre, with whom he played. He was a Championship runner-up with Dax in 1956, 1961 and 1963.

Othats, a centre, was twenty-seven and had played two matches for France in 1960. He was also a runner-up with Dax in the 1956 and 1961 French Championship finals, but he won the Yves du Manoir with the club in 1957 and 1959.

The third, Émile Carrère, was also twenty-seven and also a Dax three-quarter. He played in their losing 1961 final. His death was the second heartbreak for his wife Dani in 1964. That same year, their young son Thierry had also died. He was two years and four months old. Carrère's young widow attended her husband's funeral while pregnant with their unborn second child, a daughter, Catherine.

309

All Dax and the entire south-west of France mourned. It would be a harrowing precursor to the death of another famous French rugby brother, Guy Boniface.

In memory of the three Dax players, a building of ecclesiastical heritage up a steep road in Larrivière-Saint-Savin was transformed into the Notre Dame du Rugby Chapel by Father Michel Devert. It is now adorned with rugby jerseys from around the world.

It should act, too, as a warning to all young men. Speed can kill.

As for the man who waited, outside the famous Boniface brothers for his scoring opportunities, he, too, is here tonight. Christian Darrouy played eighteen seasons for Stade Montois, from 1954 to 1972. A sprightly eighty-five he may be, but the years fall away and the smile on his face suggests few regrets of a rugby life.

Darrouy was born and bred in the Landes, in a tiny commune named Pouydesseaux, close by Mont-de-Marsan. He went to the club as a spindly youngster, but one with coruscating pace. He was keen on football to begin with, and thought of joining a major club, such as Bordeaux. But rugby got there first. For club and country, Darrouy played twelve seasons with André, and captained France ten times. In all, he won forty caps for the national team and scored twenty-three tries. Wings do not return statistics of that nature without some class acts inside them at centre. Manifestly, France had some midfield operators of serious quality in that era, men like André and Guy Boniface, Jo Maso, Jean Trillo, Jean Gachassin and Jean-Pierre Lux. These were players of quicksilver moves, able to open a defence with the simplicity of the jailer, his cell. But it was, of course, another time, another era. Space was available for those who sought it. Very different from the new, defence-focused, modern game.

Christian Darrouy challenges Ireland full-back Tom Kiernan for the ball in an Ireland v France fixture at Lansdowne Road, Dublin.

Which of those renowned centres was the best? 'It is difficult to compare,' said Darrouy. 'Each had great talent.'

His greatest victory, he avows, was the July 1964 Test win by eight points to six over the South Africans at Springs, outside Johannesburg. He scored France's only try. By 1967, he was captain of France and wrestling with a major difficulty. 'It wasn't easy being captain because I didn't know half the rules! Then there was the problem of the referee. He only spoke English.

'"What did he say?" my team-mates asked me after one conversation.

'"I have absolutely no idea," I told them.'

He also found captaincy hard when it came to selecting the team, which the touring captain did in those days. 'As team

311

captain in South Africa, it was not easy. Do you choose your pals?'

In the notorious 1963 French Championship final between Mont-de-Marsan and Dax, he was a largely disinterested spectator when the violence erupted. 'I wasn't very concerned with it or interested. But I think the game has made great progress since those times. If you end your playing life with your nose over there [he signals to the left] and your jaw over here [signals to the right], it's not worth it.

'I didn't like the violence; it was idiotic. Sport is not about violence, it's a game. Sometimes there were tackles made in a bad way. I had my nose broken seven times, mostly by elbows. But that's not serious, it is part of the game.'

Here, on this warm evening in the South of France, he sits beside Boniface, his old friend in the seats outside a private box. From behind, I study Boniface closely. His gaze is focused intensely on the play. Much of it, let's be honest, is variable in standard. Yet he restrains himself. There is no gesticulating in frustration, no shouting or decrying the play before him. His is an elegant bearing. He absorbs the lessons of the play before him like a military commander studying the field.

What made him so good as a player? Christian Darrouy knew.

'He had so many physical qualities. He ran so fast, he attacked. Most importantly, he always arrived at the place he needed to be. It was his vision.'

Boniface tells an amusing tale concerning those skills.

'I was gifted to be able to look when I played the game. Guy never ran like me. My mother said to him, "Why don't you run like André?"

'When I was given the Légion d'honneur at the Élysée Palace, [the late] President François Mitterrand asked me, "How do you manage to pass so easily through the crowd?"

Toujours Stade Montois! Christian Darrouy (left) and André Boniface back at their old club.

'I said, "I am always looking at the people just beside me. They all want to catch me; that is the reason why."'

In 1966 in Cardiff, France chose André and Guy at centre, with Jean Gachassin inside them at fly half, Christian Darrouy on one wing and the attack-minded Claude Lacaze at full-back. But they still lost to Wales, albeit by just a point, 9-8. It was the Boni brothers' final game together in a French jersey. I was privileged to be there, to see it. For the finish was spine-tingling. France led, only to be overtaken when wing Stuart Watkins intercepted a pass and raced 60 metres to score. Yet Claude Lacaze had a last-minute penalty to win the match, but cruelly, the wind blew it just off target and Wales scraped home.

I know we're all getting on a bit and, my word, that happened fifty-seven years ago. But if only we could all turn back the clock for who wouldn't want to be the scrum half inside that French back division? Feed them the ball with your best spun pass and stand back and admire the geniuses at work. I bet even Gareth Edwards would have given something to unleash that lot.

There is an essence of homeliness about the Stade André-et-Guy-Boniface. Inside the ground, there is a place called, very inventively, Le Pub, outside of which the patrons stand on the steps of old terracing to watch the game. They clutch pints of beer, doubtless more than content after a pre-match meal.

Le Pub offers an entrecôte, confit, *jambon* or piperade, the latter a Basque dish prepared with onions, green peppers and tomatoes, sautéed and flavoured with piment d'Espelette, the spicy red pepper. Add on a plate of French fries to the steak, duck or *jambon* and they'll demand a risible €10 for the meal. Such value, such fun.

To complete dinner, they have the perfect *digestif* in these parts. Some of the grapes that make Bas Armagnac are grown within just fifteen minutes of the town. Grapes have been grown in this region for this much-prized drink since Roman times.

The stadium itself is large with two good-sized stands. Yet it has the unmistakable feeling of a Pro D2 standard ground. But then, Mont-de-Marsan is a small, homely country town. It isn't a Toulouse, a Bordeaux or Lyon, never will be.

One of the great attractions of rugby in France is the contrasts between clubs like Toulouse and Mont-de-Marsan: big and small, rich and poor, big spenders and careful housekeepers of finances.

For sure, they revere and remember their former players at French clubs such as this. The previous week, they had held a banquet for the old players of the club. A hundred and forty people turned up and there was only one missing, grumbled Boniface in mock disapproval. 'Darrouy. He was hunting!!!'

French rugby today? Boniface is a positive man but he sees the need for further attention in one area. 'There are still too many foreign players in French rugby; we don't need them. They must diminish [still further] the number.

'As for SM [Stade Montois], they can do better. Biarritz and Bayonne were promoted in recent years but we are better than them. But they need to up the level of their game each season.'

What of the best French players, past and present? Perhaps an invidious question, rather like asking someone whether Burgundy is aesthetically more appealing than the Côte Roussillon region beside the Mediterranean. 'The best of all times?' he asks. 'My father would say it's me!! Jo Maso? Not bad. He was strong and elegant.'

But the present day? 'Antoine Dupont is the best, the number one. He is very gentle, very modest. He has the qualities of a great one. When one is very strong, one is modest. The worst are pretentious, always putting themselves forward.'

*   *   *

Down here in the south-west of France, you can visit all manner of clubs who proudly boasted the title 'champions of France' at some point in their long, distinguished histories. Lourdes, Biarritz, Bayonne, Bègles/Bordeaux, Tarbes, Mont-de-Marsan, Pau: these and clubs like them have, in their day, represented the beating heart of French rugby.

Indeed, Bordeaux-Bègles enjoyed a stellar season in 2021/22, just a single point short of the leaders in the Top 14 as the twenty-sixth and final league game was played. They were to lose in the semi-final, to Montpellier. But the club had made another worthy contribution at French rugby's top table.

315

Montpellier, meanwhile, would go on to lift the famed Bouclier de Brennus for the first time in their thirty-six-year history as a club. They beat Castres 29-10 in the final in Paris.

But on this bright, beautifully sunny Saturday morning as I leave Mont-de-Marsan and cruise through the Landes forests heading north, I am making for somewhere different.

La Rochelle is a gem, one of the great travel jewels in the French crown. As for seafood, if you like that there is hardly anywhere better.

In the old town, where the architecture is a treat, there is a seafood specialist restaurant named Le Tout Du Cru. It means, literally, everything is raw. You will find it near the old market, in Rue Thiers. It is simple, unpretentious but fantastic.

We sit outside on a warm, early summer evening. Jonathan Danty, La Rochelle's French international centre, strolls by with a friend. It's that kind of place, La Rochelle. Small enough to be familiar.

As for our restaurant, if you order a mixed seafood platter, expect oysters, a large crab claw, whelks, big prawns and clams.

The iconic port entrance at La Rochelle, home of the 2022 Heineken Champions Cup Winners.

Sip a glass or two of Sancerre and you have the quintessential French seafood platter. Then there are the moules from Marennes.

As for the local rugby club, on 28 May 2022 La Rochelle toppled Leinster to win the Heineken Champions Cup. It was their first-ever major trophy. As the club's big Australian second-row forward Will Skelton said after the triumph in Marseille, 'We are only a small town; we are not supposed to be here. But we got the job done.'

Biarritz's great Basque prop Pascal Ondarts always insisted, 'At La Rochelle, you will find the best atmosphere at a rugby ground in France. The people running the club are real rugby people.'

But things mature slowly way out west. The rugby club at La Rochelle was one of the first founded in France. In 1898. The United States Consul of the time in the city, George Henry Jackson, developed the rugby section of the original club. Today, at the Stade Marcel Deflandre, a stand is named in his honour.

There was the promise of some early success when Stade Rochelais reached three quarter-finals of the burgeoning French Championship, in 1906, 1907 and 1914. Alas, they lost the lot.

Down the years, they won some regional titles but never the national championship. Then, in the 1930s, with the French national team suspended from the Five Nations, Stade Rochelais, like many others, became a rugby league club.

Vichy completely undermined the game of XIII. So by the start of the 1940s, Stade Rochelais was back in business as a rugby union club. But the war years cost outstanding French lives at this club, like so many others. Club president Marcel Deflandre, a resistant, was arrested by the Germans and shot in 1944.

By the beginning of the 1960s, the club once again reached French Championship quarter-finals, in 1961, 1962 and 1969. But again, lost them all.

In season 1987/88, a famous name played a single season for the club on the Atlantic coast. Future New Zealand World Cup-winning coach Steve Hansen.

Enfin, the club lifted silverware in 2002 and 2003, winning the Rugby Union Cup which had replaced the old Coupe de France. Alas, they were stuck in Pro D2, the second division, from 2002/03 until 2010. But euphoria at rising to the Top 14 was fleeting. They suffered immediate relegation and stayed another three seasons at the lower level.

But by now, some serious rugby people had become influential. Vincent Merling was never a top-line player for the club, but always a keen rugby man and devotee. Once he'd hung up his boots, he became the driving force that dragged the club initially back into the Top 14 in 2014, and then to the verge of titles. They lost the semi-final of the French Championship to Toulon in 2017 and lost another semi-final two years later. Also in 2019, they were beaten finalists in the European Challenge Cup, Europe's number two competition.

Clearly, something substantial was being steadily built beside the Atlantic.

By season 2021/22, Stade Rochelais not only reached a second successive Heineken Champions Cup final. On their books, they could boast three members of France's Grand Slam-winning team from that winter, three former New Zealand All Blacks, three South Africans and one Australian Wallaby. Expensive personnel to recruit and keep.

So how on earth has the club that had never won a major trophy until 2022 and never been 'champions of France' done it?

It is not a club run on the largesse of a single individual, as Toulon was under Boudjellal, or Mohed Altrad at Montpellier or Jacky Lorenzetti at Racing 92. Furthermore, the La Rochelle club has two supervisory bodies. One is the Management Board, the second the Supervisory Board. It ensures real rugby people are involved in decision making. Vincent Merling may be the figurehead, but a lot of other people play their part, not least some of the true fans.

Merling was born in the town and began playing rugby for them as a seventeen-year-old. Yet he never won a thing in his own playing days.

But by 1991 the club needed his contribution in a different sense. They were in extreme financial difficulties with a debt of 1.2 million francs. Merling set up a financial restructuring plan to pay off the debts. He has been club president ever since and his success in his own business, in the world of coffee, has been vital in the rugby club's renaissance.

Under his presidency, Stade Rochelais drew up a scheme to tap into the many businesses that populate this part of France. They may not have Airbus on their doorstep, like Stade Toulousain. But they drew a map with towns and cities up to 100 kilometres from La Rochelle. This included some quite sizeable locations, the likes of Rochefort, Niort, Royan, Saintes, Cognac, La-Roche-sur-Yon and many others. They then targeted the businesses, large and small, of all those towns.

Some agreed to put in serious amounts of money, up to €250,000 each per season. Other, bigger companies may well have put in more. The smaller, individual businesses, less. But then there was also the support from their own *municipalité*.

This exercise succeeded handsomely. In all, it is believed that today La Rochelle has the financial support of an incredible 650 businesses, big and small, in the region, not just the city itself. That is a very substantial financial base from which to operate. The club has cleverly nurtured and built a large, regular following from the whole region.

But it's not the only successful part of the story. Since season 2016/17, the club has had a 100 per cent occupancy rate for its Top 14 matches. In 2021 for a match against Union Bordeaux-Bègles, the ground was sold out for the sixtieth consecutive time. To achieve that and then maintain it, is phenomenal.

Stade Marcel Deflandre, just a short walk up the road from the sea at La Rochelle, is not a big ground. Its capacity is just over 16,000. But when it is full, the atmosphere is extraordinary and the noise shattering.

The club also built a 7000-square-metre professional training centre close by its stadium, costing €7 million. This is a club going places.

The man now charged with putting them firmly among the best in the land is a great man of Irish rugby. If anyone ought to know about and understand passion, it is him.

Ronan O'Gara, renowned player for Munster, Ireland and the British & Irish Lions, is excelling in the coaching world. He has done the hard yards learning his trade; kicking coach at Racing 92 in Paris, then two seasons as assistant coach to Scott Robertson at the Crusaders, in Christchurch, New Zealand. From there, he returned to Europe in 2019 as assistant coach to Jono Gibbes at La Rochelle.

His impact has been substantial. In season 2020/21, as Gibbes's assistant, he helped guide Stade Rochelais to the finals of both the Heineken Champions Cup and the French Top 14. Both ended in disappointment. But O'Gara is a character who doesn't do 'down times'. Not for any lengthy period, anyway. A new challenge always awaits, a trait I find infectious.

The next season, 2021/22, as head coach, he promptly steered his club back to another Heineken Champions Cup final. A rare feat. This time, the glory was theirs.

What O'Gara was engaged in was a building exercise. He is seeking to take Stade Rochelais to the next level. In other words, his task represents the pursuit of excellence. He wants them beating on a regular basis, the cream of French rugby: Stade Toulousain, Racing 92, Montpellier, etc. Not to mention the best in Europe, too.

And this is a man who never stops, a driven man.

O'Gara was born in San Diego, California, where his father, Fergal, worked as a professor of microbiology. From the father comes the son. O'Gara junior's attention to detail is microscopic.

With a family of a wife and five children – thirteen-year-old twins, an eleven-year-old, a ten-year-old and an eight-year-old – you'd need to be organised.

So, I get a text on Sunday at 12.51, almost lunchtime, at my hotel in the old city centre. 'I have an hour at 13.30. That work?'

This isn't a bloke who's lounging around a bar and sinking a few cold ones on a warm, sunny day...

He arrives in what must be the biggest 4 x 4 any vehicle company makes. It is enormous.

But in typical fashion, he cuts to the quick.

If he thought helping bring up five youngsters was a task, then he'd revised his opinions somewhat on some of those in the Top 14 rugby domain. 'It's tough when other people's ambitions don't match up with yours. I tell them, "If you don't perform for me, you get a gig at somewhere else. Bordeaux, Castres, Agen..."

'These guys end up taking your energy rather than concentrating on the good guys. For me, it's very frustrating.'

There's another thing, too. 'There is a lack of understanding and lack of respect for how competitive this league is. It's only when you get into it, you realise.

'But I have an absolutely huge love for the Top 14. It's such a dog of a competition. You get tested in every single facet of the game. Your durability and squad harmony and disharmony really are other things.

'The capacity to keep them going for ten months of the year for season after season with worries about relegation, promotion, finishing in the top six... it's only when you get stuck into it, you appreciate how tough it is.'

What of that hoary old chestnut, French flair? 'Some of the games are inspirational. But not always because some of the results are so, so important due to factors like relegation and the economic devastation that can happen to a local team.

'But then, when you come to the "barrages", the quarter-finals weekend, the quality of the rugby goes through the roof. There are some incredibly good players in this league. I underestimated how much they like to play the ball out of the tackle. Their capacity from a young age and how they are taught to play the game are incredible.

'To create space, they sometimes take on their man and they play one off one and get their arms free. In most parts of the northern hemisphere, the ball carrier would be blamed if they didn't catch the ball. In France, the recipient would be blamed because he was not anticipating the pass. If you go to ground here it is seen as a failure. That occupies a lot of my attention.

'When you work up close with Dan Carter [as he did for Racing 92], you saw that what separated him from others was his capacity to throw passes to create space and keep the ball alive. The French are great at exploiting space but they tend to run to the touchlines. Carter ran at the goalposts [in other words, straight]. He didn't eat up the space for those outside him.'

Where has he learned the most on his coaching journeys? 'I have learned so much everywhere and especially here. The benefit of France is, you get a better appreciation of the different requirements needed.

'In New Zealand, you could play three Super Rugby Championships in the time they take to play a single Bouclier campaign in France. The idea that you can copy and paste what the Crusaders do (and use the philosophy all around the world) would never work because Super Rugby is like a Grand Prix. It's bang, bang. Whereas the Top 14 is the survival of the fittest. You have to be mentally and physically more durable compared to others.

'The environment of the Crusaders is very different to anything in France. Here, because of the history and the rules, you have got to keep a group going.'

In Super Rugby, teams have fourteen regular season matches, with three knockout games for whoever reaches the final. O'Gara says you might get by with thirty players for a season. In France, you need forty because teams play twenty-six games in just the regular season. Then there are the knockout rounds.

'The big learning curve for me has been the struggle to keep as many of them as you can fully engaged so they feel very valued towards the project.

'Individual management of them is important so you have to forward plan. Like saying, "Look, you won't be playing this week but get yourself ready for Brive in two weeks' time" sort of thing.'

Then there is something else. 'You are battling against the history of the French system where it is imperative that they win at home but when they go away they think, "Well, OK, we will have a look at the away game."

'You think to yourself, "What is this attitude about?"

'I would be the most sought-after coach in the world if I could crack that. It's just always been that way. You are talking about 130 years of history. Whatever it takes, they have got to empty the tank for a win in a home game. The feeling is, we will do the business at home. That is what matters.

'I think it is tribal, that is very much the case. Parochial, too. It is like protecting your town against someone looking to come in and raid.

'You have got to remember the history of so many French coaches setting up their team to succeed at home. They want to get into the play-offs and to do that, if you win your home games and maybe poach two or three away wins, that gets you into the top six.'

As for the violence, once endemic in French rugby, it is but a shadow of its former self. 'There are high shots now in the game. But I can't recall the last time someone threw a dig [punch] which is very surprising. It doesn't happen any more because of the cameras in the game.

'But given the number of hotheads playing the game over here, that's remarkable,' he says.

He found a different coaching environment when he got to La Rochelle, compared to his life and times in Paris with Racing. The level of accountability is low in Paris, he says. 'You get the RER into Paris and no one knows who you are. It's a much more varied society. Ordinary people are doing their own thing. But it's very difficult to hide here in La Rochelle. When you arrive at the training ground, you'll find people waiting to give out about what you did (or didn't do) at the weekend! That makes you much more accountable.

'In the rugby towns of the south and west, the minute you go there you see posters, the flags, etc. Take La Rochelle, down by the port. The bars are lively, people are talking. The locals are very, very proud of their team.'

Will France eventually lose its individualism and its unique spirit and attitude towards the game, I ask him?

'I don't think so because of the strength of the Top 14. Also, the volume of players, the vibrancy of the game and the interest. Rugby has become hugely popular in France. Maybe it always was, but now it seems to be going to a different level.

'Enthusiasm for it has taken off and with the World Cup in 2023 it's only going to get more popular. What is great about the French people is they have a lot of character. Also, different personalities are immersed in their team.

'There is a little bit of a mad side to them which I think is needed.'

But it's not all a bed of roses. He foresees one paramount difficulty. 'The biggest challenge for them going forward will be, they have a lot of amateur referees in the Top 14. When it comes to playing under professional refs and you're playing at home, you get 50/50. Playing away, you don't.'

He rates 2016 and the French Top 14 final as one of his best moments in rugby (well, until the 2022 European Champions Cup triumph, anyway). Racing 29 points, Toulon 21 in the final, played in front of 99,124 fans at Barcelona FC's Camp Nou stadium. Racing triumphed despite having to play more than three-quarters of the game with fourteen men after scrum half Maxime Machenaud was sent off for a dangerous tackle on Matt Giteau.

'Winning the Bouclier in the Camp Nou... I felt privileged to have done that. When Machenaud was sent off, I threw my notebook with plans and tactics into the waste bin. We thought it was over. But that summed up coaching and perhaps French rugby. Somehow, the players found a way.'

Mind you, having Dan Carter as the General at number ten to marshal his remaining men certainly helped. So did a strong constitution when it came to the celebrations.

'The party went right through the night and ended at 6 a.m. the next morning. But that's why you get involved in sport. You have to celebrate the good times.'

At the end of a long day, when he manages to steer the giant 4 x 4 out of the club's training centre and heads for the bridge across the estuary to Île de Ré, his home, what goes through Ronan O'Gara's mind? Isn't he bemused at times by the French character and traditions?

Yes. But ask him if French rugby still excites him, and the words almost pour out. 'Oh, yes. I have always been attracted to it. But once you are here, you understand it and get a better idea of their mentality.

'There are days when it is incredibly frustrating when you feel you are banging heads but not making any progress. Then a few weeks later, you are watching your team playing with a spirit and vision of what you are trying to put into them. So when it comes together it is very, very fulfilling.

'The support is huge. Having that every two weeks of your life becomes a great buzz. But that's the beauty of the game, especially the Top 14. It is an unbelievable championship. It has people on the edge of their seats. Coaches included.'

In December 2021, South African Johann van Graan announced his decision to quit as coach of Munster, Ronan O'Gara's beloved homeland. Many assumed their champion former player would be booking tickets home for his family before buying the Christmas turkey. But they misjudged their man.

'This is a spectacular place to live. And the wife and kids love it. Which is the most important thing.'

Does that sound like a man itching to get home? Munster had to look elsewhere in their search for a new coach.

CHAPTER 13

A Golden Era

Toulouse–Castres–Narbonne–Perpignan

You could slip past Castres, a small country town 80 kilometres east of Toulouse in the rolling hills of the Tarn department, and not give it a second thought.

Yet there is plenty of history here – the town's name meant a 'fortified place' in Latin.

There was an early Gallo-Roman camp, built around a Benedictine monastery which was founded in AD 647. But the modern-day population, approximately 40,000, has been declining for some time. In 1860, there were fifty woollen mills in the town. Today? None, really.

Remarkably, Castres is the only town of this size in all France not to be connected to the motorway network. The local rugby club runs off a tight budget, mainly supplied through the sponsorship of the Pierre Fabre Foundation. You would hardly know of its rugby pedigree unless you were a true follower.

And yet... Castres Olympique contested the final of the French Top 14, four times in nine years from 2013 to 2022, winning twice. It is an incredible achievement, a tale of the smaller club punching far above its weight. It is why French rugby at the top level forever remains competitive.

I drive up from Toulouse early on a quiet Sunday morning, heading for the marketplace where I will meet one of the club's most consistent, effective players these last ten years. South African scrum half Rory Kockott.

He first arrived in the South of France in 2011. Since then, he has twice been a French Top 14 champion with Castres, besides playing for the French national team. But he shook his head at his earliest memory.

'Sometimes in my first year, it was a nightmare to think I would be here that long. But you come to terms with the challenges, and you rise above them and adapt.'

What is the toughest thing to adapt to in French rugby, for an overseas player?

'The culture of rugby in France, the way they think about the game, the way they live rugby. It's different to every other country. The South Africans have a very ingrained, disciplined and focused culture, almost a cold and direct approach to success and failure. Contrast that with the emotions, hot-blooded nature and depth of human interaction that French rugby comes with, and its passion.

'It's all like a big washing machine with a mix of emotions that you roll through especially on the weekend, but even more so during the week. Foreign players are not used to that, it is what puts you out of your comfort zone. It is something you have to adapt to.'

Kockott demonstrated a loyalty to unfashionable Castres many others would have scorned. After their surprise victory in the Top 14 final of 2013, their first title for twenty years, he received offers from Toulon, Toulouse and Racing 92. These clubs represented the cream of French rugby: richly laden with history, repute and finance.

Yet Kockott turned them all down. Why?

'Those massive teams are certainly constant threats, constant performers in the Top 14. So to win two Championships at Castres, in 2013 and 2018, then get to another final in 2022 with the club as it is, with the budget we have... it's difficult.

'I am proud of the way the club has stuck to its culture. We had two difficult years. In 2015 we were almost relegated. We had a bunch of players and a mix of coaches that just didn't gel. But we had a club that was capable of bringing new people in and fixing those situations.

'So, do the maths, look at the teams, compare them. Go to a club like Racing, Toulouse or Toulon – that would have been great. But would I still have been playing up to 2022? Probably not.

'I have no regrets about not going. Definitely not. It was meant for me to carry on my career here, not just the longevity but the personal relations that you build up along the way which are far more important after rugby than one realises.

'A lot of young players tend to chase the money when they're younger. But if you can build good relationships in that process and are capable of working in an environment that suits you, what French rugby does reward you with is loyalty. They are very loyal and very passionate about loyalty within the club's structures.'

The South African is firm in his mind about something else, too. He says foreign players and coaches have had a massive influence in changing the French game.

Kockott insists a large part of the French DNA has always been flair, that attacking mindset. Even so, he claims it is not the strongest point of the French national team at the present time. 'If you look at them today, defence is their strong point, which has always been a southern hemisphere or an English mentality. They have adapted to that.

'Maybe that is why they are performing at the level they're at. I think they have done extremely well in adapting to the needs of the higher levels of modern-day rugby. Whether it comes to player profiles, ideologies and philosophies or vision in terms of planning and structure in rugby, they have adapted to a lot of that.'

What of the violence which, these days, has at last retreated after being a central element of the sport for decades in this land? Kockott, who announced his retirement from playing in May 2022, suggests another quality has held the key to this aspect of the French game.

'One of the biggest things about French rugby is the emotional side of it. Getting emotional is a great empowerer. It's a great ignition. Controlling those emotions shows great discipline. I don't think the French have been able to do that for a very long time. But they are much better now than they used to be. The process of people talking about it, being transparent and open about it has improved things.

'Being able to prepare themselves mentally and psychologically in a constant, sustainable way is something that is key to French success. When I say sustainable, I mean it must be something that has positive energy. You can get extreme energy sometimes which overflows. It was something I experienced in my time in the French jersey [he won eleven caps]. It overflowed in a way that wasn't good for the team or the individuals within the side.'

Like other overseas players such as Jack Isaac at Biarritz, Kockott believes that trait is an innate characteristic in the French that is bred, nurtured and fed from a very young age. 'I help out with the Under-15s at Castres and I see that already within the individuals. It's what they see, what they hear and what they understand. It's what they feel is right. It's a case of juniors watching the senior teams, seeing what can happen and implanting in their own minds that's what they are going to do. It is so mentally intact within their thought process, culture and beliefs that it will be a longer evolution than the sport itself before that changes.'

Eleven years in the South of France, living the life, being paid to play the game you love. What a deal! Kockott grins.

'It's massive how the South of France is the bread basket, the birthplace of French rugby. You can go as far north as you like in rugby, searching for this. But it's just not going to happen.

'When it comes to kids training at clubs, in the north you are going to have parents who drop the kids at training, go off to work and come back later.

'In the south, you will have ten fathers standing on the touchline watching the whole training session in the rain! Then, after training, they will come and talk to you if you're the coach.

'It's that passion, involvement and connection to the game in the South of France from east to west that is the ignition to all the rugby talent and the future of rugby in France.'

It is the great glory of France and French rugby.

I could talk rugby all day with people like Rory Kockott. But I have another passion in this country. Driving. The scenery is majestic, the motorway system fast, open and inviting. But then there are the country roads.

I jump into the car and roll out of a rainy Castres. Behind me, above the dark foothills of the Massif Central mountains, loom heavy, threatening rain clouds. I shudder, find the D118 road and head south-west towards the Mediterranean.

You approach Narbonne on this road almost through the vineyards of places like Lézignan-Corbières. It is an enchanting drive, climaxed by the frisson of excitement at first glimpsing the great sea.

LE COQ

To maintain the southern hemisphere link, I am here to talk with Michael Cheika, now coach of the Argentine national team but a former player with Castres and Stade Français. After that, he coached the Paris club, too, before coaching his native Australia. With his many commitments, the guy's feet rarely touch the ground.

He's just bought a house near here and I'm intrigued as to why. 'Mate, of all the places I have played rugby in the world and coached, France stands out.

'It is a place I have always loved being and living here. The game is very interesting here; it has a lot more character than many other countries and the game plays a different role in terms of the psyche of club and country.

'It's a really interesting place to play your rugby and to be involved in the game.'

He sipped a *café* and looked out of the window. Below the level of the café, just across the road in a culvert, the gentle waters of the famous Canal du Midi flowed by.

Cheika might have an unmistakable Australian accent. Especially in the middle of a Narbonne café/restaurant. But what is equally distinguishing is his knowledge of this land, gleaned from his times as both a player and coach.

Cheika sees some key elements in the way French rugby has changed since professionalism.

'The advent of the billionaires created the new turbulence in French rugby. Their arrival has depowered the guy who was always the most important in the club, the coach. Now, the coaches are no longer the bosses. The owners want to be in charge in everything. The outcome is there for everyone to see.

'But the emotional return, which is what they are in it for I assume, and which they get for their money, is generally poor. In French rugby there was always a hierarchy on which you never messed with the coach. You did what the coach said and that was it. But the advent of the owners has changed the dynamic of French rugby.

'People like Boudjellal at Toulon played a role and in my view it was a positive one. He brought them a welter of advertising they would never have got and also brought over a terrific collection of foreign players. That encouraged other owners to get involved doing that.'

But it is not just the owners who have had a profound effect. 'One of the things that has changed the face of French rugby is the input of foreign coaches. Also, the factor of relegation. A lot of teams will start playing defensively because they are scared of going down. Relegation here is one of the worst things that can happen to a club and a town involved in French rugby. That has certainly damaged the flow of the play. But on the other hand, it has added a lot of interest to the competition.'

What of French deeds on the field? 'The French can get into that rhythm of doing the unexpected, so that they expect it to work. That's why it looks so fantastic when it comes off. Like Ntamack against New Zealand in Paris in November 2021, running from his own goal line. They just expect it to work. To me, that is when they are at their best, when they're not worried about stuff.

'Their problem is that sometimes, they worry too much about things which are not relevant to rugby. But that's perhaps down to the town and the expectations. But if you don't have that, you can't have that vintage style of play if you're too consistent.

'It's not feasible for them to play like that all the time. That's why it's so great when it does come off.

'It's like a vintage year in the vineyard. When it's special, it's fabulous. That attitude is what has made them successful as a rugby-playing country. And they are successful in various ways.

For example, they have got one of the biggest rugby economies anywhere in the world and there is a huge popularity for the sport here.'

Yet why is it France has often seemed on the fringes of the world game? 'Rugby is an Anglo-Saxon dominated game,' says Cheika. 'It's run by the countries of the Six Nations. It's true, France has had the only non-Anglo-Saxon president in Bernard Lapasset. So I think their place in the game is pretty unique. They are there but their influence has not been as strong as the countries of the four Home Unions.'

But a simple phrase Michael Cheika spoke as he departed, somehow encapsulated almost every view, each opinion expressed among these great rugby men.

As the Argentina coach said, 'France is an incredible country and the rugby is just crazy at times. Yet all the time you have this feeling that you want to go back. There is something there in your mind telling you to return. It is that special.'

Someone else who quickly spotted this passion for rugby in the land is the three-time Grand Slam-winning defence coach of Wales, Shaun Edwards, one of the most successful rugby men the games, rugby league and rugby union, have ever known. The former Wigan and Great Britain rugby league player has now added another Grand Slam title as defence coach of France in 2022. Edwards was instrumental in that Grand Slam triumph, France's first for twelve years.

After 2019 and the conclusion of the Rugby World Cup in Japan, Edwards joined France and made his home in Catalonia, near the beach at Canet-Plage, close to Perpignan. Before that, he had always lived in Wigan or London.

I get back in the car at Narbonne and join the A9 motorway heading due south to Perpignan. Great rugby towns, a multitude of vineyards, views of the sea spectacularly lit by the afternoon sunshine. All in about forty-five minutes. It is idyllic.

'To live near the beach is a different experience for me,' Edwards tells me.

But he soon became aware of something else that was different about French life in the south.

'Since I have been here, I have hardly seen any youngsters kicking a football around. I don't hate football but it's good to see that. Rugby is a very, very popular game here.'

Like everything he has ever done in his life, Edwards took to the huge challenge of his new job with great gusto. He's that kind of guy. The glass is most emphatically half full, opportunity dawns. The phrase 'pursuit of perfection' describes all these rugby men.

How has he negotiated the omnipresent language difficulty, I asked him? For it is not every Frenchman who has always gone out of his way to understand the vagaries and challenges of the English trying to master the French tongue.

Typically, Edwards took the bull by the horns. He cheerfully admits he was no good whatsoever at languages at school. So, he marched into his first meeting with the French players after his appointment to the post and delivered a speech. In French.

'I was very, very determined to give my first presentation to the players in French. I made sure I did that. I am not a natural student and languages have never been my forte. But I wanted them to see I was serious and that I respected the French people and language.'

How did it go down? 'You'd have to ask them that,' he said. 'But I think you could say they didn't expect it.'

But Edwards confesses he is not a coach who expects to spend hours drilling his players out of a textbook. 'I am much more for repetition of practice on the pitch than talking about it. That is how you improve as a rugby player. This is my job, to help them do the practice, not talk about it. I learned that from the great Wayne Bennett [the Australian rugby league coach].

'But even as a player, I liked it when coaches were precise and got out there to practise. I am a big believer in that.'

From inside the French camp, it appears that the French players are big believers in Shaun Edwards. Philippe Rouge-Thomas, Director of Training with the FFR, said, 'Individually, Shaun brings out the best for defence in each player. We are talking about the desire to defend. Players who are far away from the action, normally they wouldn't be interested in the game. But he has brought new thinking. There was a lot in terms of tackling and technique. Shaun brought a sort of rugby league concept and British culture, a rigorous spirit.'

Did the French players accept this? 'Yes, because he transmits his passion, mastering the technique. The French players like being connected to their coach. They insist on knowledge of the rules from young ages like sixteen or seventeen.

'You have to respect the way of living and the way of playing. Also, the vision of the game. It is the same for the women and the youngsters.'

Just how England and the RFU allowed Edwards to go off and coach first Wales and then France, is simply incomprehensible.

The Lancastrian is determined to emphasise that in the modern game, your job title should not be totally restrictive. 'I am called defence coach. But defence helps with attack. If you have 60 per cent possession that means you only have to defend for 40 per cent of the time. It's pretty simple. So if we (the defence) can win the ball for our attack, that can create opportunities for them. That is how defence assists attack.'

But does a significant focus on defence not weaken or undermine France's great traditional forte – attack? 'I totally disagree with that,' he said. 'My job is to create turnovers for the attack as well as defend. In the 2022 Six Nations, we created more turnovers than anybody else. We also want to create a system where the main attacking players don't have to do too much tackling.

'I once made thirty-six tackles in a single rugby league Test match and missed two. I have been there; I understand how tiring tackling is. My attacking game certainly suffered that day. I was very tired. But at least I didn't have to hit any rucks.'

But there is something else a man like Edwards brings to any task he undertakes. A sheer will to win. France's 2022 Grand Slam success may have been their first for twelve years. But even soon after the success, Edwards was looking far beyond that. 'I want to win every Six Nations. We are not happy winning just one,' he insisted.

'I am a competitive person. We [France] have not won every game [since the new coaching team was formed]. But we have only been beaten once by more than one score. That is a pretty strong record in two and a half years.'

But what kind of initial response did he get from the French players? He shrugged. 'Players are the same the world over. What you find with the top players is they always want to improve. If you give them information and the drills to help tackling and defence play, they respond well.

'I have had no problems at all with the attitude of the French players. They may be young but also experienced and they all want to improve. That is one reason why they are the best.'

Like myself, Edwards has been mightily impressed by the knowledge young French players of the present time have of their predecessors' achievements. 'Antoine Dupont, for example, is quite a person. Once we were speaking about the history of French rugby and his knowledge was absolutely amazing. He knew the Grand Slams won, the years and many of the players involved. Absolute class.'

But why does Edwards think young men like Dupont show such respect for past players? 'It's a thing that is inbred in rugby here. Not every young player I have known has had that knowledge of the past. Not everyone remembers those details. Antoine is a true student of the game. It is not essential you have that knowledge. But it would help in your motivation, etc. Because you want to be remembered in the same light as the great players of the past. After all, your legacy lasts forever. Antoine is very, very aware of that.'

Edwards has wide experience of the game in a multitude of countries. Yet was there anything that surprised him about the French set-up compared to, say, the Welsh?

'Not really. I knew it would be very professional. I knew they would have a very professional way of doing things. I wanted to join them having been an international coach for twelve years with Wales. I thought my experience would help.'

Could this be a golden era for French rugby? They have as much chance as anyone else, he thinks. For there is, he says, real back-up to the familiar names already in the squad. 'But one reason we won the Six Nations was, we had a consistent team and didn't have that many injuries. Consistent team selection is always important. Even the All Blacks' great teams had that. Your best players are your best players.

'But we have back-up because everybody wants to wear that jersey. We want young people in France to be the next Fickou, the next Dupont.'

Poor old England, Scotland, Australia etc. Isn't one Antoine Dupont enough for the French?!!!

So let's reflect on what the French have given this pulsating game down the years. A simple game invented, it is said, by the British, that can make the hairs on the back of your neck stand up straight at its climactic moments. It is, indeed always was, the essence of *liberté, égalité, fraternité...*

The French have infused rugby union with their strands of drama, of vivacity. They have taken onto the sporting field elements of beauty, creativity and invention. Entertainment? At times, it has blown your little cotton socks off.

For sure, rugby union in Gallic hands has mirrored the frustrations and myriad personality traits of their nation. Bruising, beautiful, illegal, vicarious, enigmatic. Yet the glass always seemed half full with the French. It may be the Latin influence.

Soaring highs or catastrophic lows. There hardly seems much more than a thin strip of paper between the two as far as the French are concerned. They embrace drama, don't shy from it. It is them, it's their DNA.

On the rugby field, when they're in their pomp, they play with their rivals. The ball is their toy, like the favourite toy of a small child. It is embraced lovingly, caressed, gently passed among close friends, moved mysteriously beyond the grasp of outsiders. In these moments, there is a rhythm, an elegance, timing and flow to their play. It seems effortless, yet beyond the capacity of ordinary mortals.

To see this almost private game played at times by a succession of French rugby teams down the years has been captivating, a treat as rich as the chocolate cake in your local patisserie. There is a corollary to this supreme skill and touch, in another sport. At his best, the England cricketer Joe Root is another in this elite class, a batsman who can simply ooze such qualities.

It is a world few inhabit, whatever the sport.

This spirit which the French have brought to rugby has lit up the entire scene. In their dark times, when the inspiration has ebbed away, they have failed. Miserably. Great expectations have fallen silently on fallow ground. In those sullen times, they have sought easy scapegoats whom they could chastise. Referees, coaches, club presidents, even media men. All have felt the lash of their tongues amid the widespread dismay.

But these are the human feelings that surface so powerfully within French rugby men. They reveal just how much they care about this great game.

But particularly when the Gallic sun has shone on their backs, especially when the calendar has flicked over into springtime, they have run free, like cheetahs released from the cage. The wind streaming behind them, onlookers enraptured, human souls stirred and throbbing with excitement at the spectacle.

A privilege indeed to have seen this.

Around the early 1990s, it seemed as if French rugby had lost its way. Its great values appeared to have been sacrificed upon the altar of efficiency, bruising physical power and a dour approach underpinned by kicking. Mostly opponents, but sometimes the ball, too...

The mentality had changed. Perhaps irrevocably, we thought, on the other side of the English Channel.

Yet those in power in French rugby disagreed. Their defence was launched most publicly by the highly charismatic French coach of that era, Jacques Fouroux. You would seldom see Fouroux in a crowd. At 1.62m, he was too small. But if he lacked size, he was certainly not insufficient when it came to stature.

'France,' he told me once in forthright tones, 'will always be faithful to its traditions.'

It's fair to say Fouroux was no dreamer, still less a fantasist. 'History will always be more beautiful than the reality ever was,' he said. 'Respect these men [of the past], yes, but believe in the present is my creed. I believe in pragmatism.'

Oxymoronically, the Fouroux coaching years represented an era of almost unrelenting success for the French national team. Grand Slam winners in 1981 and 1987, Five Nations Championship winners in 1989 and shared winners in 1983, 1986 and 1988.

Yet Fouroux divided opinions right across France. Was he not obsessed with the use of forward power, at the expense of French style and elegance? While he was still alive, Fouroux always mounted a stirring defence of his methods. He pointed to France's outstanding 1987 Rugby World Cup semi-final performance over Australia in Sydney. Not to mention the five tries they scored against Wales in Cardiff in the 1990 Five Nations Championship. But he had certain non-negotiables in his lexicon.

'Always, the group must be the key element, not the individual. I have fought for this all my career.'

It is instructive that as France of the present day prepares for another Rugby World Cup, similar values are established within the contemporary French team. Individuals such as Jaminet, Marchand, Dupont, Ntamack and Alldritt may command many of the headlines. But those in charge preach the collective. Just like Fouroux all those years ago...

CHAPTER 14

The Rugby-Loving Abbot

Clermont Auvergne–Toulouse–Albi–
La Rochelle

Т he journey is almost done.

The southern summer sun is now almost too strong for rugby men, except deep into the evening. Which is why the French Top 14 semi-finals and final in June seldom begin before 9 o'clock at night. Even then, given the high temperatures and great humidity in the south, the ball becomes like a piece of soap. Handling errors proliferate. Add on the pressures inherent in knockout rugby and the play suffers.

So often in this land at that time of the year, kick-off is accompanied by a golden sunset sending shafts of brilliant light across the stadium. God's own floodlights?

The warm Eden Park rugby jerseys, winter coats and scarves have been packed away, replaced by, well, very little. A T-shirt or short-sleeved shirt. A pair of shorts. It is the life of the south in this land, post-May.

Yet the passion remains.

Right up to the final kick or pass of a marathon ten-month season, emotions remain inflamed, nerves frayed at clubs right across the nation. Either in victory or defeat. It doesn't much matter which level you are discussing. Teams renowned and others largely unknown vie for the play-offs and an exclusive end-of-season ticket to glory that is promotion or a Championship title. Or they seek that miracle win which saves them from the dreaded relegation.

I went to one of these play-off matches, in the round they call the 'Barrages' a few years ago now, up in the hills of the Auvergne. Stade Toulousain were the visitors to Clermont and I was there for a couple of interviews and to watch and assess a certain player.

Bath, the rugby club of the city where I lived at the time, asked me to help in a new role. They wanted to beef up their player recruitment. The number one country they wanted to target was France.

So I made my way to the Auvergne region for a match that was sure to be a tough test for both sides. If you used the phrase 'full on' you'd be close to its understanding.

Bath were interested in recruiting one of the Clermont props. But his problem on the day was his Toulousain opponent, a man by the name of Cédric Soulette. Try to formulate in your mind an image of a bear half crouching, ready to attack a foe. In terms of height, Soulette wasn't that tall. Nor was he any kind of speed merchant around the field. But by God, he could scrummage. He was born in Béziers, never a bad starting point in life for a front-row rugby player.

They called the first scrum after just three minutes, and it took about three seconds to break up. By which time, Bath's prospective signing was laid flat out on the ground. Eventually, he was helped off and never returned. Cédric Soulette stood around with the casual, disinterested air of a man just waiting for a bus. By contrast, the Clermont man looked like he'd been hit by one. Or something, anyway...

At the end, when I'd managed to inveigle my way into the Clermont official reception, I sought out a couple of the home players to see how our man was. One shrugged and just walked off. Another, rolled his eyes and made a pained expression. It seemed this wasn't the first time Bath's desired prop had departed the scene in distress.

All of which was in my mind when my mobile rang in the car the next morning.

'How did he get on? Does he look a good player?' asked the eager Bath chief executive?

'He's a pussycat, not worth considering,' was my response.

'Oh dear, I'd better get that message to Michael Foley,' the Australian who was by then Bath's head coach.

The call from Bath's CEO to his coach was lively, it seems.

'Michael, we can't sign him. Peter Bills was at the game and says he just isn't up to it.'

'Mate, who exactly is the coach of this club? Peter Bills, or me?' was Foley's reply. 'I can make him a good player.'

I wonder how many coaches have said that down the years.

Anyway, Bath got their man, signing him for two years at a handsome salary believed to be six figures per season. He started only a handful of matches in two seasons, was often injured and made no impression. Then he left.

Michael Foley and I still laugh about it when we talk. That's the meaning of rugby friendships.

Another friendship developed, directly from that occasion, with Soulette. I told Bath to bring him over, sit him down and tell him he was wanted. His pedigree was sound. He was a member of France's 1998 Grand Slam-winning squad in the Five Nations Championship and a murderous scrummager in the best French traditions.

345

Soulette arrived with his wife and was keen on striking a deal. He loved the place. Bath were keen, too, except, alas, only at a cut price. They simply wouldn't pay anything near what the player wanted.

But time proved that wasn't Soulette's fault. I brought over two more Frenchmen, Serge Betsen and Sylvain Marconnet plus Corné Krige, the South African. All wanted to sign and live in Bath. But all were offered miserly sums that made it impossible. Bath didn't seem to want to pay the going rate. They departed and I quit.

But then relationships with French rugby men especially have a tendency to endure. They really are very special. Years later, I flew into Toulouse late one Friday evening, ahead of a match the next day. Straight to the hotel and bed? Or a swift bevy with an old mate? Tough call that.

My pal and I agreed to meet at J'go restaurant at 11 p.m.

When I arrived, you could hardly see the restaurant for the hordes of people eating and drinking al fresco. It was a warm spring night and Toulouse was hopping.

Quietly sipping a glass, I was suddenly aware of two huge arms wrapping themselves around me from behind. My body kind of crumpled as a bear of a man seized a fulsome grip on me, my head disappearing into an enormous chest. My assailant let out a roar. 'Pierre...'

'Monsieur Cédric Soulette...'

Fresh glasses arrived, and more red wine was poured. We hadn't seen each other for years but the friendship was unimpaired.

Although, I have to say, some friendships prosper rather more than others.

Back in the day, France had a pack of forwards all presumably fathered by the Jolly Green Giant. One of them was a man from Perpignan named Jean-François Imbernon and he played twenty-three times for France between 1976 and 1983. He stood 1.97m and weighed 105kgs.

Modest by modern-day standards but at that time, decidedly confrontational.

Together with Michel Palmié of Béziers, he formed the French equivalent of Michael Corleone's hit squad. Whether they left sawn-off horses' heads in opposing coaches' beds, I cannot tell you.

But they sure didn't take prisoners.

Anyway, Imbernon came to grief in one French Five Nations match on a winter's afternoon at the Parc des Princes, Paris. It wasn't an assassin that finally caught up with him, or some dastardly deed. He broke his leg quite accidentally.

Whatever, fast-forward to late that night. The official dinner for the two teams is over, the players have gone their own ways into the Parisian night. I am told that the French are in a nightclub named Crystal, near the Arc de Triomphe. So I head for it, manage to evade the mob queuing outside and squeeze in. All of which was *une part de gateau* compared to my next task.

I wanted to find Jean-Pierre Rives for a few quotes for a Monday morning newspaper piece I had to write. But the place was so dark, lit only by the dimmest of lights on every floor, that you'd probably have missed the President of France and the Queen of England if they'd walked past you.

I certainly couldn't see much. So on about the third floor, tired and fed up with this wild goose chase, I tried to negotiate my way between two large sofas but found something heavy sticking out. So I gave it a good kick.

Immediately, there was an almighty roar from a figure seated on one of the sofas. The figure was seen to crouch over a leg. Yep, you got it. Monsieur Imbernon and his plaster-encased broken leg...

LE COQ

Since that night, I've seen him, very occasionally, at a match somewhere in France. But I've never quite had the courage to ask him if the leg healed properly. But nowadays, Imbernon often attends Perpignan matches with an old foe, England's 1980 Grand Slam-winning captain Bill Beaumont, now the head of World Rugby, who is a frequent visitor to Catalonia.

Old friendships enduring once again.

*　*　*

When I come to think of it, I'd struggle to tell you the precise moment I fell in love with French rugby. French women, yes. But rugby is an even more capricious seductress. All that emotion, all that drama. How could a 100 per cent Englishman cope with all that nonsense?

But then I realised. I am not 100 per cent English. I'm 25 per cent French. My maternal grandmother came from Normandy in the late nineteenth century.

This may go a long way to explain the lunatic driving, the love of spontaneity, wine, champagne, Provençal cherries in May, fresh seafood on the French Atlantic or Mediterranean coasts, pain au chocolat to start the day, a simple espresso... and, god of all French culinary gods, cassoulet.

But the theme of rugby friendships remains omnipresent. Conceive in your minds an image of a youngster, not yet in his teens, but already crazy on rugby, hanging around outside a London club's dressing room, as the gloaming of a winter's afternoon descends. Yours truly. And we're talking way back in the day. The 1960s.

My focus was on the holy grail. Autographs. But a surprise awaits me. One of the Blackheath team, prop forward Tony Horton, played the previous weekend, against France at the old Colombes stadium outside Paris. Horton has signed many a time for me in my small autograph book, back at his London club.

But now, he beckons me into the home dressing room. Undoing his kit bag, he lifts out the dinner menu from the after-match banquet in Paris with almost reverential care. On the cover, there is a drawing of the Eiffel Tower and Big Ben. Open the menu and either side of the details of food and wine for the banquet, are the names of the two teams.

Just about every single one is personally signed. I am simply captivated by the autographs of those mythical French players of whom I have read so much but seen so little. The great Michel Crauste, the legendary André and Guy Boniface, Jean Gachassin, Benoît Dauga, Christian Darrouy, Élie Cester, Lilian Camberabero, Arnaldo Gruarin, Walter Spanghero, Claude Lacaze... men from far away, indeed another life, down in the South of France.

More than fifty years later, I still recall the frisson of excitement in that moment.

There are plenty of England players' autographs too. But somehow, they just don't capture my imagination in so vivid a way as the French. Studying proudly my gift from the Blackheath, England and British & Irish Lions prop forward, I seem to envisage an image of every French player just by seeing his name and signature.

I'm not sure, but it could have been, I believe, in those moments, where I discovered my lifelong love for French rugby.

But I wasn't alone in being captivated by the French rugby men. Consider these words, written about the French performance, after France's 13-0 win over England at that match in Paris in 1966, in front of a crowd of 37,660.

The *Playfair Rugby Football Annual* reported, 'France gave an outstanding exhibition of rugby football absolutely at its

349

best. England... were almost dead weight (through a couple of injuries) and France were consequently able to turn on some scintillating rugby – bobbing, weaving, criss-cross pattern play with scissors thrown in for good measure, which left most spectators breathless.

'France were bound to score sooner or later and towards the end they produced a picture try with Lacaze and Gachassin the instigators and André Boniface going like an electric train, taking the final pass and tearing over.'

I defy anyone not to be moved by such sporting poetry in motion.

Furthermore, I'd defy anyone to deny a few basic facts that separate France from other nations where the game is played. Rugby in France was always a game for the masses, for everyone. It wasn't like in England, elitist. It still isn't.

The garage hand, the lawyer, the guy in the computer shop, the doctor – all share a love of this game. Rugby is a universal language throughout the southern half of France. It dominates the sporting life, just as soccer dominates the headlines in English cities like Manchester and Liverpool.

In France, this love for the game is like much of the *terroir*. Earthy. It explains the many decades of intense passion for the sport all over the south and west of the country.

Happily, this game without social boundaries has spawned great friendships among those from all sections of society. Even the church. Especially the church in the case of Henri Noel Jacques Pistre, better known in France as just 'Abbé Pistre'. Now there was a man who loved his rugby. So much so that they called him 'the Pope of Rugby'.

He was born in Mazamet in 1900, in the heart of great French rugby country. The growing boy ran, hurdled, swam and indulged in many sports. But he loved rugby like God loved all men. He played for SC Albi from 1920 to 1922, starting on

350

the wing, then moving to the back row of the pack before settling in the second row.

The French rugby writer Henri Garcia once penned a glorious line about him, stating, 'He discovered that rugby adapted marvellously to the texts of the Holy Gospels because, in the heart of a scrum, it is always better to give than to receive.'

In 1922, after one final appearance for his beloved Albi, against Perpignan, he accepted his calling and took his place at the seminary in Albi.

A year later, in December 1923, he was ordained a priest in front of his former Albi rugby colleagues. One of the players, Jean Vaysse, handed the new abbot a package. Wrapped in the yellow and black cape of the Albi club were twelve pieces of silver cutlery.

The new abbot revealed, when he disrobed after his ordination, his old, faded Albi rugby shirt, the other great love of his life. He told his friends, 'I was wearing it for the last time as a gesture in the renunciation of a love.'

Later in life, he would even coach the Castres rugby team and then form a rugby side which he would coach himself. He died in 1981 at the age of eighty, beloved of all at the Albi club.

It just so happens that I have personal experiences of Albi and a gentleman in Holy Orders. Well, a dog collar, anyway. Whether it was genuine or worn as part of a fancy dress outfit, I was never quite sure. For this was a strange night.

I had motored to Castres sometime in the 2000s to write on a European Champions Cup game against Munster. Straightforward except that, because the Munster men were in town, there was nowhere to stay. They had booked out just about every room in the vicinity.

The game had even started and I was working when the mobile buzzed. My office had at last found a room for me. But it was in Albi, 22.7 miles away. But better than nowhere.

So, long into the night, after the game and post-match interviews, I drove through the silent, deserted and sleeping countryside of the Tarn *département*, to Albi. It's quite a sedate place, dominated by the cathedral, even in the middle of the day.

At ten minutes before one in the morning, it definitely is not throbbing.

But I found the hotel, albeit in total darkness, and tapped in the code to open the front door. My room key was just inside, in the reception area. Except that the code I'd been given for the outer door wouldn't work. I tried it and tried it. Nothing.

So, at 1.15 in the morning, I started to return to the car park to spend a fitful night in the hire car, doubtless wrestling with a gear stick for a bit of room.

Except that, I thought I heard... no, it couldn't have been... hold on, I'm sure it is... the sound of singing. Not raucous singing, but something of a gentle lilt. It got nearer and nearer.

A people carrier-type van pulled up right outside the hotel, and six or seven gentlemen poured out, you might say just a tad the worse for wear. Merry, but a little muddled, perhaps? It didn't take very long to work out this could be the Munster cavalry arriving over the hill.

It didn't take long to explain my predicament, either. But friendly arms wrapped around my shoulders and soothing words were uttered. All would be well. Indeed it was...

Someone did have the proper code and in we went. Alas, there was one more slight hurdle to overcome before the welcoming sight of a bed. The bar. And it was well stocked.

Suffice to say, we just stopped for a single nightcap. Which ended, as it does, when the red wine ran out. At 4.30 in the morning. Somewhere in amongst the throng, even at that late hour, was our friend in a dog collar. Ah, but then, he was surely only honouring the memory of 'Abbe Pistre'.

* * *

Someone once asked me, 'What has French rugby given you?' I'd answer that by saying, 'What does a lifelong love for anything give you?' whether it be opera, gardening, cooking, caring or anything else.

Put simply, it fires your imagination, it brings a smile to your face on a dull day. Plus the warmth of lifelong friendships. Even amid the worst times. The simple, basic human emotions that we all associate with whatever pleasure we choose.

Like any relationship, mine with French rugby has weathered some difficult days. I hated the wilful violence that all but threatened to overwhelm the game at one stage. I simply could not understand why, with so much skill and quality omnipresent in the sport in this land, thuggery was allowed to become so major an issue.

As someone said, such violence was ridiculous. This is a game, not a war. Sure, men played for pride and at times it might have boiled over. That happens. It's about emotions. But some traded almost their entire careers on the physical violence they meted out, tarnishing the great name of this game.

However, not every miscreant was French. The sport world-wide accepted for too long acts which had no place in this terrific game.

Happily, there was a saviour at hand. Television. Fist fights, kicks and illegal assaults have been largely eliminated from the game due to the role of the TV cameras. You might think it a strange way to have arrived at policing a game. But for that, we should all be grateful.

Manifestly, one rugby-playing nation has benefited more than most from that process. France. With the skulduggery now mostly banished, the French have been able to focus on their natural talents for this game. *Quel dommage*, as they say, for the men of other rugby nations lacking the supreme skills and vision of so many Frenchmen for this sport. As winter 2022 and the winning of a first Six Nations Championship Grand Slam for twelve years showed, when the French cut out the shenanigans and focus on elements such as skill, concentration and discipline, they really cut the mustard. They are a far tougher team to beat.

A golden era beckons for French rugby and it is sure to be a pulsating spectacle.

But France can offer this marvellous game an even greater legacy than just winning a Six Nations or even a World Cup. Even in this now professional game, they can remind the whole rugby world of some of the values that always underpinned the sport; like being humble whoever you are, respecting those who have gone before you, remaining the same person you always were; embracing qualities like dignity, humility and consideration for others. Not someone struggling to get their head through the dressing-room door. Happily, I ran into a huge number of people in the world of French rugby who espoused these meritorious values.

For whether a game is amateur or professional, one thing remains the same. Courtesy and civility cost nothing.

In too many countries under professional rugby union, the doors have been firmly shut to outsiders, even youngsters seeking just a sight of their heroes, or perhaps an autograph. Too many nations have allowed their top players to become remote, distant from their base. Too many have forgotten their roots and overlooked how essential it is to nurture them by whatever means.

France hasn't done that. I was immensely impressed with young men like Damian Penaud, Antoine Dupont, Greg Alldritt, Romain Ntamack and others who clearly understand rugby's traditional values and seek to preserve them. To watch Dupont cheerfully shaking a sea of hands and posing for pictures with so many supporters long past midnight after one exhausting Toulouse Top 14 match, was to see the game and its future in great hands.

Others, not as good at this, can and must do better. They can learn much from those in French rugby truly offering a warm welcome to anyone, friend or outsider.

In essence, perhaps that is the key message from this story. The ordinary rugby-loving people of France who go out of their way to welcome outsiders are the ones who really make this game and the country unique in rugby terms.

In every region, they demonstrate the values that were always the bedrock of this sport.

In spring 2022, I came scrambling out of the La Rochelle ground after a game. Late, as usual, this time for dinner in town.

'Where can I find a bus or taxi back into town?' I asked a guy getting into his car with a friend, in the most basic use of the French language.

A hand waved in a direction towards the sea. I hurried on, only to be overtaken moments later by the car. It pulled up and the back door was opened.

'*Allez, allez,*' said the driver.

And amid a mixture of faltering French and English by which means we swapped stories, we drove back into town where I was dropped close by my hotel. It wasn't the way they were going. But for a visitor and a fellow rugby devotee, they were more than happy to do so. A friendly 'deviation' we might call it.

This rugby spirit. This shared love of the game. Rugby people do these things. Not only in France. But especially in France. Real rugby people. The true rugby spirit.

Acknowledgements

Inevitably, as with any book, a huge number of people behind the scenes have contributed generously to achieving the final product. In myriad ways. The author's name adorns the cover, but so many others merit mention. All have played a role to some degree in creating the final product you now hold in your hands.

To Averil, who masterminded the lengthy process of translations and shared much of the journey, my grateful thanks. Likewise to Katie, thanks for the creative input that has made the book's appearance special. And to Rolan Knezevic for his thoroughly helpful appraisal of the text.

Thanks too, to Dan Carter for penning a highly interesting foreword.

Several people read parts of the manuscript and offered valuable advice and encouragement. In no particular order, many thanks to Serge Manificat, Mark Baldwin, Yvon Dille, Michael Lynagh, Peter Franklyn, Bob Dwyer, Darina Clancy, Andrew Collow, Ian Malin, Tim Arlott, Ronan O'Gara, Olivier Romanelli, Steven Nel, Christian Berthault, Gérard Bertrand, Jean Alcalde and Dave Rogers.

I also thank my agent David Luxton, for all his help and advice. And thanks, too, to Lorène Guillot at Stade Toulousain for her great help and professionalism in setting up interviews. Thanks, too, to the manager and excellent staff at the superb Maison des Ambassadeurs in Rue du Minage, La Rochelle, for their special help and assistance.

Those I interviewed, and therefore thank for their time, include Antoine Dupont, Romain Ntamack, Jerome Kaino, Pierre Villepreux, André Boniface, Christian Darrouy, Pascal

ACKNOWLEDGEMENTS

Ondarts, Serge Blanco, Guy Camberabero, Jean-Pierre Rives, Scott Robertson, Jack Isaac, Rory Kockott, Gareth Edwards, Donal Lenihan, Willie Anderson, Shaun Edwards, Tony Ward, Graham Mourie, Pierre Berbizier, Murray Dawson, Simon Gillham, Michael Cheika, Michael Lynagh, Tim Lane, Joe Schmidt, Jean-Pierre Garuet, Michel Cremaschi, Alain Lorieux, Christian Trallero, Jean Gachassin and Walter Spanghero. You could definitely pick a very decent 1st XV out of that lot!

Thanks also to my editor at Atlantic Books, Ed Faulkner, for his calm mastering of the whole process plus his enthusiasm, encouragement and helpful advice with regards to the text. I greatly appreciated that. Thanks too to Carmen Balit for the wonderful cover illustration, to Ian Greensill for his meticulous work on the manuscript and to Kate Ballard for all her endeavours on the production process.

Bibliography

400 at 5.30 with Nannies by Peter Bills, published 2015 by Pitch Publishing.

Deano by Dean Richards with Peter Bills, published 1995 by Orion.

Jean-Pierre Rives: 'A Modern Corinthian' by Peter Bills, published 1986 by Allen & Unwin.

Mud in Your Eye by Chris Laidlaw, published 1974 by Howard Timmins, Cape Town.

The Rise of French Rugby by Alex Potter/Georges Duthen, published 1961 by A. H. & A. W. Reed.

L'Équipe, assorted newspaper editions.
Midi Olympique, assorted newspaper editions.
Playfair Rugby Football Annual, assorted editions.
Rothmans Rugby Union Yearbooks, assorted editions.
Rugby World magazine, assorted editions.